PROPAGANDA A
IN THE OLI

Propaganda
and Subversion
in the
Old Testament

———

Rex Mason

First published in Great Britain 1997
Society for Promoting Christian Knowledge
Holy Trinity Church
Marylebone Road
London NW1 4DU

British Library Cataloguing-in-Publication Data

A catalogue record of this book is available from
the British Library

ISBN 0–281–05015–5

Typeset by Wilmaset Ltd, Birkenhead, Wirral
Printed in Great Britain by
Arrowsmiths Ltd, Bristol

Contents

ACKNOWLEDGEMENTS

I am indebted to several people for their help in producing this book.

First to Alex Wright, now of SPCK, whose enthusiasm when I first mentioned the germ of the idea of the book and whose gentle enquiries since as to how I was getting on with it have proved just the stimulus and encouragement I needed to complete it. With thanks to him I couple all those at SPCK whose friendly expertise have played such a large part in its production.

I owe an incalculable debt also to my friend and successor at Regent's Park College, David Reimer. In the midst of a very busy teaching and administrative schedule he has found time to look out for me books and articles which I might easily have missed in my semi-detached state of retirement, making many available to me. In him encyclopaedic knowledge and great generosity of heart meet, and I have been only one of many who constantly benefit from such a rare combination of qualities.

I am also grateful to my friends and relations by marriage Oliver and Ruth Stanley. I have had many stimulating discussions with them on many topics but not least those related to my study of the Hebrew Scriptures. It occurred to me they were just the kind of people I wanted to address in this book, intelligent, of ever active and questing mind, but who would be the last to claim to be experts in the specialized field of biblical studies. So throughout the writing of the book I have pictured them sitting just across the room from me and have tried to make it as near a conversation with friends as a book can be. I should explain that it is because I have wanted to address an audience of which they are representative that I have tried to avoid technical jargon, or, where I have used it, to explain it. I have also avoided endless debates in the text about every point, since it is impossible to make any point at all over which there is not profound scholarly disagreement! I have merely tried to indicate something of the range of opinion and then, with an arrogance which has been thoroughly enjoyable, simply stated my own view. For the same reason I have avoided building barricades of footnotes, confining myself in them mostly to works which would be accessible to the non-specialist and which would contain further bibliographical information for those who wanted to pursue any particular point further.

I am also deeply grateful to Audrey, my wife for many years, for her constant support and encouragement. And also for her patience when I shuffle off to my study yet again to pen a furtive footnote usually – quite by chance of course – when it turns out that there is some garden or household chore awaiting the attention of one of us.

None of these is to blame for the many shortcomings of this book. But without any of them it would been even worse than it is.

ABBREVIATIONS

AV *Authorized Version*
BCE Before the Common Era (= BC in Christian use)
BZAW Beihefte zur Zeitschrift für die alttestamentliche Wissenschaft
CBQ Catholic Biblical Quarterly
ch. Chapter
chs. Chapters
CE Common Era (= AD in Christian use)
CBQ Catholic Biblical Quarterly
CUP Cambridge University Press
f. The verse, chapter or page following the one cited
ff. More than one verse, chapter or page following the one cited
Hb. The Hebrew text
HUP Harvard University Press
JB *Jerusalem Bible*
JBL Journal of Biblical Literature
JSOT Journal for the Study of the Old Testament
JSOT Supp. *JSOT Supplementary Series*
LXX The Septuagint (the Greek Version of the Old Testament)
MT Massoretic Text (the received Hebrew text)
NEB *New English Bible*
NIV *New International Version*
OUP Oxford University Press
op. cit. *opere citato* (= 'in the work cited')
REB *Revised English Bible*
RSV *Revised Standard Version*
SBT Studies in Biblical Theology (SCM Press)
SCM Press Student Christian Movement Press
SPCK Society for Promoting Christian Knowledge
SOTS Society for the Study of the Old Testament
Supp. VT *Supplements to Vetus Testamentum*
v. Verse
vv. Verses
VT Vetus Testamentum
YUP Yale University Press

CHAPTER ONE

Propaganda in
the Ancient Near East

I am old enough to have gone to school in the days when, even at what was then called a 'County High School', we all did at least some Latin. As with all languages, the reward for stewing over declensions, conjugations and the rules of grammar and syntax was to advance to the literature. It is, perhaps, unfortunate that pupils always seemed to be started on Caesar's *Gallic Wars*. These do, of course, have the advantage of being fairly simple Latin. Presumably, like military men of all ages, he got so used to barking out terse, instantly comprehensible orders that his written work, while bristling with historical interest, lacks literary embellishment (although it is only fair to say that Cicero, no mean stylist himself, approved of the *Gallic Wars* for that very reason). Like the military memoirs we have become used to since the Second World War, they seek to justify the methods and achievements of their author, although Caesar was so successful a commander that he had no need to try very hard. And he was also concerned to show the superiority of his Roman troops and of authoritative established government like that of Rome itself. To that extent this writing was 'propaganda' of a fairly obvious and simple type.[1]

In due course, however, we advanced to Virgil's *Aeneid*, and in the course of my somewhat sketchy classical studies we read Books II and VI. This was much more to my literary and aesthetic taste, and one revelled in the imagery with its marvellously extended similes (to be met with again in Milton) and its gripping dramatic and epic character. It did not occur to me that it had other than literary qualities, however, until a few years ago when I decided to read through the whole work with which before I had only fragmentary acquaintance. I regret to say that those early scholastic endeavours had not been so thorough or successful that I could dispense with the excellent English translation by W. F. Jackson Knight in the Penguin Classics series which I use when quoting here. Reading through that I got a shock. Nothing in our earlier studies (at least nothing my wit was quick enough to perceive nor my memory reliable enough to retain) had prepared me for the fact that this was not only a superb work of literature but also an out-and-out piece of political propaganda.

It was Virgil's aim to show that the foundation of Augustan Rome could be traced back to the earlier days of myth and legend, to the flight of 'pious Aeneas' from the city of Troy. Of course, Aeneas himself could not have founded Rome since Troy fell four centuries before the time at which legend attributed the founding of Rome to Romulus. Yet the establishment of the city is shown to have been in the mind and purpose of the gods from even so long a time before. In Book VII Aeneas comes to the land where one day the city of Rome would be established. Landing where the river Tiber flowed through a forest to the sea he finds some chance words of his son 'Iulus' to confirm the fulfilment of an earlier prophecy, and this leads him to burst out, 'Hail, Land which fate has reserved for us! Hail, Gods of Trojan Homes, who never fail us! It is here that your homes are now to be. This is your Fatherland.' Throughout the work a number of such 'prophecies' both foretell and justify the later rule of Rome. One example is the 'prophecy' of Jupiter to Venus, who is distressed by the fate which has befallen Aeneas and his people who were her especial care:

Spare your fears, Cytherean. You have your people's destiny still, and it shall not be disturbed. You shall see your city, see Lavinium's walls [i.e. the city which Aeneas founded after landing at Latium] for I have promised them. And you shall exalt to the stars of Heaven your son Aeneas, the great of heart. There is no thought of changing my will. But now, because anxiety for him so pricks you, therefore I shall speak of the more distant future, and, turning the scroll of the Fates, awake their secrets. Know, then, that Aeneas shall fight a great war in Italy and overthrow proud peoples ... But Ascanius, his young son, who is now given a second name Iulus ... shall complete in royal power each circling month for thirty long years. Active and vigorous, he shall build Alba Longa to be strong, and thither shall he transfer his rule from its old seat, Lavinium ... Here kings shall reign for a period of three hundred years until one day Ilia, a priestess of royal blood, shall bear twin sons to Mars. Then shall one Romulus ... inherit the line. He shall build battlements of Mars; and he shall call his people Romans, after his name. To Romans I set no boundary in space or time. I have granted them dominion and it shall have no end. My decree is made ... And then shall be born, of proud descent from Troy, one Caesar ... a Julius bearing a name inherited from Iulus his great ancestor. (Book I, ll. 257–88)

Such 'prophecies', purporting to 'predict' events which have already happened are known as 'prophecies after the event' (or *vaticinia ex eventu*, to give them the Latin name by which scholars often refer to them). They are a recurring device in *The Aeneid*: other instances are to be found in Books VI, VIII and XII. Summarizing the political purpose of the epic, Jaspar Griffin says, 'The message of the poem is that the domination of Rome over the world is willed by heaven and that it will impose peace and civilization [*mos, ius*].'[2]

I came to my reading of *The Aeneid* as a whole after many years of studying and teaching the Old Testament. Virgil's poem is later than the great majority, if not all, the constituent parts of the Old Testament, since he was still working on it when he died in 19 BCE. Yet the purpose of some of the Old Testament literature and the devices it uses to achieve that purpose struck many echoing chords with *The Aeneid*. There also the reign of a particular line of kings, the right of a certain people to occupy a specific city and a land with clearly defined borders, are all claimed to have their roots in very early, even 'prehistoric' times. These will all be the result of divine choice and divine sanction, a purpose which is evident in the way the history of the people of Israel is presented, and in the utterance of 'prophecies' (*vaticinia ex eventu*) to certain ancient heroes revealing the future fulfilment of that divine purpose.

So the idea for this book was born. How far must at least some of the Old Testament literature also be classified as 'propaganda' and, if it may be to any degree, how does this affect claims for both its 'historicity' and, more seriously, its religious value and authority? These are the issues we shall be considering.

They become all the more urgent when we take on board what sociologists have said about the function of religion in the propaganda of social and political institutions and 'establishments'. We may let Peter Berger speak on this for the moment: 'Let the institutional order be so interpreted as to hide its *constructed* character' (he has been referring to the fact that all social and political organizations are of human design and fashioning – to that extent they are 'constructs'). 'Let that which has been stamped out of the ground *ex nihilo*' ('from nothing', or 'from scratch' as we might say) 'appear as something that has been existent from the beginning of time ... let the people believe that, in acting out the institutional programmes that have been imposed upon them, they are ... putting themselves in harmony with the fundamental order of the universe. In sum, set up religious institutions.'[3] Or again, 'Religion legitimates social institutions by bestowing upon them an ultimately valid ontological status, that is by *locating* them within a sacred and cosmic frame of reference' (p. 42). And finally, '... the political structure simply extends into the human sphere the power of the divine cosmos. The political authority is conceived of as the agent of the gods, or ideally even as a divine incarnation. Human power, government, and punishment, thus become sacramental phenomena, that is, channels by which divine forces are made to impinge upon the lives of men. The ruler speaks for the gods, or *is* a god, and to obey him is to be in a right relationship with the world of the gods' (p. 43).

All this may seem rather grim for religious truth claims. Does it mean that religion is *never* more than an elaborately woven garment made by those in power to cloak in respectability the nakedness of their claims to power and privilege? This will also have to occupy us in this book. For now we may content ourselves with a couple of remarks by way of anticipation. It is necessary to emphasize that to say that something 'is a work of propaganda' is not to say that it is invariably, or necessarily wholly false. We saw that Caesar's *Gallic Wars* were a simple kind of propaganda in that they portray Caesar himself as an outstanding and victorious general. In fact, he *was* one of the most able and successful generals of all time. Further, a particular political, religious or social order which claims divine sanction might indeed be 'within the will of God'. Or, to put it more empirically, the particular authority for which the claims are being made may evince many fine qualities which greatly benefit those who come within its control and influence. It may be shown, in the light thrown on it by the subsequent events of history, to have been a good order, or, at least, to have been one of the best available at that time and in the prevailing circumstances. If not ideal, it may have been the most available 'good'.

But, more than that, it often turns out that 'religion' is an extremely awkward genie to try to bottle up with the stoppers of official propaganda. It proves to have an almost Pygmalion-like power of its own which causes it to come to unexpected life. Often, it has burst out of its official containers and turned on those who tried to control it in their own interests. Again and again it has un- leashed energies and powers of the human mind and spirit by which the absolute claims of human orders or the abuse of their position have been challenged, with the result that they either became profoundly modified or were completely overthrown. And this has been justly noted by Peter Berger, who pays full trib- ute to the role of Israelite prophecy and the witness of the Old Testament in such a process. Having traced the part of organized religion in justifying the *status quo* of the ruling order, he acknow- ledges that 'religious perspectives may *withdraw* the status of sanc- tity from institutions that were previously assigned this status by means of religious legitimation' (pp. 104f.). He finds the criticism of David by Nathan, as if the king were just another man subject to the laws of God, to be indicative of an influence which 'may be traced all through the Biblical tradition, directly related to its radical transcendalization of God, finding its classic expression in Israelite prophecy ...' (p. 105). He concludes that '... religion appears in history both as a world-maintaining and as a world- shaking force' (p. 106).

The 'Old Testament'[4] gives some remarkably vigorous ex- amples of this latter process. These will also be the proper object of our study, and that is why the title of the book is 'Propaganda *and Subversion* in the Old Testament'.[5] Of course, even so, the idea that there may be striking parallels between the kind of religious and political propaganda to be found in the literature of the ancient Near East and the Old Testament may trouble some readers. I do not think there is any real reason why it should. In the light of the scholarly study of both Old and New Testaments for more than a century now it has become recognized even by the most sincere religious believers that there are what they would call both 'human' and 'divine' elements in our scriptures. The 'human' element is found in the obvious individuality of the various writers; the extent to which their outlook has been shaped by the historical, political, religious and social contexts in which they have lived and worked; and the limitations they shared with their contemporaries in the realms of scientific and historical knowledge. All this is accepted by all but some very 'fundamentalist' and 'literalist' believers. It is assumed as a matter of faith that divine revelation can adapt itself to each given human situation and so is 'incarnational' in principle. If some of this human context is also apparent in a shared common heritage of using literature for 'propaganda' purposes it does not seem so very different. It is true that this aspect of their writing has received little systematic attention.[6] But it seems to me that its study only highlights further the fascinating interaction between what is often termed by believers as 'divine revelation' and the part played by its human agents and interpreters.

Yet there is an aspect to the topic which makes it of more relevance, of more urgency even, than merely providing the material for a theological debate on the niceties of the interaction of the divine and the human in any concept of 'revelation'. The failure to distinguish in any way between 'human' and the 'divine' elements in the writings of the Old and New Testaments[7] can lead to some very disturbing consequences. A widely acknowledged gain from academic study of the scriptures for the past century and a half has been this recognition that they have to be grounded in the full historical context of their writers, that the 'human' element has to be taken seriously. This has enabled some clear distinctions to be made in the content and substance of the material itself. For some of what the Old Testament has to say about God is simply unthinkable for many people today. To imagine that God really is the kind of Being who wishes to see all Canaanites, men, women and children, exterminated, just because they happened to be Canaanites and, very understandably, fighting in defence of their own territory, is shocking. We rightly recognize now that in this the Israelites shared very much the same religious outlook as their contemporaries. The remarkable fact is that the same Old Testament records a growth in religious understanding on the part of at least some, who did not remain satisfied with such a nationalistic, limited view of God. They began to glimpse that he cared for all people and that he looked for high standards of ethical conduct from his own people as well as others. The Israelites' privileged 'election' would not protect them if they refused to respond to his call and his demands. There are then glaring differences of level of religious awareness and insights in the Old Testament, and the perception of this has enabled us to judge one piece of it by another, the more bloodthirsty parts of the book of Joshua, for example, by the insights of a prophet like Amos or the author of the book of Jonah. If we use the language of faith to describe what scholarship has shown to be happening, we say that God takes his people where he finds them, with all the historical, social, religious and political conditioning of their setting, but he does not leave them there. He leads them on to greater heights of religious awareness. Why should not this understanding, now widely recognized and accepted, apply to the use of 'propaganda' in certain of the writings?

If, on the other hand, all the 'propaganda' elements to be found in the Old Testament are taken at their face value and not subjected to the critiques which are to be found within the writings themselves, then they are liable to be credited with full divine sanction. The result is that it is assumed unquestioningly that it is the will of God that one particular group or nationality has rightful claim to a particular area of territory, with the implications that others do not and have no business being there. It is assumed that God looks with especial favour on the people of one particular ethnic or social grouping and that they are therefore entitled to privileged treatment which may safely be denied to others. If it is believed, on a literalistic reading of the biblical texts, that there are first- and second-class citizens in the Kingdom of God, it is not long before the favoured act as though there are first- and second-class citizens in the kingdoms of this earth. And when *different* ethnic, social or political groups lay claim to the same piece of territory and the same favoured status, then the seeds of war are sown, all the more frightening because each group may see the war as a holy crusade waged in the name of God. 'So may all your enemies perish, O Yahweh'[8] has become a convenient battle cry for too many since it was first uttered by Deborah in her song following the defeat of Sisera (Judg. 5.31). And it has proved amazing to see what inhuman treatment has been meted out over the centuries to the unfavoured by those who considered themselves to be acting in the name of God as his special 'elect'. It is, perhaps, not going too far to say that a biblical fundamentalism, which insists on taking every part of the text as equally a valid word of God for all people for all time, might well be one cause of a future war. Another way of reading and understanding the scriptures seems necessary and desirable. It is my hope that this book may be seen as a preliminary attempt to face up to some of the issues raised by the use of propaganda in the Old Testament and by the remarkably powerful subversive elements there too. And even if some of the diagnosis offered here of what is going on in various parts of the biblical texts does not prove to command full assent, perhaps it will at least initiate a discussion which must be of relevance in the contemporary international situation.

So far we have glanced at one work of outstanding literary merit which also served a propaganda purpose. We shall be looking more closely for any possible parallels with this, and other types of literature from the ancient Near East, when we examine the biblical material. But literary 'epic', such as *The Aeneid*, is by no means the only genre of literature which could serve as propaganda. Religious texts exist which seem to have had similar aims. One which is very well known among Old Testament scholars because of the influence it has often been claimed to have had on the Israelites is the Babylonian *Enuma Elish*. It contains an account of the creation of the world, and the title comes from the opening two words, which mean 'When on high . . .'[9] Although the earliest manuscripts of it date from only the first millennium BCE, it is usually thought to have originated in the Old Babylonian period early in the second millennium. It tells how the god Marduk championed the cause of the other gods in battle against Tiamat, the dragon symbolizing the chaos ocean, slew her and, tearing her body in pieces, formed out of them the earth below and the firmament above. As a reward the gods decide to have a palace/temple (the terms are synonymous in the ancient world – the same Hebrew word indicates both, another indication of the close linkage between royal rule and the rule of the gods) built for Marduk. And where is that temple built? It is hardly a breathtaking surprise to learn that it is to be built in Babylon. In Tablet VI we read (in Stephanie Dalley's translation), 'Create Babylon, whose construction you requested . . . build high the shrine'. This locates Marduk's dwelling in Babylon and so legitimizes, not only the temple there, but, of course, the reign of the priest-kings who ruled over the whole territory of Babylon in his name. Thus the myth serves as propaganda to bolster the divine nature and authority of the kings of Babylon.

However, the mere existence of the 'story' does not exhaust its power in maintaining the *status quo*. We know that the myth formed the written text (often called the *legoumena*, meaning 'spoken words') of a religious ritual (the *dromena*, which here means 'the repeated symbolic acts' – one has only to think of the 'words' and 'acts' which are combined in the Christian sacraments) which was enacted at the time of the annual New Year festival. This was designed to 'renew' the primeval victory of Marduk over the forces of chaos, so that regular rainfall would again make possible the annual fertility of the land. In this way 'creation order' was brought out of 'chaos', and, in this ritual, the king played a central role as the one through whom Marduk's original victory was continually renewed. Thus the whole community depended entirely on the duly consecrated king to mediate the order by which alone its life and continuance could be sustained.

This brings home strikingly the force of some other words of Peter Berger on the role of religion in preserving the 'order' of society: 'Just as religious legitimation interprets the order of society in terms of an all-embracing sacred order of the universe, so it relates the disorder that is the antithesis of all socially constructed *nomos*' ('law', or more generally and appropriately, 'the order which is ordained') 'to that yawning abyss of chaos that is the oldest antagonist of the sacred' (*Social Reality of Religion*, p. 48). In other words, the king, and the established order which he epitomizes and makes effective, is the divinely appointed flood barrier against all natural and human forces which threaten to engulf the community. And religion not only provides the 'story' which sanctions all this, but provides the means for its continuance. It releases the power by which the order is kept effective. Priest and king are the twin pillars supporting 'the establishment'.

This basic myth was known in many differing forms throughout the ancient Near East. Parts of the Old Testament show unmistakable knowledge of some form of the story of a primeval conflict between God and the dark, watery forces of chaos. Apart from the disputed territory of Genesis 1 (to which we shall return), some psalms allude to some form of it (Pss. 74.12–17; 89.9–14 (Hb.10–15); 93; 104.1–9) as well as other passages such as Isa. 51.9–11. Scholars today think the most likely immediate source of influence on the Israelites was the Canaanite version which is known to us from the Ugaritic Texts[10] (although in an incomplete form). Ba'al is imprisoned by Yam. *Yam* is the Hebrew word for 'sea' and so Yam must be seen as some kind of sea-god, a little reminiscent of Tiamat in the Babylonian myth. But Ba'al is encouraged by the divine craftsman Kothar-and-Hasis, who gives him two clubs with which he strikes Yam. Both are needed, for only the second deals the final blow:

> The mace whirled in Ba'al's hands
> Like an eagle in his fingers

> crushed the pate of Prince Yam
> the forehead of judge Nahar (= 'River').
> Yam collapsed and fell down to the earth,
> his face quivered and his features crumpled up.

It appears that Ba'al also scattered Yam's broken body as Marduk scattered Tiamat's. After the victory Ashtarte, the goddess, cries out in triumph, 'Verily Yam is dead! Ba'al shall be king.' Later texts tell of a palace-temple being built for Ba'al by Kothar-and-Hasis just as one was built for Marduk.

There are many problems in interpreting these texts, partly because they are incomplete and fragmentary and we cannot reconstruct anything like as continuous a story as we can from *Enuma Elish*. Other parts tell of a conflict with the god Môt (= 'Death') and of a great sea-monster Lotan, who appears in the Old Testament as 'Leviathan' (e.g. Isa. 27.1). At one point Ba'al is defeated by Môt and goes down to the underworld, but he is rescued by his sister, Anat. The conflict with Yam is not explicitly linked with creation, as the battle between Marduk and Tiamat clearly is, although in the texts dealing with the struggles between Ba'al and Môt and Lotan the connection is made. The whole cycle seems linked with the renewal of the seasons, with the 'death' of vegetation during the hot, arid summers and the renewal of life with the coming of the rains. The victory of Ba'al by which he is re-established as king is a guarantee of the renewal of 'order' and 'fertility'. And the exercise of that kingship is again associated with his rule in a temple-palace. As Walsh has said, all the elements of divine kingship come together in these texts, 'house, throne, mountain, feast, acclamation by the gods' (*The Mighty from their Thrones*, p. 24). But all these were reflected in the rule of the kings of the city states of Canaan. They too ruled from fortified cities usually situated, for obvious reasons, on a raised eminence. They were the ones who were responsible for establishing 'order' in their realm, food and water for the people and defence against the attacks of enemies which threatened always to reduce the order of the realm to chaos. For all the gaps in our knowledge, we may assume that the Ba'al epic gave sanction to the kings who ruled in his name and as his agents. As I say, it is now generally agreed that it was the various Canaanite forms of this ubiquitous myth which exercised most direct influence on the Israelites and on their writings in the Old Testament.[11]

So, not only could a literary epic like Virgil's *Aeneid* serve propaganda purposes, but religious epics could serve the same ends as well. Their influence was more than merely that of providing a literary record of a powerful story. By serving as liturgies in continuing religious worship they exerted a powerful influence in perpetuating the religious, political and social 'order', an order which the myth explained and justified by vesting it with divine authority.

Yet these are by no means the only types of literature which served as propaganda in the ancient Near East. There are all the literary products to which we might give the very general and not very scientific title of 'court writings'. Obviously these could vary enormously in genre, from historical records and inscriptions to 'wisdom' texts, legal codes, decrees, prayers and invocations of the gods and so on. Kings in those days were no more given to undue modesty than modern-day politicians. Like politicians of all times, they did not like to hide the light of their victories and beneficent care of their subjects under a bushel, nor to leave the people in any doubt as to the utter perfidy and baseness of their opponents. The equivalent then of the modern radio or television interview was the victory stela, the inscription on a prominent building, or even on their tombs which they ensured became, in something of a literal sense, favourable obituary columns. The stela or inscription boasting of military prowess was a fairly obvious and simplistic form of propaganda which need not detain us here. But some of the 'court writings' are of interest and may again afford possible links into some of the 'history' writing in the Old Testament.

Take, for example, the Hittite king Hattushilish III, who reigned in the 13th century BCE. Since he became king by murdering his nephew who was already on the throne, one might think that he, or the PR firm he hired, would have faced something of a tall order in putting it all into a favourable light. He (or his ghost writers, one can never be quite sure whether any one court scribe was merely the equivalent of a modern stenographer or more like a top Civil Servant who actually drafts his Minister's speeches) was more than equal to the task, however. He produced what has sometimes been called (by later scholars) a 'royal apology'.[12] We need not spend long over the most fitting scholarly label to give it, but the contents of the document are interesting. Hattushilish III tells the story of his life, showing how he owes all his advances and his survival, in the face of the envious and felonious misdeeds of others, to the favour of the goddess Ishtar. He was son of a king, and on the death of their father, his brother Muwattilish came to the throne. Muwattilish advanced his brother Hattushilish to high favour in the kingdom but, as always, heights are dangerous places and his influence aroused the envy of others, especially another high-ranking official Armadattash, who spoke against his loyalty to the king. However, 'My lady Ishtar always rescued me' and so, finally, truth broke through the slanders and his brother, the king, became convinced of his honesty. The result was that he rose even higher, becoming the chief military officer of the Hittites and marrying a priestess of Ishtar. With such powerful lines of influence, it is hardly surprising that he won a legal victory over his old enemy Armadattash and was thus vindicated from all charges.

His brother when he died had no legal heir, so that a son born of a concubine succeeded him to the throne, one Urhi-teshub. Hattushilish maintains that he gave this upstart nephew his full support, although human nature being what it is, it would not surprise us if a little sense of outrage did not occasionally flicker through his mind. There is no hint of it in his 'apology', however. But something aroused his nephew's suspicions, for over a period of time he stripped his uncle of rank and possessions until, after seven years, 'he tried to destroy me'. Had we access to the nephew's memoirs, no doubt we might feel a little sympathy for him with the shadow of a powerful uncle, blood relation to his royal father, looming over him.

If, in fact, he had no suspicions he should have done, because Hattushilish declared open war on his nephew. Probably, as former commander-in-chief, he still had friends in the regiments, and we might attribute his victory to the powerful camaraderie of former companions in arms. He, himself, ascribes it to a higher and more righteous cause. His justification for attacking his nephew was that Ishtar 'had even before this been promising me the king-ship' and, with the powerful backing of a goddess 'who marched with me', his nephew Urhi-teshub had no chance. He was defeated, and his uncle, a little wiser with the years than his nephew, took care to banish him from the kingdom. Apparently, even with Ishtar on your side, you cannot be too careful. Unsurprisingly, the memoir ends with a pious exhortation to his descendants never to abandon the worship of Ishtar.

So there is a story of one who was not the rightful heir but who was fully justified in all he did because he was the divine choice and all his opponents were unworthy of office. Indeed, none of what happened was really due to the scheming and plotting of real political life. It was all the working out of the god's will. How very convenient the divine will can be when we happen to be the ones who have rigged the results so that we always draw the winning lottery number!

It may seem surprising at first glance that propaganda, at least of the political type, is often as much a product of weakness and uncertainty as of strength and super-confidence. Or, where it would be inappropriate to speak of 'weakness' it may nevertheless indicate a power not yet so fully established in the respect and admiration of all its subjects as to be secure. One group of various types of literary propaganda which illustrate this comes from Egypt at the beginning of the rule of the 12th dynasty, a rule which extended from about 1990–1780 BCE. The last period of great strength in Egypt had been during the First Kingdom, but this had gradually weakened and was followed by the so-called 'first intermediate period' when, from about 2200, a series of competing but weak kings failed to keep the country united. Not only was it weakened by the rivalry of different kings but, in the prevailing climate, petty nobles were able to assert the independence of their separate domains. Further, bedouin from the desert, always a threat to the inner stability of Egypt, were able to infiltrate largely at will. Out of this inner chaos a powerful Theban family seized power and so began the 12th dynasty with its first powerful ruler, Amen-em-het I. They were to be most successful in unifying the whole country again, but first they had to assert their position and gain the loyalty and support of all their disparate subjects. One historian of this period has said that 'Under the Old Kingdom it had not been necessary to assert the benign power of the king. His godlike qualities had been manifest.'[13] In other words, they, and everyone else, knew they were good and they didn't need to keep on about it. But, as the new rulers began the task of asserting their right to rule all Egypt, they needed a little help. A more recent writer on the Egyptian literature of this period has said, 'The divine charisma of the Old Kingdom Pharaohs now needed to be supplemented by practical politics, and persuasion or eloquence ... increasingly came to be seen as an arm of government. A more realistic translation of this concept might be propaganda.'[14]

A scholarly and sensitive study of some of this literature was

made by G. Posener as long ago as 1956.[15] He underlines the fact
that Amen-em-het I came to the throne after a time of severe internal strife, having beaten various rivals to the throne. He moved his
capital from Thebes and favoured the cult of the god Amon. There
was a desperate need to unify the various sections of the kingdom
and to establish his right to the throne. To quote Posener, 'To
facilitate the restoration of order and to give foundation to the
authority of the State, it was necessary above all to create in the
country a climate of confidence and of respect for the established
power' and 'Both for the administrator and those administered it
was important to restore the prestige of royalty' (p. 8). Of course
strong actions and a rule which was seen to be according to clear
moral guidelines were needed, but as well, 'The familiar literary
forms were adapted to the needs of the time: they were perfected
and transformed better to serve the enduring themes of royal
propaganda' (p. 16).

And so they were, in lively literary compositions which are still a
delight to read and which, again, utilize a number of various literary genres. Incidentally, Posener has no doubt that they are the
work of official court scribes, both in cases where the work is an-
onymous and in those assigned to specific pharaohs. One of them
is 'The Prophecy of Neferti' which proved so popular (and useful!)
that it continued to be copied for three hundred years. Ostensibly
it dates back to the time of the 4th dynasty, when the ruling king
calls his seer, Neferti, and asks him what will happen in the future.
He predicts that troubles are to come upon the country, describing
them in lengthy detail. (This part takes up most of the text. It is,
perhaps, not surprising that such a work finds it easier and possibly
even more enjoyable to describe the evils and misfortunes of society than to linger on the good things. Prophecies and even sermons since have quite a track record of the same thing.) But after
all this terrible time of chaos and suffering, a king will arise who
will restore order and prosperity to the kingdom, securing the
delta region against the incursions of the bedouin. His name will
be Ameni. Several features show this to be one of those 'prophecies
after the event' we have already mentioned. The descriptions of
the long period of trouble are 'banal or imprecise and carry no details by which we can fix any date' (to quote Posener), but once we
come to the reign of Amen-em-het I, everything becomes much
more specific. (It is exactly the same state of affairs in the 'prophecy' to be found in Daniel 11, which enables scholars to know

that the present form of the book is to be dated in the time of Antiochus IV, 'Epiphanes', in the 2nd century BCE). But by 'prophesying' the advent of the first king of the 12th dynasty in such times, Amen-em-het is made to appear in an almost 'messianic' role. The whole work is, in fact, a political tract with 'the intention of favouring the founder of the 12th dynasty' (p. 29).

Another literary genre which can be made to serve a similar aim is that of the didactic instruction, and an example of it is found in this period in 'The Instruction of Amen-em-het I'. If the prophecy of Neferti fitted the beginning of the king's reign, this work seems to belong to its end. It has a bitter and disillusioned tone. He is ostensibly addressing his son, Sen-usert I, speaking of himself in the first person, and giving almost an autobiographical account of his reign rather than the more conventional wisdom-type teaching. He describes in full detail the great achievements of his reign. He has cured famine and created economic prosperity. He has undertaken great building programmes and seen off the land's enemies from within and without. In fact he sounds remarkably like any modern-day politician telling us just why we should vote for him again after a period of office. Yet far from being 're-elected' (not necessary for a pharaoh of course) he has met only constant ingratitude culminating in an uprising against him. Nevertheless, he counsels his son to learn from his experience. Let him be careful whom he trusts. 'Fill not thy heart with a brother, nor know a friend. Create not for thyself intimates – there is no fulfilment thereby. I gave to the destitute and brought up the orphan. I caused him who was nothing to reach [his goal], like him who was somebody. [But] it was he who ate my food that raised troops [against me] . . .'[16] One cannot help but remember David's instructions to Solomon to eliminate those who had plotted against him (1 Kings 2.5f., 8f.). So the hurt king (indeed, he appears from the text to be a *dead* king, slain by his enemies) gives instruction to his son and confirms his position on the throne: 'I have made a beginning and you have set in motion its completion' (his son was in fact co-regent with him for some years). So, in Posener's words, 'The author uses the ancient didactic genre to honour the work of the founder of the dynasty, to confound its opponents and to affirm the position of the successor to the throne.' After all the upheavals associated with the revolt and his father's assassination, Sen-usert I had to consolidate his position on his father's throne. It is even quite possible that it was he who had the document composed.

15

A quite different genre, that of the narrative, is used in *The Tale of Sinuhe*. This takes the form of a remarkably lively and vivid first-person account of the fortunes of someone who served in the court of Amen-em-het I but who, in all the upheavals associated with his assassination and the threat from possible rival claimants to the throne, decides to flee Egypt. The account of adventures which befell him in his wandering in the desert and in various countries has something of a *Boys' Own Paper* air about it or, if some readers are too young to find that comparison illuminating, like a tale out of *The Arabian Nights*. After being befriended by a band of Arabs he comes to Qedem (the name just means 'the East' and may be vague either because of the writer's lack of geographical knowledge or deliberately so for the sake of the narrative). There he is questioned about his motives for coming and about the political situation back in Egypt by a ruler of Upper Retenu (probably highland country in the area we know as Syria) much as today he might face an interrogation from an immigration official at the airport. This gives an opportunity for a long eulogy of Amen-em-het I's son and successor Sen-usert I, and Sinuhe recommends that Syria enter into an alliance with the new pharaoh who is so powerful and trustworthy.

The story has enough happy endings for a television soap opera. The Syrian ruler gives his daughter in marriage and a large tract of fertile land to Sinuhe, who rises to high position in the land of his adoption by his military prowess. He arouses the usual envy from a powerful rival, whom he successfully despatches in a duel. Yet, in spite of all this, as he grows older he becomes homesick and longs to return to Egypt. When Sen-usert I hears of this, he showers him with costly gifts, invites him to come back and provides him with a house with a garden, as well as an ornate and splendid pyramid tomb – which might sound a bit ominous but is actually a sign of great royal favour.

The story takes the form of some tomb inscriptions and might indeed have appeared as one. It is equally possible, however, that the whole thing is a skilful and imaginative invention. But the real significance of it is in the portrait it paints of Sen-usert I. He has established order and unity back at home; he is of a strength and rank to be courted by foreign kings who think it worthwhile to enter into alliance with him; he is a man of warmth and generosity who is in excellent rapport with his subjects. All of which serves to make this a work serving the ends of political propaganda, even if it is an unusual and popular one – a kind of 'tabloid' rather than 'broadsheet' journalism.

The other genres of the literature of propaganda which Posener describes need not detain us here. Royal inscriptions from Israel have not been found in anything like the numbers in which they have been uncovered and deciphered in Egypt and other surrounding lands. Hymns in praise of the kings can be moving but are not found in Israelite literature in quite the same way. Perhaps this is because, in Egypt, each pharaoh was thought to be a manifestation of a god, or the son of a god who repeated in his reign the miracle of creating order and plenty out of chaos. So a hymn written at the accession of Rameses IV praises this miraculous renewal of fertility:

> A happy day! Heaven and earth are in joy, for thou art the
> great lord of Egypt.
> They who were hungry are sated and gay; they who were
> thirsty are drunken.
> They who were naked are clothed in fine linen ...
> Ramses Heqa-maat – life, prosperity, health! – has taken
> over the office of his father![17]

The so-called 'royal psalms' of the Old Testament share the joy but show significant differences, for the king in Israel, while regarded as a 'son' of God who ruled in his name, was not himself a god. Therefore the hymns celebrating kingship are much more God-centred than 'king-centred'.

There is another example of Egyptian court literature cited by John Ray[18] which is an extraordinary instance of the 'royal instruction' genre. Moral teaching and 'instruction' is, as we have seen, a kind of propaganda in itself because it is testimony to a particular king's concern for justice and right order in his kingdom. He is firmly on the side of the 'goodies' and makes life hot for the 'baddies'. The very unusual one which Ray cites is known as the 'Instruction for King Meri-ka-re'. In this, he actually admits a fault in his own conduct. This is as unusual in the Egyptian court literature as a modern cabinet minister admitting that one of his policies was wrong. In the version to be found in Pritchard, *Ancient Near Eastern Texts* (p. 417), it runs as follows:

> Behold, a misfortune happened in my time. The Thinite regions
> were hacked up. It really happened through what I had done,

and I knew of it [only] after it was done. Behold, my recompense [came] out of what I had done.

This might seem a fatal admission for one who is supposed to be divine. Once admit a chink of doubt into the doctrine of the infallibility of the pharaoh, and what might be the consequences? But, in fact, the writer makes good use of it, for on the basis of his experience he can pass on sage advice to his son.

> Generation passes generation among men, and the god, who knows [men's] characters, has hidden himself. [But] there is none who can withstand the Lord of the Hand ... Revere the god upon his way ...

In other words, this king is not too proud nor too stubborn to have learned from his mistake and, on the basis of that experience, he sagely counsels his son to honour God and keep to his ways for there is no way anyone, not even the king, may escape the divine justice. Such an example is well worth bearing in mind when we come to consider the fairly frank admissions of sins and mistakes on the part of kings in the Old Testament's historical literature. Everything depends on the way the king reacts. The report of a humble submission and repentance may itself be a piece of favourable propaganda showing the ideal piety of the king concerned.

It must be stressed again that it is not being suggested that Israel simply borrowed some or all of these forms of propaganda or that these forms had a direct influence on them. These are merely a few randomly chosen examples of the kind of thing that is meant by propaganda in various parts of the ancient Near East at various times, the periods ranging over several centuries. But they do reflect something of the world in which Israel lived and show something of the need for, and the aims of, official court propaganda. Nevertheless, there are certain underlying general characteristics, not only to the specific texts we have mentioned, but to propaganda of all times. In demonstration of this it will be instructive to conclude this chapter by noting some very interesting observations by Mario Liverani on the underlying rationale of Assyrian court propaganda.[19] The book in which Liverani's article appears is concerned as a whole with the history of imperial expansion and its underlying sociological, political and religious motivation. As such it is not immediately relevant to Old Testament studies, for

Israel was seldom in a position to become an imperialist power and was never a major one. Her experience of imperialistic drive was to be mainly on the receiving end of it. Nevertheless, Liverani's analysis of the underlying 'ideology' behind Assyrian expansion and the ways in which she justified it, while recalling much of what Peter Berger has to say more generally on the relation of religion and politics (see above, pp. 3f; 9) certainly does afford parallels to some of the theology of the Old Testament. Liverani points out that every war is regarded as a 'holy war'. To quote him, 'The war is always a holy one if fought by us, always a wicked one if fought by the enemy: therefore, "holy" means only that which answers our social values, it means Assyrian. A king is not legitimate because of the approval of god Assur: a king, while he rules in Assyria, is always legitimate, and his legitimacy is expressed in religious terms (in fact, the less obvious it is, the more it is emphasized). In a broader sense, the divine approval is not the *cause* of the legitimacy of the act, it is clearly its *expressed form*' (p. 301).

Underlying all imperial expansion and the way this is justified in the literature are four almost subconscious assumptions which have to do with the concepts of space, time, people and goods. The concept of space is that 'the world is divided into a central zone and a peripheral zone' (p. 306). The inner is 'normal', it is 'us'. The outer is 'abnormal', strange and dark. There is, in fact, in the world a cosmic centre, structured and ordered, Assyria and its territory, and a 'chaotic periphery'. I suppose the old medieval maps with outer spaces simply labelled 'Here be dragons' would sum up Liverani's point nicely. Yet it is a triumphant adventure to launch out from the security of the central zone to the dark periphery. Imperialistic expansion is almost a mission. It is to establish the order and light of cosmos in the surrounding chaos and darkness. It is the divinely given responsibility of the enlightened centre to take the benefits of civilization out into the barbaric outer areas. Such a view has informed more than Assyrian imperialism in the ancient Near East. Much British imperial expansion was justified in the same way, and popular expression of the mood could be caught in some of the earlier missionary hymns:

> The heathen in his blindness
> bows down to wood and stone.
> Can we, whose souls are lighted
> With wisdom from on high.

Can we to men benighted
The lamp of life deny?

The concept of time among the ancients may be a little more difficult for modern minds to grasp. It was believed that creation took
place by some act or acts at the beginning of time when the light
and order of the created universes were brought out of a pre-
existent chaos. But this was a process which needed constant renewing, a renewal to be achieved only by means of the right
cultic worship. So in the proper religious rites, in which the king
took a leading part, order was being constantly renewed; chaos,
which always threatened, defeated again and again. By securing
this, and securing safety for his people from aggressors, both
within and outside the realm, and by creating the conditions in
which society could know prosperity, the king 'puts himself in the
wake of the founder heroes and, ultimately, in the wake of the
creating gods' (Liverani, 'Ideology', p. 308). So time is a constant
renewal of the established order. Yet there is also a contrasting
sense in which the king is always pioneering advances into new
achievements in time, by enlarging the boundaries of the empire,
building new cities, winning ever more victories. The king, with
his successful imperialistic campaigning, therefore, is always re-
peating the original miracle of creation, subduing the dark forces
which threaten.

A third underlying concept is that of the diversity of peoples in
the world. There are Assyrians, the epitome of order and civilization, and there are the strangers beyond the borders or outside the
beneficent shelter of Assyrian rule. By advancing out towards
these 'others' and bringing them, when they submit, into the
order and light of the Assyrian empire, the king is again bringing
order out of chaos. But if they resist, they must be eliminated. They
have shown themselves unfit for a civilized world. They represent
the ever-present menace of chaos. In such a case 'the enemy is abnormal, unnatural – we must eliminate him. He is wicked . . . it is
his fault if we kill him' (p. 311).

Finally there is the concept of the material goods of the world.
Assyria, as the centre of civilized order, is the centre of processed
goods, of wealth, culture and all truly noble human achievement.
It is the role of others to supply the raw material, the tax and the
tribute and, where appropriate, the manual labour, by which this
superior civilization can be fed and may flourish. The reward of

'the hewers of wood and drawers of water' is the protection of the great power.

It is not a long nor an arduous task to think of parallels in the Old Testament to these four underlying concepts of imperialism. Jerusalem is seen as the centre of the world (it can even be described as being 'the apple of God's eye', Zech. 2.8). Indeed, the rule of the Davidic king there stretches from 'sea to sea' (Ps. 72.8), a concept which does not mean merely from the Mediterranean to the Persian Gulf, but the whole earth encompassed by the cosmic sea.[20] We shall see plenty of evidence that the sacred worship in the temple in Jerusalem was seen as the means of the renewal of the original reality of creation as it is described in the first chapters of Genesis. We shall see the way some of the Old Testament literature, particularly the so-called 'Deuteronomic' literature, regards foreigners, especially Canaanites and Philistines, as 'lesser breeds without the *Tôrah*' whose resistance to Israel deserves their elimination because it is really resistance to Yahweh. And often the longing is expressed in the Old Testament that the day will come when Yahweh rules from Jerusalem, the centre, as universal king of the whole world, his kingship acknowledged by all nations who bring their tribute to swell the wealth of Jerusalem. So the benefits of his reign will be extended to all peoples and Israel will have accomplished the divinely given role of being the means by which 'all the families of the earth shall bless themselves' (Gen. 12.3).

These then are some examples of the use of propaganda in the ancient Near East and some account of the rationale of the actions of the powers it was designed to justify and promote. With these in mind we can the better turn to begin our examination of 'Propaganda in the Old Testament'.

CHAPTER TWO

Royal Propaganda in the Old Testament

It might seem as though the story of Israel begins in Genesis 12 when Abraham walks on to the scene. His appearance on the stage is a little abrupt: 'And Yahweh said to Abraham, "Leave your country, your own people and your father's household, for a country which I will show you."' But there has been a Prologue to the play in the first eleven chapters of the book. These chapters, sometimes described as 'the primeval history' bring together a number of different mythological and legendary motifs to describe the creation of the world, the story of the first human beings, the flood which came because of their increasing wickedness, and the descendants who came from Noah and his family who were miraculously preserved during the flood in the ark. It is shown how from these descendants all the (then) known nations of the earth sprang, including the line of Shem (the Semitic people), from whom eventually came Terah, the father of Abraham. The development of all these different nations brought complications, however. One result of the attempt to build the tower (ch. 11) was the division of languages, in a way symbolic of the rivalries and tensions which divide people of different nationalities. And so the stage scenery is set for the sudden entry of Abraham and God's call to him, a call which is backed up by a promise which, through him and his descendants, will prove to have ramifications for all the other divided nations of the world.

At this point I could take quite a long detour to explain (and justify) to the general reader certain things many scholars claim to have discovered about the Pentateuch (i.e. the first five books of the Old Testament). That is as nothing to the length of the detour I would have to take if I were to justify to other scholars the general approach to the biblical text on which I am basing my discussion in this chapter. So I propose to take a ruthless short-cut through what is a veritable scholarly minefield, and leave it to others to decide whether I make it safely to the other side or get blown up on the way.

What might be called the 'classical' scholarly consensus, developed over the last 150 years, is that the Pentateuch as we now have it is a combination, or a 'redaction' ('redactor' being a word for 'editor') of four written sources. These sources were identified by a combination of features, linguistic characteristics, use of vocabulary, stylistic peculiarities, theological views, supposed historical allusions, and so on. The fact that the text did not represent a continuous and unified piece of writing was evidenced partly by these differences, partly by the appearance of accounts of the same incidents in different versions, and by inner inconsistencies within the text. The net result was the hypothesis that we had a 'Yahwistic' source which was the first layer. It got its name from the belief it expressed that God was known by the name 'Yahweh' from the first (see Gen. 4.26). It is believed, because of its main interests and allusions, to have stemmed from the southern state of Judah and to have been composed (even if formed from various and earlier component parts) in the royal court during the time of the united monarchy, that is, in the time of the reigns of David and Solomon sometime during the 10th century BCE. Beginning in Genesis 15 and interwoven with the Yahwistic (or 'J' source, from the German form of the name Yahweh) there is another comparable source, labelled 'Elohistic' (E). This source, contrary to J, believed that in the early days God was known only by the name 'Elohim' and that the name 'Yahweh' was revealed first to Moses in the incident recorded in Exodus 3 (see especially v. 15). This source appeared to reflect more the viewpoint of the northern kingdom of Israel, and its profounder theological and ethical insights showed some prophetic influence. This was usually dated later therefore, in the 8th century BCE, the time when Amos and Hosea were active in the north. Deuteronomy (D) seemed to be a source all of its own, and the close parallels of its legal requirements with those enacted in the time of Josiah when a lawbook was 'found' in the Jerusalem temple leading to Josiah's religious reform (2 Kings 22.1—23.30) encouraged the belief that this lawbook was some form of Deuteronomy which must thus have been composed sometime in the 7th century BCE. Finally there was a source detected which is woven throughout the Pentateuch from its beginning in Genesis 1 to the end of the book of Numbers (some scholars believe it continues in the books of Joshua and

Judges). It comprises both narrative and legal material. The fact that the legal material is concerned mostly with matters of priesthood, sacrifice, temple matters, and cultic measures mainly designed to secure ritual 'holiness', led to its being called the 'Priestly Writing' and its viewpoint was believed to be that of priests in exile in Babylon, or even the post-exilic priesthood in Jerusalem. Thus it was dated in the 6th–5th centuries BCE. Some believed that it was this source, 'P', which formed the basis and framework of the final redaction of the Pentateuch as a whole, which was thus, in its present form, a post-exilic work.

That thumbnail sketch, it will surprise no one to learn, disguises a most complex and varied range of scholarly opinion. Even if these four 'sources' were admitted (and a large number have always doubted at least the separate existence of the 'Elohistic' source), how they came to be composed, how far each represented any kind of unity in itself, and how they all came to be put together and over what length of time, all of this was fiercely argued. Just when the broad outlines might seem to have been agreed, however, fires of new controversy have broken out. Even those who still work with the broad concept of four such strands in the Pentateuch have begun to debate anew their date, some putting the 'J' source, not in the time of the united monarchy, but in the Babylonian exile.[1] Some have dated it even later.[2] Others have rejected the whole approach.[3] Others have said that it is high time we studied the Pentateuch as a whole in its final form (however it achieved this).[4]

I am going to turn something of a Nelsonian blind eye to all this by saying, in common with a number of contemporary Old Testament scholars, that something of the various outlooks, style, and approach associated with the claimed four 'documentary sources' *are* to be detected in the present form of the Pentateuch and need to be explained. Most of us are content to remain agnostic about the exact process by which they came there, and are not unduly worried about whether we can identify any one 'source' down to the last half-verse. Whether there ever were four documents; whether, if so, each source ever existed as a continuous and consciously shaped whole; how far they themselves represent the accumulation of a great number of different oral and written traditions over a long period of time, an accumulation achieved only by a very complex process of growth; how far the Pentateuch itself has grown like a giant snowball by gathering more and more material to an original 'core' of traditions; all this may be left open for legitimate and continuing discussion. Nevertheless, when all is said and done, one can detect much material which represents something of the features and outlook claimed for the 'J' source (perhaps we can only speak of a 'JE' source) and this is observedly different in many respects from the so-called 'Priestly' material. One of the easiest tasks for students in text classes is to differentiate between the two in, say, the Flood story in Genesis 6—9.

This affects our matter in hand because, as I mentioned above, the 'J' source has traditionally been associated with the royal court in Jerusalem and is believed to have come from the time of, and even to justify, the united reign of the Davidic monarchy. If, in fact, it comes from the time of the Babylonian exile as J. van Seters has argued (see n.1), this will affect the argument. It could not then have had the justification of the reign of David and Solomon and their successors primarily in mind. However, many scholars have questioned the wholesale dating of J in the exilic period. (The existence of certain 'anachronisms' and later historical or topographical references is another matter. These can easily be explained by supposing that the material, like much in the biblical books and sources, was subject to constant editing, updating and reapplication in new circumstances. This is most clearly the case in the present text of the prophetic books, but it applies equally to the historical and other books.[5]) The difficulty of dating it in the time of the Babylonian exile is that, as we shall see, it sounds such confident and optimistic notes about the rightful possession of the land of Canaan by Israel and the gift to them by God of the monarchy. This is a point made recently by E. W. Nicholson in an article on the Pentateuch in the new Göttingen theological encyclopaedia, *Evangelisches Kirchenlexikon*, in which he says, 'In sharp contradiction to all the literature recognised as exilic, it [J] lacks any hint of the catastrophe of the exile' (p. 1119). When I once raised this point with van Seters in the discussion following a seminar, he replied that its optimism reflected the period of the prophet of Isaiah 40— 55 (since his name is unknown he is often referred to as 'Second Isaiah' to distinguish him from the prophet of chapters 1—39, 'Isaiah of Jerusalem'). Second Isaiah looks forward in glowing terms to the restoration of Israel after the exile in Babylon. It is this optimism, from a time late in the exile, which is shared by the Yahwist, according to van Seters. But that answer is unsatisfactory. For, while Second Isaiah does see the dawn of God's new day about to break, its radiance is all the brighter because it is viewed against the background of the exile. The experience of the exile and its causes loom large in these chapters, which are heavily influenced by it as an historical reality. It is extremely unlikely that, if the JE material came from the same time, the experience of exile itself could have left so little mark on the work.

However, we can afford a little of our general agnosticism about the nature and composition of the Pentateuch some rein here as well. It is the material which forms its contents which must speak for themselves, and in the light of that we must each form our opinion of what interests it may best be seen to be serving.

To return, then, from our detour, to the Prologue of the first eleven chapters of Genesis, we must see that they do far more than serve merely as a formal introduction so that we recognize Abraham when we meet him. They serve to set the story of Abraham, and therefore of Israel, whose ancestor he is seen to have been, in a universal setting. The J account begins with its version of the beginning of things in 2.4b. God formed man (the Hebrew is 'the *'ādām*', so that it is the creation of what we should call 'humankind' generally which is being described and God is said, in a play on words, to have formed him from the dust of the 'ground', *'ǎdāmah*) and then plants a garden for human beings to live in, filled, not only with the functional, the food-producing, but also the beautiful, trees and plants 'attractive to look at' as well as 'good to eat' (2.9). The writer does not intend us to try to identify the exact topography of this garden – that would be far too pedantic and literalist. It is 'in the East', and that is really quite enough. Genesis 2.10–14 might seem to identify a place, with its description of the four rivers, but only the Tigris and Euphrates are known. We must be careful about immediately labelling this garden as Paradise with echoes of Milton's *Paradise Lost* in our ears, even though the later Greek and Latin versions did call it that. All we can say is that it is a place of beauty, of harmony, of work certainly, but not of hardship. The name in Hebrew is associated with 'delight', 'happiness', and some have seen in the rivers an association with the concept of God's presence in Jerusalem, where it is described in terms of a cosmic river in Psalm 46.4 (Hb. v. 5).

There is a river there and its waters make the city of God rejoice

This is the psalm which celebrates God's presence in the city with the repeated refrain, 'Yahweh of hosts is with us' (vv. 7, 11,

Hb. 8, 12) and its bold assertion, 'God is in its midst' (v. 5, Hb. 6). Some even believe the phrase 'in the East', denoting the place of the rising sun, also has mythological overtones about the 'presence' of God in the garden.

But the idea of 'Eden' could be understood in some traditions as depicting an original blissful and ideal state of the world as God meant it to be, and this is shown by Ezekiel 36.35. After saying that God will intervene to rescue and redeem his people after the judgement of the exile upon them for their sin, it continues: 'And they will say, "This devastated land shall become like the garden of Eden." ' And, further, this will have repercussions for the other nations as well: 'And the nations which are left round about you shall know that I, Yahweh, have rebuilt what was torn down and have replanted what was devastated. I am Yahweh: I have spoken and I will achieve it.'

To such a view, then, God intends to restore the world to the ideal state of Eden, and he will achieve it by his restoration of Israel. Certainly the Yahwist shows that something goes wrong in Eden when Adam and Eve are tempted by the serpent and eat the fruit of the tree. And he shows through the rest of these early chapters the growing consequences of this act of *hubris*, by which human beings attempted to cross the boundaries of their humanity and usurp the realm of the divine. These consequences are increasingly disruptive of relationships, their effects being more and more widely felt like the ever-increasing shock waves of a nuclear chain reaction.

So, the people whom God created for friendship with himself hide from him in shame when he comes. The husband and wife, created for their mutual help and enjoyment (Gen. 2.18–24), begin to blame each other for what has happened (3.12f.). Pain, the burden of toil, stress between people, all follow (3.16–19). In the next chapter the first murder is recounted, when a man who felt no special responsibility or obligation for even a brother ('Is it my job to watch over my brother?' 4.9) lets his anger spill over into fratricide (4.8). The repercussions of that spread wider in the boast of Lamech that he has repaid a mere wounding blow with murder and, whatever the origin of the 'Song of Lamech', it is linked with the Cain and Abel incident by Lamech's boast,

> If Cain has been avenged seven times over
> Lamech has been avenged seventy-seven times. (4.24)

(This boast, incidentally, is almost certainly in the mind of the evangelist when he reports Peter's question to Jesus, 'Lord, how often am I to forgive my brother if he goes on wronging me? As many as seven times?' with the reply, 'I do not say seven times but seventy times seven' (Matt. 18.21f., REB). There is even some textual witness to that saying as being 'until seventy-seven times', which would make the words of Jesus a direct allusion to the Song of Lamech.) It is not without its irony (probably intentional, such is the sophistication of the Yahwistic author) that this example of still further human violence and even deeper disruption of human relationships occurs in the context of mankind's development in technology and culture, city-building, the achievements of the bronze and iron ages and the development of musical skills (4.17–22).

All that leads on to the story of the Flood in Genesis 6—9, a story in which both the Yahwistic and Priestly accounts are interwoven in a way they are not elsewhere, but in which each is easily distinguishable. It is introduced by the Yahwist with one of his rare 'theological' statements (normally he lets the story make the theological point: he is forerunner of the 'narrative theologians' in fact). 'And Yahweh saw how the wickedness of humankind ['ādām] had multiplied on the earth and that every purpose he formed in his heart was never anything but evil' (6.5). So came the flood which seemed all but to wipe out the creation which God had made. Yet God preserved Noah and his family and enough livestock to start again and promised that, thereafter, the regularity of the blessings of nature would remain for all people for all time (8.21f.). Not a great deal seemed to have changed, however. Even by the end of the chapter which completes the story of the flood, Noah, who began to dabble in viniculture, tasted a little too freely of its fruits and, while he was dead drunk, one of his sons saw his nakedness. We are already into a note of propaganda here. For, in the very convenient genealogy given in the story, Ham was the father of Canaan. What else could anyone expect of the *Canaanites*? And the incident provided a good opportunity for a round curse from the righteous Noah on all Canaanites, in the person of Ham, whom he condemns to permanent slave status to his brothers Shem and Japheth, Shem, of course, being the patronymic ancestor of the Semites. For, in contrast to Ham, Shem and Japheth put their drunken father to bed and covered him with all due decorum and seemliness (9.20–27).

The climax of this story of the grandiose overreaching of themselves by human beings with its consequent disruption of relationships, comes in the account of the Tower of Babel (11.1–9). Here they wish to build a tower whose top reaches the heavens. What is in mind is probably one of the ancient temple towers which consisted of a series of platforms connected by a stairway leading to the highest one on which a temple was erected. This was, therefore, the abode of the god. 'Shinar' is the archaic name for 'Babylon', which means, 'Gate of God', and so this is probably a somewhat contemptuous allusion to the religion of other peoples in the ancient Near East. In any event, the story is told with fine irony. This temple, whose top was to reach to the heavens, is such that Yahweh has to '*go down*' to take a look at it (v. 5). Their aim is to make sure that they are not 'scattered' all around the earth (presumably because of military defeat). Religion as a means of unifying (and so strengthening) a people was, as we have already seen, a powerful political tool in the hands of those who governed, something the Israelites themselves were to discover. The irony is, of course, that the result is the very 'scattering' they had aimed to avoid, the differences in languages symbolizing the divisions and tensions between different races. (This is another theme from the Old Testament taken up in the New Testament. Luke, in his account of the Day of Pentecost, says that, with the gift of the Spirit of God, people of all different nationalities suddenly found they could 'understand' each other (Acts 2.5–11)).

One aspect of their claim is not mentioned again in irony in the story itself. That is when they say 'Let us make a name for ourselves', which is really to say 'let us establish a reputation for ourselves', or 'let us cover ourselves in glory' (11.4). We shall see, however, that the Yahwist by no means forgets this. It is one of the vital links between his 'Prologue' and the beginning of the dramatic action when Abraham comes on to the scene.

So the Yahwist pictures this growing disruption of that which God had meant for his creation, a disruption with terrible consequences for all humankind. It is, in effect, a reversion to chaos from the order and purpose of creation. Of course, that is not all he shows. In spite of all that happens, God by no means abandons his creation. When Adam and Eve are ashamed of their nakedness after eating the fruit of the tree, God goes into the tailoring business and makes them clothes from animal skins (3.21). It is possible that even the barring of Eden to them is to be seen as an act of kindness rather than punishment, to protect them from the danger to which they have exposed themselves in the garden. Even after Cain has killed his brother, God spares his life and puts a protective mark on him (4.15). When the Flood comes, God spares Noah and his family together with enough animals to ensure the survival of his creation and makes a promise that all people will continue to know the benefits of his providence (a promise which occurs in two forms, 8.21f., J, and 9.8–17, P). And even the genealogies of chapters 10 and 11 tell the same story, of how God provides for the perpetuation of his purposes through Noah, from whose family come the Semites, i.e. through Shem, from among whose line comes Terah, the father of Abraham.

So the appearance of Abraham (the first form of whose name is Abram) comes in the course of God's purpose to rescue his creation from the disruptive chaos which has been threatening it and to restore it to its original 'paradisaical' condition. He calls this man and his family from the region where they have been living, promising him a 'land which I will show you' and that he will be the progenitor of a 'great nation'. The parallels with the promises to Aeneas are striking (see above, pp. 2f.). God will so bless Abraham and his descendants (which really means here that he will cause them to prosper) that their fame will become widespread. The Hebrew idiom for this is literally, 'I will make your name great' (12.2), which immediately recalls, as the Yahwist intends that it should, the vain ambition of the nations in building the tower of Babel, 'Let us make a name for ourselves' (11.4). God gives by grace to Abraham that which the nations strive in vain to achieve by their own effort. The story of the call of Abraham, of course, does immediately follow the story of the Tower of Babel (only the inserted genealogy breaking the direct sequence), and this connection is strengthened by the further promise to Abraham that there is a purpose for 'all the families of the earth' in his call, for those very 'families', indeed, which have been dispersed around the earth and separated from each other by the barrier of language (11.9).

But just what is this purpose? There are, perhaps unfortunately, two different ways of translating the Hebrew of 12.3b, both of which are quite legitimate. We can render it as 'In [or 'by'] you shall all the families of the earth be blessed,' or we can read it 'By you shall all the families of the earth bless themselves.' The form of the Hebrew verb used here (the *Niph'al*) can indicate either a passive or a reflexive sense. This ambiguity is reflected in the different translations offered by different versions of the English Bible. The old Authorized Version took it as a passive, a sense in which few more recent versions have understood it, an exception being the somewhat theologically conservative NIV, which has 'all peoples on earth will be blessed through you'. Otherwise, RSV uses the reflexive form, a sense also found in JB ('All the tribes of the earth shall bless themselves by you'), and implied by the NEB and REB, 'All the families on earth will pray ('will wish', NEB) to be blessed as you are blessed.'

Does it matter? It affects the sense quite markedly in fact. The earlier passive rendering suggests that God has a saving purpose for all nations whom he intends to reach through Abraham/Israel. That is the way it was understood by the AV, and it is not surprising that it is still the way it is taken among more theologically conservative Christians. It fits very well with the theological view that God revealed himself to Israel in such a way that a knowledge of him became available to other peoples as well. Israel was the instrument of divine revelation. Of course, this also suits Christian apologetic, since it tends to remove some of the 'scandal of particularity', to cite a phrase which has often been used when speaking of God choosing the Jewish people in particular, and to justify the New Testament claim that Christians are the true 'faith' descendants of Abraham (so Paul, for example, in Romans 4). We shall see that there *are* similar insights in the Old Testament itself among those who believe that Israel has been called, not for itself alone, but as a means of revelation to others. But a reflexive sense of the verb here offers somewhat different implications. At best it implies a subordinate role for other nations if, in fact, it implies any role for them at all. What it means is that God is going so to bless Abraham and his descendants that others will use him as a kind of 'measure' of blessing: 'May you/we know the same prosperity that Abraham has known.' The supremacy of Abraham/Israel in the matter of blessing is intended to invite something akin to envy among others who will be forced to acknowledge the superior status of Israel, and Israel's God, in the divine order of things. With such a reading, the issue of whether or not there is likely to be any chance of other nations sharing such blessing is not touched upon.

Is there any way of deciding between the two ways of translating Genesis 12.3? The same promise in some form is repeated three times in the Pentateuch – in Genesis 22.18 to Abraham, 26.4 to Isaac, and 28.14 to Jacob – and, for good measure, it is alluded to again in Jeremiah 4.2. Of the five instances where it is used, twice (Gen. 12.3, 28.14) the passive form of the verb is used, the *Niph'al*, which, as we have seen, can indicate either a passive or a reflexive meaning. But the other three times a form of the Hebrew verb is used which can indicate *only* the reflexive sense (the *Hithpa'el*). Perhaps thus the balance of probability tilts towards this being the way the saying is to be understood in each instance.

Another indication is offered by the opening of 12.3, however. God will either bless or curse other nations by the way they treat Abraham and his descendants. At the very least, therefore, the superior status and role of Israel is firmly maintained in this account of the call and promise to Abraham. God's answer to the division and chaos among the nations, described in chapters 1— 11, is to call Abraham/Israel out from among the nations, and make them into a great nation, inhabiting a land of his choice for them. Their superiority will bring its own kind of order to the earth. There will, later in the Old Testament, be those who challenge such a 'privileged' reading of divine choice, but the Yahwist is not among them. This is 'propaganda' explaining and justifying the special place of Israel in the divine order of things and their divine right to the land of Canaan.

The fluctuating fortunes of Abraham and his descendants in the patriarchal stories which follow (which we cannot and need not follow in detail here) remind us repeatedly of the fluctuating fortunes of Aeneas. Often, the divine purpose and the divine promises appear threatened, by the opposition of other powerful forces, by the weakness of the human instruments of the divine purpose, by the absence of a child through whom the promise can be continued, and so on. But always there is a miraculous intervention on hand, overcoming all obstacles and exceeding the weak faith of the protagonists. At strategic points of the story the promise is renewed in another 'covenant', or a 'prophecy' confirms the eventual fulfilment of the promises.

One such passage is to be found in Genesis 15.1–16. In his journeyings Abraham has come to the land of Canaan which he and his descendants have been promised, just as Aeneas came to the shores of Italy. Genesis 13.18 shows that he was near Hebron. Of course, he is as yet only a nomadic wanderer in this land, not yet its rightful owner. Further, he has no legitimate heir since his only child is one born, not of the ancestress, Sarah, but of a servant girl. Again God promises, however, in the face of Abraham's misgivings, that the promise will be fulfilled. He will have an heir through whom a nation as numerous as the stars of heaven will spring. Further, he has been brought on his journeyings because it is God's purpose to give him 'this land' (v. 7), i.e. the land of Canaan, to possess. Then, as evening falls and Abraham sleeps, God appears to him in a dream and speaks a 'prophecy' to him, 'foretelling' all the misfortunes which will befall his descendants, including their slavery in Egypt for 400 years. But he also foretells their exodus from that land in triumph, carrying the wealth of their oppressors. Four generations after Abraham's own death, his descendants will come back to the land. If Abraham (and the modern reader) wonders why it was necessary for all that waiting around when, after all, it is God who is arranging it all, it is because 'the sin of the Amorites is not yet complete'. The blood-curdling meaning of that is that the Amorites (i.e. the pre-Israelite occupants of the land) have not yet got to quite that pitch of evil which would justify God judging them by driving them out of the land before the Israelites.

Here, of course, is another instance of a *vaticinium ex eventu*, a prophecy after the event. And here is just the kind of political propaganda which we have encountered elsewhere in the ancient Near East. The land belongs to one racial group because it has been allotted to them by God, and, if that appears a bit rough on its previous owners, it is quite all right because they are so wicked that they *deserve* the fate which has befallen them.

To this point, it might be conceded that we are dealing with national propaganda, but can we justify treating it under a chapter headed *royal* propaganda? Here we must note that Genesis 15, in its present form, ends with a second 'prophecy' given to Abraham at night.[6] Again it concerns the promise of land to his descendants but this time some actual borders are mentioned: 'To your posterity I have given this land from the river of Egypt as far as the great river Euphrates,' and then follows a list of the nationalities who originally occupied such a wide expanse of territory: Kenites, Kenizzites, Kadmonites, Hittites, Perizzites, Rephaim, Amorites and Canaanites. In that list there is a large mixture of fancy as well as fact and a good dose of wishful thinking. But what is significant is that these are the very borders ascribed to Solomon's rule at the height of his fortunes: 'And Solomon exercised rule over all the kingdoms from the River [i.e. the Euphrates], to the land of the

Philistines, that is, as far as the border of Egypt, and they brought
tribute and served Solomon all the days of his life' (1 Kings 4.21,
Hb. 5.1). This is also very largely fancy, for Solomon's 'empire' (if
such it may be called) certainly did not extend as far nor did he receive tribute from as many nations, but the parallel between the
ideal boundary claimed in royal propaganda for Solomon and the
extent of land promised to Abraham in the 'prophecy' cannot be
coincidental.

But there are further indications that the stories about Abraham
have an element of royal ideology in them. Long ago R. E. Clements demonstrated a number of strong connections between the
stories of Abraham and David.[7] As with Abraham, David's
career was closely associated with Hebron. It was among the
cities which he sought to placate with gifts plundered from his
raiding parties (1 Sam. 30.26–31). Small wonder, then, that the
men of Judah came at Saul's death to anoint David king over
Judah at Hebron (2 Sam. 2.1–4). Seven years later, when it
became apparent that Saul's weak son and successor in Israel, Ishba'al, was no match for David, Abner and the men of Israel came
to Hebron to 'make a covenant' with David by which he would
reign as king over the whole nation, north and south (2 Sam. 5.1–
5). David, who had no blood descent from Saul, nevertheless dis-
played his usual sagacity in ensuring that Michal, Saul's daughter
to whom he had earlier been married, was restored to him, so that
he could claim descent at least by marriage (2 Sam. 3.12–16).
Thus, both Abraham and David are shown to have entered into
covenants which were regarded as vital to the emergence of the
nation state of Israel, both covenants being enacted at Hebron.
Further, as we shall see when we consider the covenant between
God and David, both the Abrahamic and Davidic covenants are
of what is often termed a *promissory* nature. They do not demand
the fulfilment of certain conditions by the recipients before the
promises of the covenant operate (as with, for example, the Sinai
covenant, which more or less stipulates '*If* you keep these conditions *then* I will be your God, etc.'). Further, the promise to Abraham that other nations would be affected by God's special blessing
of him and his descendants could be seen to have found partial fulfilment in the bringing of surrounding peoples under David's control. As was promised to the forefathers of ancient Rome, Israel
could be seen as the instrument of a divine rule and justice (*mos,
ius*) in the world. Taken together, then, with the near parallel of

the territory promised to Abraham and the idealistic account of the extent of the Davidic/Solomonic empire, it does seem as though the Abraham story has been presented in such a way as to 'foretell' and so to give divine sanction for, the Davidic monarchy. As Clements says, 'The Yahwist's purpose was to show the divine providence which brought into being the Davidic Kingdom, by which Israel became a nation, and took possession of the land of Canaan' (*Abraham and David*, p. 16).

Questions about the actual historicity of Abraham and the other patriarchs are therefore irrelevant. There may well have been such people, although we lack any of the precise and verifiable historical allusions by which we could date or place them. But the important thing about them is not who and exactly what kind of people they were *in history*. The important thing about them is the role they came to play in the later tradition of Israel and the way that tradition expressed, and even helped to shape, later Israelite self-understanding. A similar example might be seen in the person of King Arthur. There may indeed have been such a figure in history, but details about him which enable us to portray him *historically* are lacking. But that has not been his function in later use of the traditions about him. It is how he came to be shaped in those traditions, and how those traditions helped both to create and express the self-understanding of later generations, that are informative about Arthur. See what a people admires in its heroes from the past (or in the present, for that matter) and you will learn a great deal about them even if you are no wiser about the heroes. So we find various forms of the Arthurian traditions in Geoffrey of Monmouth, in Malory and – that prize source so often neglected by the English! – the Welsh *Mabinogion*.[8]

A further example of how the material in the patriarchal stories has been shaped to express and foster *later* Israel's self-understanding can be seen in the so-called 'Blessing of Jacob' in Genesis 49. Of course the idea that there was once a patriarch who actually had twelve sons whose names all corresponded to the later tribes of Israel has no historical foundation. The concept is, however, a valid testimony to the way at least some later Israelites expressed their belief that their unity had its origins in the purposes of God and was founded in the distant past. The material in Genesis 49 is of diverse origin, and the composition of the chapter is much debated, but all which need concern us here is that it includes an exaltation of Judah and thus forms some kind of royal propaganda in that it gives early patriarchal authority to the emergence of the Davidic monarchy from Judah:

> Judah, your brothers shall praise you,
> your hand will be on your enemies' neck;
> your father's sons shall prostrate themselves before you . . .
> the [royal] sceptre shall not depart from Judah,
> nor the [law-giver's] staff from between his feet
> until ———— comes;
> and the people's obedience is his by right. (49.8, 10)

The missing word makes the meaning of the line unintelligible to us as it stands, reading 'until Shiloh comes'. If it is not some obscure reference to the old sanctuary of Shiloh, then the word needs emendation, and there has been no shortage of scholarly suggestions! They may safely be left to the commentaries, however, since enough of the 'blessing' is clear to assure us that it is another *vaticinium ex eventu*. The sovereignty of the royal line which comes from the tribe of Judah has patriarchal, and therefore divine, sanction. For good measure the material usually assigned to 'J' has one more such prophecy, to be found in Numbers 24.17–19. The speaker of this is Balaam, who 'foretells' that,

> A star shall march out from Jacob,
> a sceptre shall rise from Israel;
> it shall crush the heads of Moab
> and the skulls of the Sethites.

Again the sense is clear, although the words rendered here as 'heads' and 'skulls' are unusual and require some emendation to make sense. The important point is that it bodes no good for these surrounding peoples, who will be dealt crippling blows by a ruler who comes from the tribe of Judah. It is no great surprise to read in 2 Samuel 8.2 that this is exactly what David did: 'And David smote Moab and measured them with a rope, making them lie down on the ground. He measured two ropes of those to be killed and one rope of those to be kept alive. So the Moabites became David's subjects and paid him tribute.' Had not such action been justified by the divine word of 'prophecy', allegedly spoken long before by Balaam?

These, then, are some of the 'royal propaganda' elements in the traditional material in the Pentateuch, generally referred to as the Yahwistic tradition. But royal propaganda is to be found not only there, but, naturally enough, in the history books of the Old Testament, especially in the books of Samuel and Kings. There is general agreement among scholars that these books utilize a number of early, written sources, much of which must have emanated from the royal court, where it was traditional and customary in the ancient Near East to keep 'official' records, although there would also be much material of interest to temple personnel which had to do with the religious life of the nation. These two interests were so closely interwoven in a 'theocracy' that it is often difficult (and pointless) to try to separate them. In the present form of the history books, however, all such disparate and varied 'source material' has been woven together and presented and edited in such a way as to bring out the particular theological interests and concerns of those who are often referred to as 'the Deuteronomists'. They are called this because their language, style and theology are so close to those found in the Book of Deuteronomy that both that book and the history books appear to have come from similar circles. As we saw above (p. 23), Deuteronomy has often been dated in the 7th century and is believed to have exercised influence on the Josianic reform of 621 BCE (or, at least, on the account of that reform we have in 2 Kings 22f.). Some scholars believe that a first form of the Deuteronomistic edition of the history books originated in the reign of Josiah, while a second edition was made during the Babylonian exile explaining just why it was the disaster struck.[9] Others have believed that the whole of Deuteronomy—2 Kings is the result of a single editor's work in the time of the Babylonian exile.[10] Still others have found several editorial layers in the work, but these are not those of Cross and Nelson. They believe that the basic text was formed during the time of the exile and that subsequently this was expanded by both prophetic and priestly sources.[11] A complete and final decision on all such matters is not necessary for our purposes here. We shall need to examine the work of the 'Deuteronomists' when we come to consider various forms of 'subversion' of the royal and priestly propaganda, but for now, our task is with the earlier source material. Even here, scholars are by no means united in the 'sources' they claim to find there, but it is often felt that much of the material in 1 Samuel 16.14—2 Samuel 5.10 forms a coherent story of 'David's rise to power'. Others have claimed that 2 Samuel 9—20 together with 1 Kings 1—2 form a united source which has been called 'The Succession Narrative' since its main interest is in how and why Solomon came to succeed his father David. As with our examination of the so-called 'Yahwist' in the Pentateuch, it is by no means necessary for us to be able to identify a clear 'source' with exact verse numbers to be able to see some of the things which are going on in the biblical text. The contents tend to speak for themselves and decisions about whose interests they serve and represent can be debated when we have examined them. Nor can we by any means be sure just how far even the earliest source material is historically reliable. There are indications of 'interpretation' of history from particular points of view from the first, and there is little external material by which we can verify them. Again, all we can do is observe what is there and try as far as we can to see 'who is saying what to whom'.

The first thing to notice is that our text is markedly 'anti-Saul' and 'pro-David'. One is forcibly reminded of the apology of Hattushilish III (see above, pp. 11–13), who is able to represent all he does in a favourable light, acting as he does under the favour and within the purpose of the goddess Ishtar, and to paint the nephew whom he supplanted on the throne in the worst possible guise. It is difficult to know exactly how the 'kingship' to which Saul was appointed was understood. There are conflicting accounts of how he came to be made king. In 1 Samuel 8, the people come to Samuel and demand a king, much to Samuel's displeasure. In 1 Samuel 9.1—10.1, Samuel, the prophet, is directed by God to anoint Saul, who turns up at his house asking for an oracle to guide him to his father's lost sheep. In 1 Samuel 10.17–25, Saul is chosen by lot at an assembly of the Israelites convened by Samuel. In 1 Samuel 11, Saul is designated because of his military prowess against the threat of the Ammonites and is 'made king' at Gilgal (v. 15). Not only do the accounts vary in detail but they differ profoundly in outlook. In 1 Samuel 9, monarchy is God's idea which he reveals to his prophet as his chosen means of delivering his people. But in 1 Samuel 8 and 10, the choice of a king is represented as rebellion against God's direct rule over his people, and Samuel is instructed to warn the people of the tyrannical nature of the centralized power to which they are subjecting themselves. Probably the actual events were not recorded in official detail and became blurred in people's memories. As we shall see, monarchy evoked strongly differing reactions in Israel, and the different accounts represent some of these different views. There is no

indication that the people were consciously initiating a continuing, dynastic monarchic line when they appointed Saul. He probably differed little from the 'judges' of whom we read in the book of
Judges, who were apparently chosen for their charismatic gifts.
Saul was probably chosen by a number of tribes since they all
faced increasing military pressure from other peoples trying to
enter the land, and, in particular, from the Philistines, who were
settling in the south-western coastal strip, and he showed considerable military skill in staving off those threats for some time. There
is no indication of any large 'court' or settled 'palace'. But those
who are elected for charismatic gifts of leadership may be in
danger when those gifts begin to fail – or have no chance of success
against increasing power from outside, and such seems to have
been Saul's fate. Finally he was defeated by the Philistines at
Mount Gilboa (1 Sam. 31.1–10). It is nice to know that at least
the people of Jabesh-Gilead, whom Saul delivered from the cruel
threat of the Ammonites (1 Sam. 11), remembered him with grat-
itude (1 Sam. 31.11–13).

However, Saul's failure, probably inevitable as it was, is shown
in our records to be due to his increasing moroseness (described as
an 'evil spirit from Yahweh' which came because Yahweh's spirit
had left him, 1 Sam. 16.14), and his disobedience to the word of
God as it came through the prophet Samuel (two instances are
given for good measure: his failure to wait for Samuel to come to
conduct the sacrifices (1 Sam. 13.8–14), although it was quite
common for kings to do this, as, for example, Jeroboam was later
to do (1 Kings 12.33); and his failure to carry out the divinely ordered total extermination of the Amalekites (1 Sam. 15.1–33)).
Because of this, God rejected Saul as king (1 Sam. 13.13f.; 15.11;
16.1). One might think that this raised questions about God as
judge of character but, of course, such passages are there, not to
raise or answer such awkward theological questions but to justify
the switch of monarchy from Saul to David, who is pictured as the
one really worthy of God's choice.

David is portrayed as an increasing threat to Saul. Indeed, his
relentless and calculated hunt for the throne makes some campaigns for the re-election of the President in recent American history look like Sunday School tea parties. There are fanciful stories
of his introduction to the scene of power. One story tells of his musical abilities which leads to his being brought to court to cheer up the
melancholy Saul (1 Sam. 16.14–23). This worked so well and Saul

was so pleased with his repertoire that he 'loved him' and made him his armour-bearer. Yet, in the next chapter, which tells the story of the young David's acting as champion against Goliath, Saul has never heard of him and David has to be presented to him (17.31–9). Even this marvellous *Boys' Own Paper* story, of the youth taking on the mighty giant while all the rest of the professional army look on helplessly, is highly suspect. Elsewhere the feat is credited to someone else, one Elhanan (2 Sam. 21.19). David was not the first, and would not be the last leader whose early career was embellished in the light of subsequent glory.

In fact he appears to have been the leader of a gang of mercenaries who acted very much in their own interests. He took service under the Philistines but two-timed them by carefully larding the way to popular support in Judah with the strategic distribution of his booty; in other words, by generous bribes. Of course, as we read, our sympathies are enlisted on David's side, for the Philistines are presented as sinful people who have no place in the land God has intended for Israel. Even when David and his gang carry out the first recorded 'protection racket', our theological sympathies are firmly enlisted on his side. Of course, such action was not surprising in the context of the time, but David gets Nabal's wife, Abigail, to give him the 'protection' money refused by Nabal ('a churlish and ill-behaved man' (RSV), but then, what could you expect, 'he was a Calebite' (1 Sam. 25.3)). Abigail's tearful attempt to gain her husband's life by trying to buy David off behind his back is portrayed as the work of Yahweh. But so too is the death of Nabal, because '*Yahweh* smote Nabal and he died' (1 Sam. 25.38), which leaves David free to take the good-looking Abigail off with him (v. 42). Nabal's death occurred a satisfactory ten days after his wife's negotiations with David (v. 38). It is amazing how all who stood in David's way got conveniently bumped off, although David was never around himself at the time.

There is no doubt that David was a supremely able military leader and one who could fire great devotion and utter loyalty among his followers. No doubt he was also a very shrewd man. He secured marriage to Saul's daughter, Michal, which would give him some semblance of legitimacy as Saul's successor. It is true Saul allowed this because he thought it would lead to David's downfall since he demanded the death of a hundred Philistines as the price for the marriage bargain. But when it came to craftiness and a show of strength Saul was not in the same league as David who easily outsmarted him (1 Sam. 18.20–29). Further, as we have seen, he carefully prepared the way for securing the loyalty of the Judean leaders by his gifts to them. But, also, he proved himself in action the obvious alternative to Saul, so that when Saul was defeated in battle and things looked black indeed, it was to David that the Judeans turned. As we have seen, they made him king at Hebron (2 Sam. 2.1–4) and he ruled there in Judah for seven years continuing his successful military campaigns the while.

Strangely enough the northern kingdom of Israel acted on the 'dynastic' principle in choosing Saul's rather weak and ineffectual son, Ishba'al, as their king under the direction of Abner, Saul's commander-in-chief (2 Sam. 2.8–10). It did not take very long, however, before military men saw that Ishba'al was no match for David, and Abner offered secretly a deal with David by which he would become king over all Israel, north and south. This was accepted, although, conveniently for David, such a powerful man as Abner was killed by Joab, David's own 'C-in-C'. Of course David was not there at the time and knew nothing about it, but Joab does not seem to have been disciplined too severely, David contenting himself with a vague wish that *God* would do something about judging Joab and his descendants. Ishba'al was obviously in the way and was murdered in his sleep. David washed his hands of the incident in the blood of those who perpetrated it, but there was no doubt that Ishba'al's very convenient death opened the way for all the people of the northern kingdom of Israel to come to make a covenant with David at Hebron so that David became king over the whole nation. With consummate diplomatic as well as military skill David captured the Jebusite stronghold of Jerusalem, a city which had belonged neither to Judah nor to Israel, and made this his capital from which to rule the whole realm. By bringing up the Ark of the Covenant to the city he was able to provide a religious focus of Yahwism in Jerusalem for all his subjects, a process which was carried further by Solomon when he built the temple in Jerusalem to house the Ark and so become the centre for the whole national Yahweh cult.

In an article on the nature and function of the giant towers Jochin and Boaz which were features of the temple in Jerusalem which Solomon built, Carol Meyers showed how such towers formed an architectural feature common to temples throughout the ancient Near East.[12] Inscriptions and iconography on them showed that they marked the entrance to the temple chosen as his dwelling by the god to whom the temple was dedicated. But, as we have seen, they thus also legitimized the rule the kings of that city exercised in his name. She summarizes:

> In building a temple for the ark, the symbol of Yahweh's presence, Solomon incorporated the Davidic covenantal traditions into a structure representing the permanent dwelling of Yahweh and thus the permanent and eternal legitimacy of his dynastic power.

This was the effect of the temple which Solomon built, but he was, metaphorically at least, building on the foundation laid by David. For David's triumph was to base his rule on the will of Yahweh, to bring religion in to buttress the legitimacy of his position. In the story of his rise to power there is nothing which is out of the way for the politics of his time. It would be quite wrong to judge his measures and actions by the ethics and susceptibilities of a later time (although one wonders whether even in contemporary politics we have become all that much more sensitive). What has to be seen, however, is the way that this rise to power is presented as the working out of the will of God who has chosen him and who is on his side throughout. The history as we have it is political propaganda of exactly the type to be encountered throughout the ancient Near East. Opponents are always evil and so have incurred the judgement of God. All successes of the victorious candidate are evidence of the favour and power of the god. People are to be subject to his authority as they would be to God. Religion becomes the ally and tool of the state. All that Peter Berger had to say about the sociology of 'state religion' finds vindication here.[13]

Nowhere is this more brilliantly demonstrated than in the tradition that God had made a special covenant, not only with David, but with all his successors. Its classic expression is to be found in 2 Samuel 7. The occasion is David's intention to build a temple ('house') for Yahweh. Nathan, the court prophet, brings an answering oracle from God, an oracle which one commentator has described as 'the title deed of the Davidic house to the rule of Israel and Judah'.[14] David is not to build a temple since Yahweh is not a deity who can be localized in one place. This failure of David to build a temple was obviously a bit of a problem for later generations. The 'Deuteronomistic Historian' suggests that David was too busy fighting wars to get it done (1 Kings 5.3). The Chronicler suggests that it was because the wars David had fought had made him ritually unclean for building the temple (1 Chron. 22.8). However, Yahweh intends to build David a 'house', says the oracle. His sons will succeed him and God will not remove his favour towards David and his line as he did from Saul. Even if David's son sins (verses 12–15 seem to refer to Solomon particularly, so that perhaps they are a 'Solomonic insertion between vv. 11 and 16 which follow on from each other quite naturally'[15]), he will be punished, but God will not remove his covenant loyalty from him. So the result is that 'your house and your kingdom will be supported before you [many versions read 'before me'] for ever: your throne shall be founded for ever' (v. 16).

So God has chosen not only David, but David's line 'for ever', and the covenant (like that with Abraham) is an unconditional one. The significance of this is not only that royal power has the sanction of divine approval, in the way of states everywhere in the ancient Near East, but, once it is granted that a certain line has permanent *dynastic* rights, much more power is centralized in the king of the day. If each new ruler is approved by popular choice on some evidence of 'charismatic gifts' (as Saul, and even David, were), then much more power remains in the hands of the people and their representatives. But if a royal line enjoys continuing divine authority, then power is much more centralized in its hands. As we shall see, this was fully recognized by whoever wrote the 'anti-monarchic' account of the founding of the monarchy in 1 Samuel 8.1–22 and also by the representatives of the northern kingdom of Israel when they rejected the rule of Solomon's son and successor, Rehoboam, because he refused to rule on their terms (1 Kings 12.1–20).

At this point a very reasonable question arises. Can the material in the Old Testament history books really be classed as 'royal propaganda' when they do not seem to have made all that good a job of it? This particularly applies to what is often regarded as another major source, the so-called 'Succession Narrative', the name given to the material to be found in 2 Samuel 9—20 together with 1 Kings 1 and 2. The source was first identified and named as such by L. Rost in 1926.[16] But, if the aim of this was to justify Solomon's succession to the throne after his father David, it does not seem to have achieved it, at least with a number of modern scholars. They even disagree about whether it is pro- or anti-Solomon! Certainly, it contains some details highly damaging to the reputation of both David and Solomon. It tells, for example, of David's adultery with

Bathsheba and his disgraceful action in arranging to have her husband killed in action (2 Sam. 11). Further, it narrates how a second child born of what began as an adulterous liaison was Solomon. Solomon was not David's oldest surviving son. Even after the unsuccessful rebellion of Absalom there was still Adonijah, who had prior claim. Solomon came to the throne, partly because of the dangerous weakness and irresolution of the ageing David, and partly because of shameless intrigue and in-fighting of the party consisting of Bathsheba, the priest Zadok, the prophet Nathan and Benaiah, the army commander. They outwitted and out-manoeuvred the party of Adonijah led by Joab, the general, and Abiathar, the priest (1 Kings 1—2). It is noteworthy that the sources are entirely silent about any ceremony by which the people conferred their approval on Solomon by making a covenant with him as, to be fair, had happened with David when 'all the elders of Israel came to the king at Hebron; and king David made a covenant with them at Hebron before Yahweh, and they anointed David as king over Israel' (2 Sam. 5.3). Further, the records are frank that, once on the throne, Solomon carried out a series of purges on his political enemies, Benaiah murdering Adonijah (an uncomfortable older brother to have had around for a successor who had no legal right to the throne), Joab (not unexpectedly since he was the military ringleader of the Adonijah faction) and, for good measure, Shimei, who had opposed David earlier (2 Sam. 16.5–14, an opposition to which, at the time, David has apparently responded with model patience and forbearance, but which apparently rankled, for, on his deathbed, he reminds his son to deal with Shimei). On the other hand, in the manner of the time, those who had 'backed the right horse' got their pay-out, Benaiah becoming commander-in-chief of the army and Zadok high priest in place of Abiathar. So began the long and uninterrupted ascent to supremacy of the Zadokite priests in Jerusalem.

It is small wonder, then, that (apart from questioning whether there ever was such a self-contained unit as Rost's 'Succession Narrative' and also whether it had any particular political purpose) scholars have disagreed about the aim and effect of this work. Some have said that there must have been an 'anti-Solomonic' editing of a work which was originally favourable to him. The details of such careful investigation of the text need not detain us here for we have seen enough to observe that it sends out somewhat mixed signals.

In response to the question as to whether such a 'mixed' portrait can be regarded as royal propaganda there are, however, one or two general points which may fairly be made. The first is that the historical books, as we now have them, have been edited finally during the time of the Babylonian exile by those whom we have seen are often referred to as the Deuteronomistic editors. By that time, the institution of monarchy had been seen to have failed. They had to deal with a theological problem. How could the Davidic line have come to so miserable an end when it had been founded on the unconditional promise of God as stated in the Nathan oracle, 'your throne shall be founded for ever' (2 Sam. 7.16)? We shall see that they have offered their own, to some extent subversive, account of the history of the monarchy.

But we must also remember that, in the propaganda literature of the ancient Near East which we considered, the faults and mistakes of a king *could* be admitted, as we saw in the 'Instruction for Merikare' (see above, pp. 17f.). Error admitted, its lessons learned in humility, and the resulting 'wisdom' passed on in moral instruction to others could also be a part of royal propaganda. So David is challenged in memorable terms by Nathan over his sin in the matter of Bathsheba and her husband Uriah the Hittite. But he responds in penitence, as a model of Yahwistic piety should: 'I have sinned against Yahweh' (2 Sam. 12.13). By submitting so obediently to the word of God spoken through the prophet, David shows himself worthy of the purpose God has for him. He is judged by the death of the son, it is true, but absolution is pronounced immediately, 'Yahweh has made your sin pass away: you shall not die.'

And this opens up yet another line of the royal propaganda. In the face of all obstacles, including that of the unworthiness of the human instruments, the grace and purpose of God are not thwarted but continue triumphantly through the line of those chosen by the divine will. So, from the union between David and Bathsheba, comes the birth of Solomon. And, above all, everything can be portrayed as being in accordance with the will of God, however dubious its morality and however much it appears to have been the result of purely human emotions and motives. So our records make it clear that Solomon was especially loved by Yahweh. They had it on the authority of a prophet, Nathan, and the baby was called Jedidiah (= 'loved by Yahweh') on the strength of it (2 Sam. 12.24f.). So, when Nathan suggests to

Bathsheba that she 'reminds' the aged David of his promise that Solomon should succeed to the throne (1 Kings 1.13, 17), they may not be completely fabricating it, even although there is no earlier record of such a promise. Certainly the record of 1 Kings 1 has David allowing that he *had* held out such a promise (v. 30). By contrast, when Adonijah begins to think of his succeeding David, as assuredly he had every right to, he is described as 'lifting himself up' (1.5, variously rendered as 'exalted himself', RSV, 'boasting', REB, 'was ambitious', JB, 'put himself forward', NIV). It is reported as a sinful presumption on the part of one who had no divine right to the throne. And propaganda of all times, as we have seen from the Middle-Eastern parallels, makes the case for X by rubbishing the character and motives of Y. Whitelam ('The Defence of David', see n. 13) cites the words of Jonathan Swift, no mean propagandist in the service of the Tories of his day: 'In all contests the safest way is to put those we dispute with as much *in the wrong as we can*' (*Journal to Stella*, pp. 54f. Politicians of all parties in our own day have certainly mastered that lesson.)

The account of Solomon's reign need not detain us long for it is full of the fancy of propaganda. The legend of his piously asking God for 'wisdom', the kind of astute arbitration in the matter of two prostitutes both claiming parentage of a child, the account of his wealth, the splendour and extent of his empire, his literary gifts, the international reputation he built for himself, all these are of the stuff of ancient Near-Eastern royal court literature. He is fortunate in having had the first real court in Israel and so the first official team of 'PR' scribes. What he did do, which was to have the most profound effects, was to have the temple built. But we have seen enough to know that this was not mere disinterested piety. The existence of a royal temple in the royal capital was a sign of the presence and favour of the god who had approved and given sanction to the rule of the king and his dynasty. It was the subjection of the deity to the service of the royal house and the nation-state in which all power and authority were now vested at the centre. It is no wonder the objection had been raised when David apparently suggested building a temple that Yahweh 'has not lived in a house since the day when I brought the people of Israel up from Egypt, but I have been moving about in a tent for my dwelling' (2 Sam. 7.6). In fact, apart from this, the records unconsciously reveal that Solomon showed remarkably little wisdom. Without his father's military abilities and yet with a

taste for luxury and splendour he engaged in a building programme and maintained a court which not only stretched the
dwindling resources of his kingdom to the limit and beyond, but
involved the mobilizing of forced labour, a practice which proved
highly unpopular. It was his high-handed, expensive and author-
itarian regime which led directly to the break-up of the two kingdoms, when, after his death, the people of the north came to his
son and successor, Rehoboam, and demanded the kind of agreement and 'consensus rule' which tradition assigned to David (1
Kings 12). Rehoboam had learned enough from his father to de-
termine to show them who was the master in the kingdom, and
this led to the north's secession and the founding of the new kingdom of Israel under Jeroboam.

It was in the south, however, that the greatest flowering of propaganda developed, and, unsurprisingly, it flowered in the liturgy
of the 'royal' temple in Jerusalem. Here the psalms which hail the
Davidic king and his relationship with Yahweh are among the
clearest forms of its expression and, while they do not address the
king, but God, they are the closest propaganda approaches in the
Old Testament to the hymns of praise sung to the kings in Egypt
and elsewhere.

So the king has been 'chosen' by God and 'adopted' by him as
his son, and he is the agent appointed by Yahweh to bring the kind
of unity among powerful and rebellious nations envisaged by the
promise to Abraham in Genesis 12.1–3.

> 'I have installed my king on Zion, my holy mountain;'
> I will recount the statute of Yahweh,
> he said to me, 'You are my son;
> today I have given you birth.
> Ask me and I will give the nations for your inheritance,
> and the limits of the earth as your possession.
> You will break them with an iron sceptre,
> like a potter's vase you shall smash them.' (Ps. 2.6–9)

The king, by virtue of his office, assumes a priestly role in the worship of Yahweh:

> Oracle of Yahweh to my lord:
> 'Sit at my right hand,
> until I make your enemies

47

a stool for your feet.' ...
Yahweh has sworn, he will not change his mind,
'You are an eternal priest,
in the same way as Melchizedek.' (Ps. 110.1, 4)

The same role of the king in subduing all his (and therefore Yahweh's) enemies, thus bringing about peace on earth under the rule of Yahweh and his anointed king, is seen here. Melchizedek is something of a shadowy figure in the Old Testament. Tradition shows him emerging from Jerusalem as 'priest-king' to bless Abraham (Gen. 14.17–20). The name suggests some kind of association with the Zadokite priesthood which came to the fore in Solomon's day. But, it is clear, the king himself is vested with priestly status and function.

Further, the psalms show that it is through the Davidic king that God's purpose, to restore the 'paradisaical' conditions described in the Yahwistic strand of the Pentateuch, is to be fulfilled, again by the defeat of the enemies who threaten that peace and prosperity.

O God, give the king your right judgement
and your righteousness to the royal son.
Then he will judge your people rightly
and give fair judgement to your poor.
The mountains will bring prosperity to your people,
and the hills righteousness.
He will judge fairly the poor of the people,
he will deliver all who are in need
and tread down the oppressor ...
He will act like rain on mown grass
like showers falling gently on the land ...
He will have dominion from sea to sea,
from the River to the ends of the earth.
Before him his enemies will bow low,
and his foes bite the dust.
The kings of Tarshish and the islands
will bring tribute.
The kings of Sheba and of Seba will bring him gifts ...
There will be an abundance of corn in the land
on the mountain peaks it will wave in the wind.
His fruits shall flourish like Lebanon;
city dwellers too like the produce of the land.

His name shall last for ever,
his reputation shall rival the sun's. (Ps. 72.1–4, 6, 8–10, 16f.)[17]

So the king is the intermediary, the channel, through whom all God's purposes of blessing are brought to fulfilment both for his own people and, by their submission to the Israelite king in Jerusalem as God's representative on earth, all other nations. Peace and order are to be fulfilled on earth in a unity between all peoples, based on Israel's supremacy. We are in exactly the same world as that described by Mariano Liverani in the ideology of the Assyrian imperial powers (see above pp. 18–21).

We are in the same world as other Near-Eastern powers also in the concept of the city and temple which the god has chosen for his dwelling, which thus becomes the centre of the world and in which the rule of the priest-kings who rule in his name is validated.

> There is a river whose streams make the city of God glad,
> the holy dwelling of the most High.
> God is in her midst,
> she shall not be moved.
> God will come to her aid
> at the first light of the morning.
> The nations rage
> the kingdoms shake:
> God utters his voice
> and the earth melts away.
> Yahweh of hosts is with us;
> our secure fastness is the God of Jacob. (Ps. 46.4–7, Hb. 5–8)

Finally, lest there should be any possible doubt, the utter immutability of the covenant between God and the Davidic dynasty, promised and given divine sanction in the Nathan oracle, was reaffirmed constantly in the temple liturgy in terms which could hardly be more absolute:

> 'Once I swore by my own holiness,
> I would never lie to David;
> his dynasty shall last for ever,
> his throne shall be like the sun in my presence;
> Like the moon he shall be established eternally,
> as sure as such a witness in the skies.' (Ps. 89.35–7, Hb. 36–8)

Such, then, is the nature of royal propaganda to be found in the Old Testament. As we have seen, we are very much in the world, samples of whose propaganda literature we surveyed in the first chapter. There can be no doubt that in Israel, as in other countries of the ancient Near East, the monarchy did confer some very great advantages on its people, advantages none the less real for there being always a flip side to the institution. It also brought some tyranny, injustice and oppression. Nevertheless, it may well be doubted if Israel as a self-conscious and identifiable people would have survived without it. It would probably have become fragmented, with the fragments absorbed into one empire and another. By the time it had run its course, a foundation had been laid on which a new understanding of what it meant to be a people of the God, Yahweh, could arise, an understanding which was to ensure the continuation of an identity which survived defeat, exile and dispersal, survived the Babylonian, Persian and Greek empires, and has survived many another empire and historical vicissitude since.

All the while monarchy could be seen to 'deliver the goods' its continuity was probably assured. But when all the political and religious hopes it aroused, expressed in its own propaganda and the worship of its own state temple, faced the terrible anti-climax of defeat and disaster, then its claims were bound to be re-examined.

Even before that, however, the monarchy in Judah and Israel faced challenges. And these came from the very religion it had sought to tame for its own purposes. As we said in chapter 1 (see above, pp. 4f.), religion is a dangerous force, a genie which often refuses to remain corked up in the bottle we have made for it, intending it to pop out only when we want to summon it to serve our own purposes. It has a power and life of its own to rise up disconcertingly to challenge, to rebuke, to threaten. In other words, it can also unleash elements subversive of the *status quo* of the political and even religious establishment. And nowhere and among no other people in the ancient Near East whose records have survived, did it do so more powerfully and with longer-ranging effects than among the Israelites, who have left us the record of such subversion in their sacred scriptures, our Old Testament.

CHAPTER THREE

Priestly Propaganda in the Old Testament

Eventually the royal nation states, first of the northern kingdom of Israel, and then of Judah, were blown away by the march of the Assyrian and Babylonian armies. At least from the time of Josiah it is probable that Judah had once more brought large areas of the former kingdom of Israel into the one realm, to that extent united for the first time since its division after the death of Solomon. But, for all the hopes obviously associated with the rule of Josiah, a rule marked by the centralizing of political power by means of religious reforms which strengthened the position of the king and temple in Jerusalem, the end was not far away. Josiah's reforms are dated in 2 Kings 22f. in the year 621 BCE. In 609 BCE he was killed in battle with the Egyptians at Megiddo and Judah passed for a brief four-year span under Egyptian control, when the Egyptians put their own puppet-king, Jehoiakim, on the throne in Jerusalem. But very soon the shadow of Babylonia was falling across this part of the Near-Eastern stage. In 605 BCE Nebuchadnezzar defeated the Egyptians at Carchemish and Jehoiakim became subject to him. Later Jehoiakim rebelled, provoking another Babylonian incursion before which Jehoiakim died, probably assassinated by some who saw his aim of independence as not only ridiculous but highly dangerous. In 597 BCE Jerusalem surrendered to Nebuchadnezzar, and Jehoiakim's successor, Jehoiachin, together with many leaders of the Judean community, was taken away into exile. In the time of Zedekiah, who was left on the throne in the Judean capital, there were further attempts at rebellion which culminated in yet another Babylonian invasion, when, after a three-year siege, Jerusalem finally fell in 586 BCE. Reprisals on the ringleaders were swift and horrific, in the manner of those days, and Jerusalem itself was fired and razed to the ground with yet more of its citizens deported.[1]

This was the end of the nation state of Judah and of the Davidic dynastic line. Apart from a brief spell under the Hasmoneans in the second half of the 2nd and first half of the 1st centuries BCE, Judah would never again be independent, but would form part of larger empires, in turn the Babylonian, the Persian, the Greek and the Roman. Of course, life in Jerusalem and Judah continued. Many people were left in Judah (although obviously the city and its immediate environs were only sparsely populated). Over time many returned, and there was a renewal of prophetic activity, especially with the ministries of Haggai and Zechariah (around 520 BCE). The temple was rebuilt, cultic activity was restored and the Persians, who absorbed the Babylonian empire into their own when Babylon fell in 539 BCE, seem to have had a policy of encouraging the religions of their subject peoples.

But major questions had now to be answered. Since Yahwism before the exile had been so much the official religion of the Davidic nation state, how was it to be defined and understood now? What did it mean to be 'the people of Yahweh' now it could no longer be explained in political terms? What had happened to the promises of God once made to Abraham and the fathers, and what of the assurance of the 'immutability' of the covenant with David that his line should last 'for ever'? A major theological redefinition was needed if Yahwism was to survive the trauma associated with the exile and the collapse of the state. And it seems to be just one such attempt at redefinition which is attempted in what is often referred to as the 'Priestly' strand of the Pentateuch ('P', see above, pp. 23f.). Of course we do not know just who these 'Priestly writers' were. Their interest in the sanctuary, in sacrifice and all matters of worship, in the importance of ritual 'holiness', in the nature and status of the priesthood, and their total silence on the question of monarchy, has led scholars to infer that they were 'priests', either those exiled to Babylon, or those serving back in the rebuilt temple after the exile. Quite probably the 'Priestly writing' represents the continuing work of both groups. But other officials of what has been termed a 'Bürger-Tempel-Gemeinde'[2] could well have been involved.

Their work must be classed as 'propaganda' in the interests of a community in which, alongside the leadership of a civil governor, the temple priesthood played a major and significant role. Yet, at the same time, it represents a bold and theologically creative attempt to renew Yahwism as a living religion after all its major institutions had collapsed.

Our best method of approach is to see what this tradition has to say in the Pentateuch and then to stand back and ask just what is going on here in religious and sociological terms. We must ask what were the strengths of this 'Priestly' construction and to what extent, just like the monarchy before it, it may have been open to abuses of power.

The Priestly strand of the Pentateuch opens with its account of creation in Genesis 1.1—2.4a. For all the differences from a work like *Enuma Elish* (see above, pp. 8f.) and the Ugaritic literature (see pp. 9f.) – there is, for example, no account of a struggle between God and the chaos monster nor is there a number of gods involved because the Priestly writers by the time of the exile were virtual monotheists – the same 'order out of chaos' theme is prominent. At the beginning, the universe consisted of a dark, watery 'chaos' with no shape and no order.[3] God subdued this by his 'word' ('God said, "Let there be" ... and there was'). The creative power of God's word is seen throughout the Old Testament in the belief that he exercises control over the affairs of men and women by the 'word' of prophecy (e.g. 'I, the LORD, have spoken, and I will do it', Ezek. 36.35, RSV). But the 'word' of the priest was also vital since it was he who pronounced on what was 'clean' and 'unclean' and so regulated and ensured the people's approach to God and their continued relationship with him. Indeed, the exclusive role of the priests in conducting all the ritual of sacrifice and establishing ritual holiness for the community was a vital element in the continuing life of the community as 'the people of God'. For, to the priests, it is clear that God's work of creation by subduing chaos was not a once-for-all act. As we shall see, they believed that chaos was always a menacing potential force for destruction, ever waiting in the wings. That is apparent in their account of the Flood, and it is a view also to be found in such a passage as Jeremiah 4.23–8 in which judgement from God is pictured as a point-by-point reversal of the creation recounted in Genesis 1, with the disappearance of light, mountains, birds, humankind and all fertility, and the reappearance of the very qualities which were used to describe chaos in Genesis 1.2, where it is said that 'the earth was *tôhû* and *bôhû*', usually rendered 'without form and void' (so RSV). So Jeremiah 4.23 reads, 'I saw the earth and it was *tôhû* and *bôhû*.' So, for the priests, the properly ordered cult is the divinely appointed way of keeping chaos at bay and maintaining God's order in creation, just as royal propaganda had seen the king to have a vital role in securing the same end (e.g. Ps. 72, see above, pp. 48f.).

Another theme of Genesis 1 is the theme of 'separation'. God 'separates' light from darkness (vv. 4, 18), the waters of chaos from the earth by the formation of the 'firmament' (vv. 6f.), and day from night (v. 14). The account of each new stage of God's work is also marked out in the Priestly strand of the Pentateuch by the phrase, 'These are the generations of ...'. It occurs at the end of the account of creation (Gen. 2.4a) but otherwise at the beginning of the account of the descent from Adam (5.1), the story of the Flood (6.9), the emergence of the nations after the flood (10.1) and the account of the descendants from Shem (the Semites), from whom Israel came (11.10) and so on. In fact, the concept of 'separation' by God in Genesis 1 is like the statement of a theme in a symphony which will reappear and be developed as the movement unfolds. For the Priests' aim is to trace the way by which God has 'separated out' Israel for himself as his special people.

But that does not exhaust the hints in Genesis 1 of what is to come. It has often been noted that the 'sun', 'moon' and 'stars' get rather lukewarm mention here. They are not named, they are merely 'a greater light to rule over the day' and 'a lesser light to rule over the night' while God seems to have thrown in the stars as an afterthought, 'he made the stars also' (v. 16). The Hebrew name for 'sun' is *shemesh*, and *Shamash* was the name of the Babylonian sun-god. The Hebrew for 'moon' is *yerah*, also the name of a moon goddess in the ancient world. The place of astrology in Babylon is well known, built as it was on a firm belief that the movement of the stars guided and fixed human destiny. It is usually thought, therefore, that the Priestly writer avoided such names in order to dissociate himself firmly from any suggestion of the religion of Babylon, where so many Jews spent the exile and where many remained after others had returned. The heavenly bodies are the creation of the one, all-powerful God and not objects of worship in themselves. Indeed, far from being objects of worship, they serve rather as witnesses to the need to worship the one God of Israel. They are said to be 'for signs and for seasons' (v. 14, RSV). The Hebrew word for 'sign' is used again in 'P'. The 'rainbow' is a 'sign', a sign of God's promise to and covenant with all creation (Gen. 9.12, 17). The exodus from Egypt, leading to their worship of him on the sacred mountain of Sinai, is a 'sign' of God's special redemption of his people (Exod. 3.12). The sabbath is a 'sign' of God's special relationship with the people of Israel (Exod. 31.13). Circumcision is a 'sign' of the same special covenant relationship

(Gen. 17.11). In the same way, the word rendered 'seasons' in Genesis 1.14 is the very term P uses for the appointed festivals at which God meets with his people when they worship him and where he offers them his grace in cleansing and renewal (e.g. Lev. 23.2, 4, 37, 44, etc.). So, far from being objects of worship, the heavenly bodies were created by God to witness to his special covenant relationship with the Israelites and to his provision of what we might term 'the means of grace' by which that relationship could be kept fresh and effective. Indeed, this account of creation ends with God's resting on the seventh day, the day which he blessed and pronounced holy (Gen. 2.2f.), so anticipating the institution of the sabbath. The origin of the 'sabbath' is obscured in the mists of our lack of records. It was doubtless of early origin but it came to special prominence during the time of the Babylonian exile when, with the sacrificial cult of the temple denied to them, Israelites could still observe a day for the worship of God. The sabbath thus became a mark of their 'separation' from the gentile world and, as we have already seen, it was identified by the priests as yet another sign of God's covenant relationship with his own people (Exod. 31.13).

The continuing threat from 'chaos' is nowhere more apparent than in P's account of the Flood. The earlier 'J' strand says that the flood came because of heavy and continuous rain (Gen. 7.4, 12). But P is more graphic: 'on that day all the fountains of the vast deep [Hb. *t^ehôm*, the same word to describe the dark, watery chaos that occurs in Gen. 1.2[4]] burst open, and the windows of heaven were opened' (7.11). This is an undoing of what God did in creation when 'God made the firmament and separated the waters which were under the firmament from the waters which were above the firmament' (1.7), so creating the ordered area of dry land on which all the life of earth could flourish. Chaos reasserts itself through the sin of humankind and creation is reversed, the dry land, mountains, living creatures and human beings, all are overwhelmed (7.19–23). Noah and his family, including Shem, from whom the Semites and so the Israelites will spring, are, however, preserved by God's grace and power, just as, later, God will preserve the true Israel through the 'waters' of the Babylonian exile (Isa. 43.1–7). Finally, all the order of creation is restored. The P account in Genesis 9.1–7 of the covenant with Noah describes all the elements of Genesis 1 reappearing: the command to 'be fruitful and multiply' is renewed (v. 1, cf. 1.28), human dominion over all

the living creatures on the earth, in the air and on the sea is promised again (v. 2, cf. 1.28), the provision of food is made again (v. 3,
cf. 1.29f., except that now the eating of meat is allowed), and the
statement that human beings are made 'in the image of God' is reaffirmed (v. 6, cf. 1.26f.). It is highly significant that Noah, through
whom all this is effected, is spoken of as a 'righteous' man (Gen.
6.9), for as we shall see, the priests believe that Israel has been
called out to be a people specially holy to God, and it is through
their 'righteousness' before God, or the 'rightness' of their relationship with him, that the earth and the land are blessed with order
and fertility.

However, they realize that Israel was not always righteous, and
needed therefore to know the grace of God to expiate their sins and
'keep the lines of communication open' as we might say. And they
provide a striking anticipation of the expiatory sacrifices in their
use in 9.4 of the words prohibiting the eating of blood, 'the life is
in the blood'. It is the 'blood', and therefore the 'life' of the sacrificial victim which expiates the sin of the worshipper. So, for example, Leviticus 17.11 reads, 'For the life of the flesh is in the blood,
and I give it to you on the altar to expiate [literally, to 'cover'] for
your lives; because it is the blood which expiates by virtue of its
life.' Of course, P does not mention Noah offering any sacrifice:
that is impossible until the duly ordained priesthood is instituted,
for they have exclusive rights as intermediaries between God and
human beings. But, already, this gracious divine provision by
which men and women may be kept 'righteous', and so experience
the blessing of the fertility and order of nature, is adumbrated in
this priestly account of the covenant with Noah.

P's account of the covenant between God and Abraham is found
in Genesis 17. Unlike the covenant with Israel made on Sinai, the
emphasis here is all on God's action and initiative. Abraham has to
respond with faith and in obedience to the divine call, but the hope
of this covenant is more on the grace of God than human qualities
of belief and steadfastness. The divine promises emphasized here
are those of a great people who will descend from Abraham and
Sarah, and of land. 'I will give to you and to your descendants
after you the land where now you are only an immigrant, all the
land of Canaan as an eternal possession, and I will be their God'
(Gen. 17.8). So the land is, as yet, a future gift in which for the
present Abraham is only an itinerant, or pilgrim. Indeed, P's
story of the death of Sarah in chapter 23, shows that Abraham

has to *buy* a grave for her. He, who is heir by the divine promise to the whole land, is forced, in the reality of the present, to negotiate even for so small a part of it. It is remarkable that, at the end, the P narrative leaves Israel only on the threshold of the land, in Moab (I am not persuaded by the arguments of those who believe 'P' continues as any kind of continuous source through the books of Joshua and Judges. Odd traces of it here and there are another matter). By the time of the priests' construction of history, Israel might be living in the land but they were not masters of it, living as they did as a subject people in a larger world empire. They are being reminded that they are heirs to God's promises to Abraham but that these are promises which, as yet, they possess only by faith.

The 'sign' of God's covenant with Abraham is circumcision (17.10–14, 22–7). It is in P that this rite receives greater attention for, like sabbath observance, circumcision is a sign of the distinctiveness, the separation, of the Israelites as a 'people of God', marking them out as different from all the other nations round about.

The real climax of everything for P, however, comes with God's disclosure to Moses on Mount Sinai of all the instructions concerning the building of the tabernacle, the institution of the sacrificial programme and the appointing of the legitimate priesthood. After having given an account of the Passover in Exodus 11f. and the story of the Exodus from Egypt in which the danger from the sea again takes on the character of a renewed threat from the waters of chaos (see Exod. 14, esp. vv. 22 and 29, where the waters of the sea are described as a 'wall on their right hand and their left'), Moses receives the revelation from God on the mountain. There is none of the emphasis on the conditional Sinaitic covenant to be found in the earlier versions. God's gracious provision of the cult for his people holds centre stage. Theoretically, the tabernacle is meant to be a kind of portable shrine which the Israelites will carry around with them on their journeyings. However, it is clearly influenced by the later Jerusalem temple. It is interesting to note the close parallels between the way its building is described and the account of creation in P. After creating the world 'God saw all which he had made and, behold, it was very good' (Gen. 1.31). When the tabernacle was completed, 'Moses saw all the work, and behold, they had done it just as Yahweh had commanded' (Exod. 39.43). 'And the heaven and the earth and all their contents were completed' (Gen. 2.1): 'And all the work of the sanctuary of the tent of meeting was completed and the Israelites did it all as Yahweh had commanded Moses' (Exod. 39.32). 'And on the seventh day God completed his work' (Gen. 2.2): 'And Moses completed the work' (Exod. 40.33). 'And God blessed the seventh day and pronounced it holy' (Gen. 2.3): 'Just as Yahweh had commanded so they did it, and Moses blessed them' (Exod. 39.43). In this way P shows a real sense of continuity between God's bringing order out of chaos in creation and the maintenance of order in the tabernacle, the place where God's presence 'comes down' to be among his people and accompany them on their journeying (Exod. 40.34–8). It is the place also where his grace is mediated through the sacrificial ritual administered by the duly ordained priesthood.

There follow the instructions about the sacrifices (Lev. 1–7) and the consecration of Aaron and his sons (Lev. 8) and the first sacrifices performed by the priesthood on behalf of the people. Just to underline the *exclusive* rights of the priests in this matter, the obscure incident involving Nadab and Abihu is recorded (Lev. 10). Although sons of Aaron, they offered fire to Yahweh which was unacceptable because 'it was not as Yahweh had commanded' (v. 1). Their instantaneous fate was dire enough warning for anyone else who might be tempted to usurp the role of the priest or try cultic procedure their own way.

But it is, in fact, more specific in its warning. While we know only a little about the development of the priesthood in Israel, it seems clear that, earlier, a wider circle of people were regarded as full priests. In the 'J' tradition, both Nadab and Abihu were included in the list (Exod. 24.1, 9–11). We know also that kings acted in a priestly manner and took a part in the worship, as Solomon did in blessing the people and interceding for them from the altar (1 Kings 8.14–66), while Jeroboam went up to the altar to offer sacrifices (1 Kings 12.33). But at the time of David's death the priest Abiathar, as we saw in the previous chapter, backed the wrong party, that of Adonijah (1 Kings 1.7). He was exiled from Jerusalem to Anathoth and escaped death only because of his earlier loyalty to David (1 Kings 2.26). Up to then, since David's capture of Jerusalem, he and Zadok had acted jointly as priests. However, from this time on, Zadok, who had supported the winning candidate, Solomon, came more and more into prominence. Originally all the Levitical priesthood seem to have been regarded as equal, with many operating at outlying sanctuaries. However, from the time of Josiah's reform, which decreed that legitimate worship could be carried out only at Jerusalem, the Levites began to lose ground, while the Jerusalem Zadokites assumed more and more supremacy. While Deuteronomy, for whom priests and Levites were the same thing, called for such centralization, it nevertheless urged that the Levitical priests of the outlying sanctuaries, now faced with closure, were to be given equal rights at the central sanctuary (Deut. 18.6–8). This ideal foundered on the reality of power and the jealousy with which it is guarded, however. The Jerusalem priests saw to it that it did not happen ('Then the priests of the high places did not come up to the altar of Yahweh in Jerusalem but ate unleavened bread among their brethren', 2 Kings 23.9). By the time of Ezekiel, not only is there a clear distinction between the Zadokite priesthood and the Levites, but it is being given a theological justification: 'The Levites who went far away from me, compounding the backslidings of Israel from me to idols, shall bear their guilt' (Ezek. 44.10). '"But the Levitical priests, the Zadokites, who kept the sacred trust of my sanctuary amid all the backslidings of Israel from me, shall approach me to serve me, to stand in my presence and offer me the fat and the blood:" Oracle of Lord Yahweh' (Ezek. 44.15).

After the exile this distinction between priests and Levites was complete, with the Levites playing only a subordinate role (although they have a champion in the post-exilic writer of the books of Chronicles, who sometimes contrasts their behaviour favourably with that of the full priests, e.g. 2 Chronicles 29.34). It is small wonder, however, that Ezra apparently found it difficult to recruit many Levites from Babylon willing to come back to such a position (Ezra 8.15). Now, after the exile, the descent of the Zadokite priests in both the P strand of the Pentateuch and in Chronicles is traced right back to Aaron so that they can claim full Aaronic legitimacy. In 1 Chronicles 6.1–8 they are said to have come from Eleazar. Eleazar and Ithamar are sons of Aaron whose full priestly authority is given divine sanction in the same passage we have just been considering, a passage which shows Nadab and Abihu to have been excluded (Lev. 10.6, 12). So this story not only stresses the exclusive role of the priests in general, but is seen to have been part of the specific priestly propaganda of the Zadokites, by which they established their special position after the exile.

59

That exclusive position can be further illustrated in the writings of the post-exilic Chronicler. The Deuteronomistic Historian tells us, with no hint of disapproval, that king Ahaz 'went up to the altar' and offered sacrifices there (2 Kings 16.10–16). We have seen, anyway, that the kings of the pre-exilic temple could and did act in a priestly manner. Further, the reign of king Uzziah (also called in places Azariah) is spoken of favourably by the Deuteronomist: 'He did what was right in the sight of Yahweh' (2 Kings 15.3). Nevertheless, Uzziah died of leprosy and, in the way of the Deuteronomistic theology, there has to be a reason. They tell us sadly that Uzziah did not eliminate all the worship in the outlying sanctuaries (they are untroubled by the fact that, until the reforms of king Josiah in the following century, there was no law requiring him to do any such thing!). But they have provided enough clue for the Chronicler to introduce a wholly new note, one completely favourable to the same idea of the *exclusive* sacrificial role of the priests as that found in the P strand. According to the Chronicler, king Uzziah 'when he became strong, got above himself [literally, 'lifted up his heart'] and went to Yahweh's temple to offer sacrifice on the altar of incense'. The priest, Azariah, challenged him and told him to leave the sanctuary, whereupon Uzziah became angry. But it does not do to trifle with a priest. That was the very point at which Yahweh struck him with leprosy (and so he became ritually unclean for any sacral act anyway, 2 Chron. 26.16–21).

Our texts therefore show how, in the absence of monarchy, the priests came to a greater position of leadership in the post-exilic community. This must not be overstressed. Obviously, there were priests before the exile who exercised great influence, especially in the temple but also, doubtless, in affairs of state. For example, Jehoiada, the priest, played a leading part in overthrowing the usurping queen Athaliah in the interests of Joash of the Davidic line (2 Kings 11.1–20). There was even then an office of high priest: the title was given to Jehoiada (2 Kings 12.10) and to Hilkiah (2 Kings 22.4, 8, etc.). Clearly they were more prominent when any king undertook religious reform, such as Jehoash (2 Kings 12.4–16), or Ahaz (2 Kings 16.10–16), and especially Josiah (2 Kings 22f.). Nevertheless, in the Deuteronomistic history recorded mainly in 1 and 2 Kings, it is the kings themselves who are centre stage and who 'call the shots', with prophets being the more actively involved in affairs of state. The picture is rather different in the Chronicler's history, where priests play a much more prominent role, advising kings and uttering homilies at every opportunity.[5]

The picture is different also in the post-exilic prophetic literature. Haggai and Zechariah 1—8 reveal a society in Judah and Jerusalem in the later 6th century BCE in which there is a joint rule of civil governor and high priest. For Haggai and Zechariah these are Zerubbabel and Joshua. Malachi, probably to be dated about mid-5th century, talks of a 'governor' (1.8), but his attacks on the Levites and priests reveal the prominent place they must have held at that time. Nehemiah, who came to Jerusalem from Babylon around the same time, was a layman appointed to be governor (and he speaks of a series of governors before him, 5.15). Yet the central role of the priests and Levites is apparent everywhere in his book. Ezra, who probably came to Jerusalem at the end of the 5th century, was himself a priest, as well as a 'scribe' (i.e. someone expert in Jewish 'Torah') and, again, the essential and central role of the priests and Levites speaks to us from every page of the book which bears his name. As we shall see, the attacks on the priests in Joel (whatever the exact date of that book may be) again show how vital they were to the functioning of post-exilic Judah when there was no king.

No doubt there were those who hoped for the restoration of the Davidic monarchy either then, or at some time in the future. Haggai seems to have held out almost messianic hopes for Zerubbabel (2.20–23). Yet even in Zechariah 1—8, that hope seems to be pushed ahead to some indefinite time. Zerubbabel is warned that any kind of militarism must be avoided (4.6b–10a) and the 'Branch', presumably the title of some royal, messianic figure, is now unnamed and his coming promised only at some time in the future (3.8; 6.12). Meanwhile, Joshua, the high priest, and his 'friends' are given quasi-royal prerogatives and are seen as those who maintain Yahweh's rule among his people, guarantors of the coming of the future messianic figure (3.6–10; 6.11–14).[6] Meanwhile the Chronicler, whether or not, with his glowing picture of the promises to David and his successors, he holds out hope of its future restoration, shows that the theocracy, under the guidance of the priests, is a true heir and successor to the royal line.[7]

Comparing the emphases of the Priestly tradition of the Pentateuch and of the post-exilic biblical literature we can see that a major revision of the theology of what it meant to be 'the people of

God' was going on during and after the exile. They were face to face with a wholly new situation when the Davidic monarchy, and the nation state whose official religion Yahwism had been, no longer existed. It is a brave and creative theological scheme. P's term for the people is *qāhāl*, the word for a religious assembly, roughly equivalent to the New Testament Greek word for the church, *ekklēsia*, 'those who are called out'. Israel is, therefore, a *religious* community, to be separated from the other nations and called to reflect by its holiness something of the nature and character of God himself. This is shown supremely in its great ethical law code, often called the 'Code of Holiness' (Lev. 17—26), from its refrain, 'You shall be holy because I, Yahweh, am holy' (e.g. Lev. 19.2; 20.26; 21.8, etc.). There is a good deal in the Code of Holiness which deals with matters of ethical conduct. Leviticus 19, for example, deals with reverence for parents; leaving generous harvest gleanings for the poor to collect; not stealing, giving false witness, oppressing a neighbour, or deceiving the deaf and the blind, etc. Yet great attention is paid as well to the idea of ritual and cultic holiness. It was this which 'separated' them from others as a people who belonged in a special way to Yahweh.

Thus the community is seen now, not primarily in political, national or, certainly monarchic terms – there is not one mention of a king – nor even in geographical terms, but in terms of a *theocracy*. They are ruled by God and the priests are the sole and exclusive mediators between him and the people. In a sense P shows them as still a 'pilgrim people', heirs to the promises to Abraham of land and great posterity, but, like Abraham, as yet possessing all this only in part. As we have seen, P leaves them on the border of the promised land, but still encamped in Moab (Num. 36.13). Nevertheless, they have the tabernacle, in which Yahweh manifests his presence when he comes down and fills it with the cloud of his 'glory' (Exod. 40.34–8) and they know 'the means of grace', the appointed religious festivals and sacrifices by which their sins are covered. By these means they experience constantly the renewal of their covenant relationship with God. And these means of grace are mediated through the duly and divinely appointed priesthood (e.g. Lev. 5.6, etc.) whose 'word' makes them effective and instructs the Israelites in the proper ordering of the cult (e.g. Lev. 10.8–11; 11.46f.; 20.25). We might borrow a term from later Christian theology and say that the priestly tradition of the exilic and post-exilic periods shows a sense of 'realized eschatology'.

That is, they hold out the promises of a great fulfilment of the promises to the patriarchs still to come, but urge the present congregation of Israel to faithfulness and obedience in the present while they await that greater fulfilment. This is exactly the position of some other post-exilic writings which have assumed their present form in temple/priestly circles, Haggai, Zechariah 1—8, Malachi, Ezra, Nehemiah and the book of Chronicles.

But much of this understanding of the world, where chaos always threatens the light and order of God's creation and has to be kept in check by the proper ordering of the cult, recalls what Peter Berger has to say about religion as a means of legitimizing the institutional order. 'Probably the most ancient form of this legitimation is the conception of the institutional order as directly reflecting or manifesting the divine structure of the cosmos, that is, between microcosm and macrocosm. Everything "here below" has its analogy "up above".'[8] Or again, 'Just as religious legitimation interprets the order of society in terms of an all-embracing, sacred order of the universe, so it relates disorder that is the antithesis of all socially constructed nomos to that yawning abyss of chaos that is the oldest antagonist of the sacred' (p. 48). And on the place, value and purpose of religious ritual: 'Men forget. They must, therefore, be reminded over and over again ... Religious ritual has been a crucial instrument of this process of "reminding". Again and again it "makes present" to those who participate in it the fundamental reality-definitions and their appropriate legitimations' (pp. 48f.). 'Religion thus serves to maintain the reality of that socially constructed world within which men exist in their everyday lives' (p. 50). By their whole religious and theological structure the priests were creating a social order which could follow the disappearance of the monarchic nation state and maintain a recognizable and authoritative identity in a totally new political context.

But another sociologist has helped us to understand the nature and reality of this 'priestly reconstruction'. Mary Douglas has studied the nature and significance of laws on ritual and cultic purity. In her book *Purity and Danger*[9] she says, 'We cannot possibly interpret rituals concerning excreta, breast milk, saliva, and the rest unless we are prepared to see in the body a symbol of society reproduced in small on the human body ... Four kinds of social pollution seem worth distinguishing. The first is danger pressing on external boundaries: the second, danger from transgressing the internal line of the system; the third is danger in the margins of the lines. The fourth danger ... [is] internal contradiction...' (p. 122). In other words, purity laws are a means of defence for any community under threat. This may afford us another insight into at least one reason for the priests' insistence on what is 'clean' and 'unclean' in their laws of holiness. Ritual 'separation' is a means of defending identity in times of crisis. Mary Douglas says elsewhere, 'Where the social system is well-articulated, I look for articulate powers vested in points of authority: where the social system is ill-articulated, I look for inarticulated powers vested in those who are a source of disorder' (p. 99).

Strangely enough, another sociologist who has studied the period of the Israelite exile in Babylon in the light of the experience and literature of other landless peoples comes to a similar conclusion about the importance of ritual, although along a different line of approach. Daniel L. Smith in his book, *The Religion of the Landless*[10] examines the experiences of groups who in more recent times have lost their land and *status quo*, South African Bantustans, African-American slaves, American internees in Japanese prisoner-of-war camps and the Bikini islanders. He lists various 'mechanisms for survival' which each has developed to cope with their condition of 'displacement', mechanisms which include 'structural adaptation', 'the rise of new leadership', and 'ritual'. So 'The very social structure of the group may evolve new configurations to deal with the new situation' (p. 75) and '... the role of ritual in minority, dominated contexts may play an important functional role in the preservation and symbolic resistance of the group in question' (p. 84). Both the rise to new power of the priests and the whole temple-based system of ritual and holiness which they developed may be said to have played a similar function in exilic and post-exilic Israel. They created the conditions in which the distinctive continued identity of the Jewish people could be maintained in the face of all political changes and upheavals. They skilfully preserved continuity with what had gone before where they could, and yet proved creative enough to forge a new system with courage and no little success.

We ended our survey of royal propaganda by concluding that, while the monarchy had grave weaknesses and dangers, it yet managed to preserve a system which continued for several centuries and provided a womb in which the faith of Israel could gestate and come to birth with vigorous life and potential for continuing growth and adaptation. The same can be said of the priestly temple community which kept the faith of Judaism alive for many centuries and forged a faith which could survive the traumas of persecution, war, destruction and oppression. For, like the monarchy, the rule of the priests was not destined to permanence. With the destruction of Herod's temple in Jerusalem in 70 CE, their system, represented then by the Sadducees, came to an end. It was the Pharisees, heirs to the Wisdom writers and teachers, who were to shape the form which rabbinic Judaism took, 'a religion of the book, the Torah', not of the altar. As we shall see, long before that the priests and their system had their bitter, subversive critics. But their achievement was no mean one.

CHAPTER FOUR

Propaganda *and* Subversion –
the Deuteronomists

The idea that a certain race, nation or group has a divine right to a particular area of territory is basic to propaganda, ancient and modern. The people's god either resides there himself, or leads his people to it and, in overcoming all heavenly and terrestrial opposition, opposition always identified with 'the dark forces of chaos', establishes them there. His temple validates the rule of their leaders and their occupation of the land and shows that their rights and fortunes are secure because he himself resides in their midst, the earthly temple being a projection on earth of his heavenly dwelling. Meanwhile, the 'king' or 'priest' who occupies the temple/palace is his chosen, authorized representative through whom he exercises his rule over that land and all surrounding nations. That was basic to much of the royal propaganda of the ancient Near East we examined in chapter 1, and we have seen that it figures largely in the royal propaganda of the Yahwist and the claims of the priests in the Priestly strand of the Pentateuch.

A forthright and uncompromising theological expression of the right of Israel to the land of Canaan is also to be found in the Deuteronomistic literature of the Old Testament. We mentioned this briefly in our study of royal propaganda as it is found in the Old Testament historical books (see above, pp. 37–46 and notes 9, 10, 11). To recapitulate, certain parts of our Old Testament show a remarkable similarity of vocabulary, style and theology. These consist primarily of the book of Deuteronomy, the historical books from Joshua—2 Kings (often called the 'Deuteronomistic History') and the present form of the book of Jeremiah. As explained above, it is believed by many scholars that the whole of Deuteronomy and Joshua—2 Kings, while made up of many earlier and varied sources, have been finally edited by those who shared a broadly similar theological outlook, and that the same circles were also responsible for the editing and presentation of the prophecies of Jeremiah and the stories about him and his times which are found in that prophetic book.

The recognition of a complicated process and lengthy period of time during which the various stages of this compilation of Deuteronomy—2 Kings went on has resulted in a great deal of complex and detailed scholarly study, with the scholars involved coming to very different conclusions (see especially notes 9, 10, 11 to chapter 2). Nevertheless, there is a wide acceptance of the fact that the major form of the work was completed during the time of the Babylonian exile. Thus its authors had not only to explain to those both at home and in exile why the divine promises about the land appeared to have been broken, but to reassure them of the continuing validity of those promises and the conditions under which their renewal might yet be experienced. This dual task has led both to an uncompromising restatement of the divine promises about the rights of Israel to possession of the land, and to a searching critique of the reasons for its temporary loss. As we shall see, this critique has given strong ammunition to the Deuteronomistic theologians for the very doctrines by which they helped to shape King Josiah's reforms, doctrines which included demands for the exclusive worship of Yahweh and the absolute rights and sole validity of the cult of the central temple in Jerusalem. In vesting such exclusive rights in the Jerusalem temple and its personnel they thus attempted to secure their own position as the sole, legitimate exponents of the true Yahwistic faith, a faith which they believed should utterly repudiate every vestige of the cults of other deities and exclude all who practised them. *Their* interpretation of Yahwism and theirs alone was valid. Anything or anyone which threatened to dilute that exclusive interpretation of Yahwism, and thus their exclusive rights as its interpreters, was anathema to them.

It was this critique which led them also to a searching assessment of the role of the institution of monarchy before the exile with its adverse effects, as they saw it, upon a view of Israel as a more equal community of 'doers of the Torah'. The same emphasis on 'Torah' as the essential element in defining Yahwism led also to some 'de-sacralization' of its cultic life, a move which could have the effect of weakening the position of the priests in favour of those who were the law's guardians and interpreters. In any case, once the temple had been destroyed and its sacrificial rituals were no longer possible, the Deuteronomists' insistence that Yahwism was primarily a matter of 'keeping the law' would give it a continuing form of expression and identity which could continue through even the changed circumstances of the exile. Exactly the same was to happen after the later destruction of the temple in 70 CE when the rabbis, under the impetus of the Pharisees, stressed that Judaism was essentially a matter of 'Torah' rather than the sacrificial cult which had been practised by the Sadducees.

It is these dual emphases in the work – the theological claims which are more insistently and even stridently asserted in a time of weakness and uncertainty, together with powerful social and political criticism of the pre-exilic monarchic state – which lead us to deal with the Deuteronomists under the heading of both 'propaganda' *and* 'subversion'.

The book of Deuteronomy largely consists of three 'sermons' preached by Moses. In presenting their work in this form, its authors are partly acknowledging that much of the law which they set out had been received by long tradition, but, more importantly, are claiming Mosaic authority for the teaching they wish to promulgate which involves the application, as they see it, of the principles of Israel's ancient law to the new circumstances of their own time. This is the same practice as that observable in the prophetic books of the Old Testament when later editors and exegetes add elements to the books bearing the name of the great prophetic figures of the past. They are not trying to be dishonest. They believe they are legitimately giving to words which were spoken to one situation, continuing vitality and relevance by applying them in new, contemporary circumstances. The practice of the Deuteronomists is similar to that in Wales long ago, where laws formulated long after his time were known as the laws of Hywel Dda, since they were seen to be the updating of the principles behind his original codification of Welsh law. Just how the Deuteronomists developed earlier laws must be regarded, as we shall see, as part of their 'subversive' activity. But nothing could be clearer than the statement of their belief that it had always been God's purpose to grant the land of Canaan to the people of Israel.

Moses wastes no time in getting on to this subject in his first sermon, which consists of an historical retrospect of how God has brought the Israelites to the very threshold of the promised land (1.1—4.43):

'Go to the hill country of the Amorites, with all its occupants in the Arabah, in the hill country and in the lowlands, in the Negeb, and the coastlands, the territory of the Canaanites, and Lebanon, as far as the great river, the river Euphrates. See, I have given you the land which is before you: go in and take possession of that land which Yahweh swore to your forefathers, to Abraham, to Isaac and to Jacob, to give to them and to their descendants after them.' (Deut. 1.7f.)

Not much chance of getting the map references mixed up there! Not only was the land theirs to go and claim in God's name, but those who were already in occupation were to be wiped out to make room for them. God would do this for them in the kind of action which has often been described as 'Holy War'.[1] Their part was to make sure that no one of the defeated people, man or woman, old or young, survived. They, and all their goods, were to be forfeited to the deity. In the words of the Old Testament they were to be subjected to a religious 'ban' (the Hebrew word being *ḥerem*). Nowhere is this made more explicit than in the second sermon of Moses, to be found in Deuteronomy 4.44—29.1. This includes the central law code of the book (chs. 12—26), an introductory section calling on Israel to keep the law (4.44—11.32) and a conclusion which sets out the sanctions of blessing when they observe the law and curses when they do not. In the section which introduces the law code we hear these chilling words of Moses:

'When Yahweh your God brings you to the land you are going to occupy, and clears away many nations before you, the Hittites, the Girgashites, the Amorites, the Canaanites, the Perizzites, the Hivites and the Jebusites, seven nations more numerous and stronger than you, and Yahweh your God gives them up to you and you strike them, then you shall put them completely to the ban. You shall not make any treaty with them and you must show them no mercy. You shall not intermarry with them, your daughters with their sons, nor their daughters with your sons. For they would turn your sons away from following me to worship other gods, and then Yahweh's wrath would be kindled against you and he would instantly destroy you. No, this is how you are to treat them. You shall break down their altars and shatter their sacred pillars, cut down their Asherim and burn their idols.' (Deut. 7.1–5)

This (utterly theoretical and idealistic) understanding of how the Holy War was to be conducted is shown very clearly in the programmatic picture the Deuteronomistic Historians give in the early chapters of Joshua of the conquest of the land under the leadership of Joshua. The picture is of all twelve tribes of later Israel marching under the united banner of Joshua, the general designated by God to succeed Moses. This shows three major campaigns delivered from the east side of the river Jordan after a miraculous crossing of it which is reminiscent of the story of the Exodus from Egypt (3.7–17). The first is in the centre (chs. 2—9); the second in the south, against a coalition of kings led by the king of Jerusalem (ch. 10) and the third in the north against a coalition of kings led by the king of Hazor (ch. 11). After a list of the kings it is alleged that the Israelites defeated (ch. 12), the whole territory on both sides of the river is divided up between the twelve tribes (chs. 13—22). Victory is thus virtually complete and is the work of Yahweh, who leaves the Israelite troops merely the task of mopping up against an already demoralized and panic-stricken army. The most familiar example is how the stronghold of Jericho is captured. There is no direct, frontal assault on its formidable bastions. The Israelites march round its walls in cultic processions led by priests blowing rams' horns, after which the walls fall down by themselves and the Israelites storm in. In (nearly complete) obedience to the commands of Yahweh we read,

> And they put everyone in the city to the ban, men and women, young and old, oxen, sheep and asses, all with the edge of the sword. (6.21)

The only interruption in this fantastic picture of sweeping victory on every side comes because of human sin. This means that Yahweh withdraws his blessing. Achan thought he would hang on to some of the spoils of war, and this leads to an inexplicable defeat first time round before the city of Ai. In a kind of decision by sacred lot it is shown that Achan is the culprit, and action is swift and total. Not only he and the 'stolen' goods, but his family and his own possessions are destroyed, an act which was seen to appease Yahweh for we read 'so Yahweh turned from the heat of his anger', and the familiar story of victory is renewed (7.1–26).

Just in case we should miss the fact that this is Yahweh's doing, and in case it should raise any questions about such treatment of people who were doing nothing but defending their own homes

and families, the Deuteronomistic Historian brings out the same
theological justification that we found in the Yahwist's work and
which has featured in other ancient Near-Eastern propaganda we
have examined: the inhabitants of the land deserved all this because they were so wicked that they opposed God himself by opposing his people:

> For it was Yahweh's idea that they [i.e. the kings and people of the
> land] should determine to come against Israel in battle so that they
> could be put to the ban, and no mercy be shown to them in their
> destruction, so as to confirm his command to Moses. (Josh. 11.20)

If all this appears somewhat breathtaking, there are one or two
points which need to be made. The first is that none of all this actually happened – at least, not in anything remotely resembling
the way it is described in this highly and artificially coloured account. It must be reckoned as part of the propaganda by which
the Deuteronomists reinforced their claim that the land of
Canaan belonged to Israel by divine right. The account of the conquest and the treatment of its former inhabitants given in Deuteronomy and the book of Joshua must be counted as nothing but an
Ayatollah's pipedream. It is a reaction to the threat to their understanding of Yahwism which the Deuteronomists saw to be coming
from various elements in the mixed population of Canaan and
amid all the uncertainty and threat of exile imposed by victorious
foreign armies.

We actually lack much hard and fast evidence by which to reconstruct just how the Israelites came to be in possession of the
land. Such archaeological evidence as has been cited is often ambiguous and the conclusions which can be drawn from it uncer-
tain. We do not know necessarily who destroyed some of the cities
of Palestine in the 13th and 12th centuries BCE. The latest consensus of archaeologists now appears to be that Jericho was not
occupied at any possible time for the entry of the Israelites, while
Ai had been uninhabited for centuries (the name actually means
'ruins' in Hebrew). But, apart from any external information by
which we can check what happened, the biblical record itself con-
tradicts this theoretical picture and reveals that the reality was
much more piecemeal, even humdrum, and much more mixed in
fortunes than the Deuteronomists would have us believe. Judges 1
shows this by telling of how individual tribes conducted their own,

much more limited campaigns, with very varying success. Further, the Deuteronomists have to devise theological reasons as to why all the Canaanites were clearly not destroyed. In Deuteronomy 7.22 it is said that God will clear away the people already living in the land only gradually so that they can give the Israelites help in meeting the threat from wild animals! Judges 2.20–23 says that God decided to leave these peoples because of Israel's sins and so that their presence would provide a kind of continuous assessment process in their religious fidelity. Joshua in his farewell speech to the Israelites warns future generations of Israelites against intermarrying with the Canaanites left among them (Josh. 23.12f.). Another rationalization is offered in Judges 3.1f., where it is said that God has thoughtfully left some Canaanites as target practice for the Israelites, a means by which they might keep their martial arts up to scratch.

Almost all serious biblical scholars acknowledge that the process by which the later whole nation of Israel came to be where they were was a very much more complex process than that depicted in the book of Joshua. For the lack of much hard historical evidence, theories about this vary. Some believe there was a gradual process of growing penetration by those who had been semi-nomads (that is, who had a settled area where they lived and from which they took their flocks out into the desert during the winter rainy season) and that this would have been a very much more peaceful process than the warlike entry the Deuteronomists describe, even if it gave rise to skirmishes with those already resident.[2] Some have spoken in more sociological terms of a kind of 'peasants' revolt' against the growing power of the city states, instigated by those for whom the whole imagery of deliverance from the power of Egypt – perhaps the tribal memory of a small group of them – would have taken on powerful symbolic importance.[3] A more 'developmental' view of the emergence of Israel has come into general favour recently. An early exponent of this was C. H. G. de Geuss,[4] who believed that Israel arose from the development of a particular social system. It was made up of a great number of family clans, and the idea of the 'tribe', and particularly a complete network of 'twelve tribes', represents only the attempt to give expression to a social coherence which developed gradually and continuously. Somewhat similar have been the views of N. P. Lemche.[5] He sees Israel as resulting from the movement of people out from the Canaanite city states into the countryside, and particularly the hill country, where they were able to keep themselves during a period of economic decline. The need to co-operate in order to husband this land more efficiently and the sense of a common purpose would have led gradually to the formation of 'Israel'. A brief and convenient summary of current scholarly views on the emergence of Israel in the land of Canaan may be found in Adrian H. W. Curtis's recent Introduction to the book of Joshua.[6]

All this is a far cry from the Deuteronomistic portrayal of the 'holy war' or 'Yahweh war' in the book of Joshua. If the absence of *any* kind of military engagement seems too far a cry from what we have there, we may consider a possible alternative. It is by no means impossible that a group of people who had experienced what seemed to them a 'miraculous' escape from Egypt, a land in which they had been severely oppressed, should, after years in the desert, launch an attack to gain a foothold in the highlands of the land of Canaan. That they should attribute their victory, or victories, to Yahweh, the very God whom they believed had delivered them from Egypt, is natural enough, and we should not ignore the very strong and apparently early tradition that Yahweh was originally thought of as a war God.[7] Some of the purely 'sociological' accounts of Israel's origins seem to me too much to ignore this strong element in her traditions. Then, as they in turn had to fight off other marauders seeking to do the same things, neighbours across local clan, tribal and locational divides would find themselves banding together with them in mutual defence. If further military successes occurred and were seen as the work of Yahweh, then these other people might well join themselves to a growing group who acknowledged allegiance to this God. Such a view would still admit a 'developmental' understanding of 'Israel's' origins – it would envisage a rolling snowball kind of effect – but would account for the 'conquest' and 'war' elements which appear so strong a part of the traditions. But, the fact is, we just do not know enough to construct anything other than an hypothesis which is based on a balance of probabilities, probabilities themselves based on the very scant evidence we do have.

What becomes clear from all of this, on such archaeological and biblical evidence as there is, is that there was nothing like Joshua's campaign described in the book of Joshua and that the Deuteronomists' bloodcurdling threats against all the former occupants of the land were never implemented. In fact the Canaanites for a long time continued to occupy the towns and the fertile lowlands while the early Israelites were confined for the most part to the more rugged highlands. Far from ridding themselves of all that was Canaanite, the Israelites were deeply influenced by them at all possible levels, technological, cultural and religious. Early Yahwism adopted and exhibited many characteristics of what we know to have belonged to Canaanite religion.[8] Further, 'all-Israel' was a long time in the developing. There is no evidence of the united actions of north and south before David united both in personal allegiance to himself when he founded his kingdom. All portrayals of the twelve tribes acting together from the days of Egypt, through the wilderness and into the settlement in the land of Canaan, are attempts to express a later sense of unity and give it validity by tracing it back into the past, claiming what was, at most, the varying experiences and traditions of different units of later Israel, as the common inheritance of them all.

So one point which can be made about the almost paranoid xenophobia of the Deuteronomists and the religious hatred for which they call, then, is that the total destruction for which they call never happened. It remained a theoretical, perhaps a theological 'ideal'. Another point to be made is that the sentiments, and the action which is called for, if only in theory, were nothing very unusual in the context of the world of the time. It would be hopelessly anachronistic for us to pass moral judgements about the severe cruelty in war for which they call in the light of what we would want to claim as the more humane feelings of a modern, educated, liberal conscience. Indeed, even as we describe ourselves in such flattering terms, we have to remember that shocking war crimes have proved to be no monopoly of the ancient world, nor, for all the propaganda to which we are subjected in times of war, of any one side in the modern world. A civilization which, among other atrocities, has produced the dropping of two atomic bombs on two cities, the gassing of millions of Jews and the burning of men, women and children with napalm, can hardly afford to claim the moral high ground of history. Wars in the ancient Near East were marked by horrible cruelty and atrocities. And, no doubt, for all we see that the Deuteronomists' wishes were never realized fully in practice, plenty of atrocities were committed by all sides in the warfare in which they did engage with their neighbours, near and far. There is no reason to doubt that the account of David's terrible treatment of the Moabites after victory is based on fact (2 Sam.

8.2). Deuteronomy backs it and like actions by calling for the total rejection of all Moabites from the people of Israel because of their past hostility (Deut. 23.3–6, Hb. 4–7. Its apparent concession in the case of Edomites and Egyptians (vv. 7f., Hb. 8f.), often cited by those who want to mitigate the xenophobia of Deuteronomy, hardly outweighs everything else it has to say about foreigners.) But all such actions were normal in the social, political, religious and cultural context of the time. The real trouble comes when the Deuteronomists' case, the product of times of special threat and uncertainty and the product of a particular propaganda to validate their understanding of Yahwism, is elevated in later ages to the status of an infallible, divine word for all time. For some, even today, 'foreigners' are to be excluded and denied basic human liberties because of the divine right to the land by one particular ethnic and religious group. For such fanatics, those who threaten to dilute the purity of this divine word for all time by 'giving away' any of the sacred territory in the interest of lasting political stability may legitimately be abused, even shot, for 'disobedience' to that word. This is the real danger to our world from those who take the 'propaganda' of the Old Testament in an unqualified way as the eternal and unchallengeable word of God, especially when others are taking what they regard as equally 'divine words' to promise exclusive ownership of the land to them in the same way.

When we turn from such propaganda claims to the subversive elements in the Deuteronomistic literature, it is important to see, as we stated earlier, that we are not dealing with something which they regarded as different from, or as inconsistent with, the propaganda element. Both the propaganda and the critique of all that they see as obstructive of the realization of its legitimate claims, spring from the same source. That does not deny all validity to their critique, however, with its criticism of some of the institutions and of what they see to be the common assumptions of their society. In these, as we shall see, they appear to owe a good deal to the prophets with whom they have at least some basic tenets of faith in common.

The most obvious element of Deuteronomic 'subversion' is to be found in their attitude towards the monarchy in Israel. We are in a different world from the kind of exalted views of sacral kingship expressed in the royal psalms. It is worth citing the Deuteronomic 'law' about kingship:

'When you come to the land which Yahweh, your God, is giving to you, and you take possession of it and live there and you say "I will appoint for myself a king like all the neighbouring nations," you shall indeed appoint a king over you, [but only] one whom Yahweh your God will choose and who shall be one of your own kinsmen, not a foreigner or one who is not your kinsman. He must not accumulate horses for himself nor send people back to Egypt in order to get horses, for Yahweh has said to you, "You shall never return by that route again." He is not to accumulate wives for himself either, in case his heart turns away from me; nor shall he amass excessive silver and gold. But when he sits on the throne of his kingdom he is to write a copy of this law for himself in a book under the direction of the priests and Levites. It shall always be with him and he shall read in it every day of his life so that he may learn to worship Yahweh his God and to keep all the directions of this law and all its requirements in deeds, so that his pride may not raise him above his fellow-Israelites nor cause him to deviate to the right or the left from what is commanded. This way he shall prolong the days of his reign and that of his successors.' (Deut. 17.14–20)

Here the king, far from being spoken of as 'son' of God, as 'royal priest' or the one who exercises rule as God's vicegerent on earth, is seen as one with his fellow-Israelites and, like them, subject to the law. Indeed his submission to the requirements of the law, the knowledge of which be it noted is mediated to him through the priests and Levites, is as binding as that required from any of the Israelites, who are his 'kinsmen', not his 'subjects'. The Deuteronomists' xenophobia is made explicit in their special stipulation that the king shall never be a foreigner, but what may seem more strange at first is the requirement that he does not trade with Egypt for horses nor amass silver and gold. It becomes far less strange when we recall the account of the reign of Solomon which these very Deuteronomists record. They tell us that Solomon had 'forty thousand stalls of horses for his chariots and twelve thousand horsemen' (1 Kings 4.26, Hb. 5.6). Where did he get them? He imported them from Egypt. 'A chariot could be imported from Egypt for six hundred talents of silver and a horse for one hundred and fifty' (1 Kings 10.29). Not only did he import them for his own use but developed a nicely profitable side-line by acting as middleman in (literally) 'horse-trading' between the Middle-Eastern kingdoms, for they were passed on 'to all the kings of the Hittites and of Syria' (v. 29).[9] There are several reasons why the Deuteronomists would have frowned on this. Their stated objection to any kind of pact, whether for purposes of trade or military alliance with foreign countries, and especially with Egypt their traditional oppressor, would fit their general mistrust of foreigners. Further, 'the horse' is so often the symbol of human military strength, and so building up this vast force of chariotry, analagous perhaps to large tank divisions in modern armies, would smack of self-sufficiency rather than reliance on Yahweh. But this criticism is found also in the prophets who roundly denounce any kind of military alliance involving 'horses'. See, for example, Isaiah 31.1, 'Woe to those who go down to Egypt for help and depend on horses ... but do not fix their gaze on the Holy One of Israel nor consult Yahweh.'

But, further, the Deuteronomists link this with 'amassing silver and gold'. When done by the king this means taxation, and taxation means the growing power of centralized government. We know this in our own time. Politicians who call for low state spending, and so for lower taxes, often use a phrase to describe their policy. They speak of 'rolling back the frontiers of the state'. They want to give greater rein to private initiative and individual responsibility, which they see being eroded by the ever more officious actions of central government in every department of social life. The Deuteronomists would have sympathized with them.

Solomon was a great 'state centralizer'. In his time the power of the central establishment became ever greater. He indulged in prodigious state building enterprises and gathered round himself a far more elaborate royal court than David, and certainly Saul, had before him. And this meant taxation. His system for raising this is described in 1 Kings 4.7–19, when he divided his kingdom into twelve tax districts, with an official responsible for raising the royal revenue in each one. Some have found it significant that these tax districts cut across the old tribal boundaries. Was this a deliberate attempt to reduce the power of the tribe? That has certainly been the policy in a number of newly formed African states, for example, where people feel their allegiance is to their tribe while the 'state' is a somewhat remote and unreal entity. The records also tell us that money came in by way of tribute from subject neighbouring peoples (subjected by David, not by Solomon) and also from his lucrative trading deals. Nevertheless, the impression of considerable luxury, something akin to the lifestyle of a successful pop star today, is forcefully depicted. 'And the amount of gold which came annually to Solomon was six hundred and sixty talents of gold' (1 Kings 10.14).

No doubt there is a great deal of fancy about this, part of the propaganda of the royal court which we discussed earlier. But this is exactly the kind of luxury, an unequal amount of wealth gained at the expense of the labour of his 'kinsmen' which the Deuteronomists were wishing to subvert. They depict it as the main reason for the break-up of the kingdom at the death of Solomon. In 1 Kings 12 they tell the graphic story of the people of the northern kingdom of Israel coming to his son and would-be successor Rehoboam and demanding that he undertake to lighten 'the heavy burden [of taxation] which his father had imposed on them' (v. 4). The older counsellors who had served Solomon advise him to meet them half-way, but not so his own younger advisers who had grown up with him and no doubt saw their chance of 'getting rich quick' (vv. 6–11). What was really at stake was the true nature of the monarchy. Was it to be an office ceded by the consent of the people as in the kind of monarchy in which kings were chosen for special qualities it was seen they possessed (often called a 'charismatic' view of kingship)? Or was it to be a more absolute kind of monarchy in which the king ruled by divine right over those who were his 'subjects' and who were required by divine law to yield him unquestioning obedience? There is no doubt which answer the Deuteronomists gave to that, and it was an answer entirely subversive to the sacral views of monarchy expressed in the royal psalms and 'pro-Davidic' propaganda still to be found in the records.

There is one final stipulation in the requirements for the king in the law of Deuteronomy 17.14–20. He was not 'to accumulate wives for himself in case his heart turns away from me' (v. 17). It is unlikely that this is merely a general indictment of polygamy. When a king married it was usually in the interests of international state relationships and to cement a system of alliances for trade and defensive purposes. Solomon is recorded as entering into the spirit of this in no half-hearted way. 'And king Solomon loved many foreign wives; the daughter of Pharaoh, and Moabite, Ammonite, Edomite, Sidonian and Hittite [wives]' (1 Kings 11.1). Indeed, we are told that he had 'seven hundred wives as [royal] princesses and three hundred mistresses' (v. 3). The Deuteronomists show their disapproval of this as clearly as they did in the law of the king in Deuteronomy 17.14–20. He broke, they say, an express divine prohibition against intermarrying with foreigners, and then they quote the very law of Deuteronomy (v. 2). They record the result, 'In Solomon's old age his wives turned his heart away in loyalty to other gods and his heart was not sound towards Yahweh his God as the heart of his father David had been' (v. 4). And they show their theological estimate of this by the way they structure the history of Solomon's reign. Up to that point all has been success and good fortune. But chapter 11 heralds trouble after trouble, troubles which dog his steps until his death – and even afterwards, as we have seen.

Indeed, this severe critique of the institution of monarchy found in the book of Deuteronomy also characterizes the Deuteronomistic History. The idea that the king is to be subject to the law as much as any of his 'kinsmen' is worked out in remorseless detail. A theological assessment exercise is carried out on each king's reign to show whether he was a 'good king' or a 'bad king' or something of a mixture of the two. And the laws by which they are all judged are those of the exclusive worship of Yahweh and the sole validity of the Jerusalem temple as the only place where Yahweh may legitimately be worshipped. So all kings of northern Israel are condemned from the start. Like Jeroboam, the first of the kings of the break-away realm, they encourage their people to worship at the wrong sanctuary, sanctuaries such as Bethel, and it is no wonder that in the eyes of the Deuteronomists worship conducted at an irregular site proves to be irregular in its nature, hopelessly imprinted with idolatry and polytheism. Judean kings receive a mixture of praise and blame but *the* king for the Deuteronomists was Josiah. He was the king, after David, who most completely fulfilled Yahweh's commands, especially instigating and carrying through a religious reform which shut down all the outlying sanctuaries throughout the realm and purified the worship of Yahweh at the one sanctuary by purging it of all extraneous and foreign influences (2 Kings 22.1—23.25).

It is because this so closely fulfils all the laws to be found in Deuteronomy that scholars have long been convinced that the book of Deuteronomy is, or contains, the 'lawbook' which was 'found' in the Jerusalem temple and which is said to have inspired the reform.[10] This, whatever the historical reality and motives behind it, forcefully expresses the religious propaganda of the Deuteronomists. The king is there to ensure that Yahwism is followed in conformity with the divine law, and for no other purpose. That law is interpreted to him by those who are expert in its exposition and practical application. The centralization of worship in one sanctuary alone allows such religious leaders, the Deuteronomists, to keep a tight check on all that goes on and keep Yahwism pure and exclusive. The king has become the servant of a religiously defined community, one of the 'brethren' or 'kinsmen', not the sovereign ruler of a nation of his 'subjects' and by no means the sole, divinely appointed and anointed mediator between Yahweh and the people.

The Deuteronomists' understanding of monarchy is seen not only in their demonstration of how the king is subject to the divine law, but also in the very mixed signals about it which are flagged from the history of its rise as an institution and its conduct thereafter. There are different accounts of its beginning, as we have seen, which can only be accounted for by their being taken from different sources, so violently opposed are their differing viewpoints. The story which is recounted in 1 Samuel 9 is strongly pro-monarchic in its attitude. Saul, together with his servant, go in search of a herd of his father's asses which had wandered off. Their search is vain until, finding themselves near the place where the prophet Samuel lived, the servant suggests consulting him for a fee in the hope of getting a divine oracle locating their where-abouts. But Yahweh had already prepared Samuel for Saul's visit. 'About this time tomorrow I am sending to you a man from the territory of Benjamin, and you are to anoint him as leader over my people Israel. He will deliver my people from the power of the Philistines for I have looked on my people and their cry of distress has reached me' (1 Sam. 9.16). Notice that it is *Yahweh* who has sent Saul. So all this is God's idea, and chooses the one who is to be ruler (actually the term 'king' is not used, but all that follows suggests that the term used is not significant. In fact, the word *nāgîd* is regularly used of kings *before* they are crowned king.[11]) Further, monarchy is God's means of delivering his people from the power of their oppressors. This is a strikingly positive view of the institution, comparable to that of the editor who added twice to the stories of the Judges the dark comment, 'In those days when there was no king in Israel each person did what was right in his own eyes' (Judg. 17.6; 21.25). While we are considering the favourable view of monarchy in the Deuteronomistic History we must not forget the whole presentation of the story of David's supplanting Saul by God's choice of him and his dynasty in place of the rejected Saul. This almost certainly belongs to original court sources from the time of the united monarchy, as we saw when we were looking at the royal propaganda in the Old Testament, but the fact is that the final editors kept these stories. They have recorded the terms of what was claimed as the divine sanctioning of the rule of David's line, culminating in the words spoken through the prophet Nathan in 2 Samuel 7.16: 'Your dynasty[12] and your kingdom shall be established for ever before me' (the MT actually has 'before you', but the alternative 'before me' in several versions, including the Septuagint, seems more likely) 'and your throne shall be founded for ever.'

Not only has the Deuteronomistic History recorded this quite unconditional promise of God towards the Davidic dynasty, but it several times returns triumphantly and hopefully to the theme in the course of the history. To take just one example, Abijam's reign is described in 1 Kings 15.1–8. He was son of Rehoboam, Solomon's successor in the southern kingdom of Judah, and so Solomon's grandson. The Deuteronomistic Historian passes theological judgement on him, as he does on all the kings. In this case it is entirely adverse. 'He followed all the sinful ways which his father had committed before him and his heart was not loyal to Yahweh' (v. 3). One might have thought this would bring him only judgement, on the basis of the historian's view that judgement inevitably follows sin. But not so: 'But for David's sake Yahweh his God gave him a lamp in Jerusalem, raising up his son after him so that he might enable Jerusalem to survive' (v. 4). The reference to a 'lamp' is to a continuing successor in the Davidic line, as 1 Kings 11.36 made clear, when Ahijah the prophet promised Jeroboam that he would reign over the northern kingdom, but with one strong proviso. Neither he, nor any king of the northern kingdom of Israel, would ever inherit the whole realm because, 'to his [i.e. David's] son I will give one tribe so that David my servant may always have a lamp before me in Jerusalem . . .'

Even after the final disaster of the destruction of Jerusalem, the exile of the legitimate Davidic king, Jehoiachin, and many of the leading citizens, the Deuteronomistic History does not seem quite to despair of all hope. It ends on a slightly up-beat note. Jehoiachin is brought out of prison in Babylon, given a change of clothes (sometimes a signal of a change of God's favour, cf. God's command to clothe the high priest, Joshua, in clean clothes after the disgrace of the exile in Zechariah 3.3–5) and a place on high table in the Babylonian court, above the place of all the other kings who were similarly exiled (2 Kings 25.27–30). Scholars have been very much divided about whether this signals any kind of hope on the part of the final Deuteronomistic editor of a restoration of the Davidic line following the exile. We need not pursue this here since it is hard to base much on such slender evidence. At least we can say, however, that it does little to dispel the favourable impression of this strand which runs through the History and is so positive about the Davidic dynasty.

The complications begin, however, when we realize that this is by no means the only strand, nor the only attitude towards monarchy in general and the Davidic dynasty in particular, which the work exhibits. Preceding the favourable account of the recognition of Saul by Samuel in 1 Samuel 9 is a far less flattering origin story. In 1 Samuel 8.1–22 the people approach Samuel with the somewhat insensitive reminder that he is getting on and they don't like the way his sons behave. So they don't want too much rule from a prophetic line. Instead they say, 'Now appoint a king to govern us like all the other nations' (v. 5). That in itself is a very suspect phrase for the Deuteronomists. We have seen something of their xenophobia, their belief that Israel has been called to be *different* from all the other nations. Monarchy starts under a cloud of suspicion, then. It is suspect just because it is what other people do. Rather hurt, Samuel goes to God and tells him what they are saying. And if there was ever a grudging response it was that which God gave to his prophet. 'Follow the people's request exactly as they have put it to you. Because it is not you they are rejecting, but me, as their true king' (v. 7). But he goes on to insist that Samuel must tell them exactly what they are letting themselves in for: 'Tell them the kind of rule they will get from the king who will reign over them' (v. 9). The word I have rendered as 'the kind of rule' (Hb. *mishpāt*) has an ironic ring about it. It is a noun formed from the Hebrew verb 'to judge', the verb used by the people when they tell Samuel they want a king to 'govern' them (v. 5). The noun *mishpāt* usually means 'judgement' or even 'justice'. It is the basis of the prayer for the king in Psalm 72, 'Give *your* justice to the king, O God' (v. 1). But it also means a 'way of life', that is a manner of life based upon a certain set of standards. When there is real 'justice' in a realm, the way of life in that realm is based upon the standards of God's requirements of justice. That is why the word can also be used of human conduct. When the angel tells Samson's father, Manoah, that a boy is to be born to him and his wife, he asks, 'What is the boy's *mishpāt* to be, and how is he to act?' (Judg. 13.12). In other words he is asking, 'On what rule of life are we to bring him up?' So there is biting irony in the fact that the kind of *mishpāt* of the king as Samuel describes it is based on a rule of centralized power which sucks wealth from the people into the establishment of court and state, on a rule of tyranny and of oppression (1 Sam. 8.11–17). That kind of satire on royal power is very close to another which has been preserved in the book of Judges and which has to be set alongside the two statements quoted above (17.6; 21.25) which suggest a pro-monarchic stance. Jotham's fable in Judges 9.7–15 ridicules the institution of monarchy. It tells of trees getting together and deciding to make one of their number king over them. They approach the olive tree, who scorns the idea. 'Shall I give up my oil by which gods and men are honoured and go to hold sway over the trees?' (v. 9). So they go next to the fig tree and are met with a similar rebuff. Fortunately for us the vine also thought its job of producing wine far more worthwhile than being king. So, repulsed by every worthwhile tree, they go to the bramble, which has no particular use at all, and the bramble graciously consents to become their king!

Further, throughout the Deuteronomistic History it is the kings who, again and again, are seen to be responsible for Israel's ills. There is a formula the editors use in passing judgement. They say, to take just one example, that Ba'asha's savage destruction of the rest of the line of Jeroboam in the northern kingdom was just judgement from God 'because of the sins of Jeroboam in which he sinned *and by which he made Israel to sin*' (1 Kings 15.30). Deuteronomy expresses the theological principle that people cannot keep the fruits of their sins to themselves. Their consequences always affect others. They put it in the well-known words that God 'visits the iniquity of the fathers on the children to the third and fourth generations' (Deut. 5.9). That is particularly true of a king who holds such a position of trust and leadership, and this is the point made repeatedly in the History. So, in spite of all Josiah's faithfulness and piety, he could not avert the disastrous consequences of Manasseh's sins, and that was why the exile of Judah to Babylon took place (2 Kings 23. 26f.).

How are we to reconcile these two different strands in Deuteronomy and the Deuteronomistic History? On the one hand there is the concept, favourable to monarchy, that it was all God's idea and that he chose David and his dynasty and promised them his eternal favour. On the other, there is the strongly negative attitude, that monarchy is really a result of human rejection of God as the one and only true king, and that, eventually, its failure was the cause of Israel's downfall.

It should be noted that some have thought them irreconcilable. This is the main reason why some scholars have argued for a two-stage redaction of the Deuteronomistic History. The first, with its strongly favourable tone, must have been produced in the reign of King Josiah when the nation's religious and political fortunes seemed to have recovered strongly through the instrumentality of a king who was a descendant of David. However, when the disaster fell, with Jerusalem burned, the Davidic king taken into exile, and all the divine promises apparently broken, someone revised the work to give a theological explanation of why it all happened.[13]

This is certainly possible. On the basis of the only evidence we have, which is the work as it stands, it is very difficult to be certain about just what editorial stages and complex redactional process it has passed through to get where it is. I do not myself believe that this theory, popular as it has become, offers a right answer, however, and I would see a rather more sophisticated, dialectical structure within the work as a whole. In any case, the 'double redaction' theory does not really solve the problem of the work's apparent inconsistency. Some final editor(s) must have left it in the form in which we now have it, and, unless they were idiots, they too must have seen that in 1 Samuel 8 and 9 they have left, not only two totally different accounts of how the monarchy began, but two totally different evaluations of its worth. Is there any reason, aside from literary and editorial incompetence, why they should have done this?

The first thing to notice is that they introduce, at three significant stages of the History, a new note into the idea of the covenant between God and the Davidic dynasty. As that was enunciated through Nathan in 2 Samuel 7 it was entirely unconditional. If David's son proved disobedient to God, then he could expect punishment, but God would not revoke the terms of the covenant: 'I will not remove my covenant loyalty [Hb. *ḥesed*] from him' (2 Sam. 7.15). In the History, however, when David is giving his dying charge to his son Solomon he tells him to keep all the law of Moses 'so that Yahweh may fulfil his promise which he made to me, *if* your descendants maintain their way of life before me in truth with all their heart and with all their energy, there shall never be wanting a man on the throne of Israel' (1 Kings 2.4). The same conditional note is expressed when Solomon himself addresses God as he dedicates the temple he has just had built (1 Kings 8.25) and when God speaks to him afterwards (1 Kings 9.4f.).[14]

In this way may not the Deuteronomists be saying something quite profound about such an institution as monarchy – and, indeed, any other human institution for that matter? Monarchy is, in fact, an ambivalent thing. Used aright and in obedience to God's requirements for justice, it can indeed be an instrument for good. In that sense, it really is God's idea. But, abused, as an instrument of oppression and extortion, where the interests of the 'subjects' are subordinated to those of the 'monarch', it becomes an evil, an affront to true human worth and liberty. This attitude in the History is exactly in line with the law of the king in Deuteronomy 17. The king is to exercise his rule in conformity with all the requirements of God's laws of justice and compassion for the little people of society. He is not to 'lift himself up above his kinsmen'. He needs constant reminding from the law that he is one with them, not their master whose interests are somehow different from theirs and which they are there to serve. On the contrary, anyone in power is the servant of his people, not vice versa. And if that is the message of the Deuteronomists, if that is the way they are subversive of what monarchy all too often became in Israel, and what any power system in human societies of all times has all too often become, is it such a trifling or irrelevant one? Whatever may be said of it, it is certainly not inconsistent or merely the result of editorial incompetence.

However, it is not only the monarchy itself of which Deuteronomy is to some extent subversive. It has often been noticed that there is what has been called a 'desacralizing' tendency in the work. It is amazing that this should be so from those who sought to give apparently such exclusive rights to the central sanctuary, namely, the Jerusalem temple. We have seen, however, that this was because of their desire to be able to keep Yahwism under control, under the same kind of subjection to what they saw to be the law to which they insist the monarchy must be subject. They saw this as the only way in which their insistence on the exclusive rights of Yahweh himself could be maintained in practice. This involves, therefore, considerable prominence for the Jerusalem priesthood (although they did try to involve those of the outlying sanctuaries which were shut down, Deut.18.6–8) and for the temple. However, they seem to go out of their way to play down the *sacral* significance of the temple building in the way it seems to be understood in those psalms which celebrate it as the place where Yahweh himself lives among his people (e.g. Pss. 46; 132). They have a certain circumlocution which they always use when speaking of the sanctuary. It is the place Yahweh has chosen 'to cause my name to dwell there' (e.g. Deut. 12.11). That seems to mean that Israelites may experience God's presence and his power there when he meets with them in worship, but they must not believe for a moment that they have him 'bottled up' there, serving their interests like some amenable genie in a bottle. He does not 'live' there in any exclusive sense.

There have been some recently who have argued that this is not all that significant. The average Israelite would not have seen the fine distinction between the 'name' of Yahweh and Yahweh himself being present. This may be true, but that it mattered to the Deuteronomists is I believe underlined by the words they put into Solomon's mouth when he prays at the dedication of the temple. It is worth quoting them in full at this point.

'But will God really live on earth? Indeed, heaven and the highest heaven do not confine you. How much less this house which I have built! But give attention to the prayer which your servant prays to you today. And hear the cry for grace of your servant, O Yahweh my God, listening to the cry and the prayer which your servant is praying before you today. May your eyes be open day and night towards this house, towards the place of which you have promised, "My name shall be there" ...' (1 Kings 8. 27–9)

That seems to argue for a real distinction between the thought of God's presence as literally and wholly embodied in the temple, and an existential encounter there with one who is by no means confined to its precincts and religious practices.

Further, while the Levitical priests do have a cultic function to fulfil, and Deuteronomy keeps all the sacred festivals and regulates about sacrifices, the fact is that the centre of gravity is beginning to be placed elsewhere. We have seen that the Levites and priests have a responsibility for teaching the law to the king. They are also teachers of the law to the people (e.g. Deut. 24.8) and this is stressed in the 'Blessing of Moses' in 33.8–10, where the responsibility of the Levites to teach the 'Torah' is put before their sacrificial duties. Moses is the supreme teacher of the law (4.1, 5, 10, 14; 5.31; 6.1). It is interesting that the 'Ark of the Covenant', which in other Old Testament traditions seems to have been regarded as a sign of the presence of Yahweh (e.g. Num. 10.35f.), the support for the throne of Yahweh in the temple (e.g. Jer. 3.16) and to have played a significant part for the Priestly writers in the rites of expiation (Lev. 16.2, 13–15), is spoken of in Deuteronomy as simply a box for containing the tables of the law (Deut. 10.2).

In the way Deuteronomy thus tends to desacralize the temple and its furnishings, and to put the emphasis much more on teaching, hearing, and obeying the word of God than on religious ritual, it really does make them sound rather more like latter day non-Conformists than High Church sacerdotalists![15] But the tendency does not stop there. For there is in a real sense a 'democratizing' process at work in Deuteronomy. It is by no means only the Levitical priests who are charged with teaching the law to the Israelites. Even more often, ordinary Israelites are called upon to discharge this responsibility. Parents are to teach their children. At Horeb God had called Moses to collect the people together that they might hear the commandments so that 'they may teach their children' (4.10). Israelites are commanded, 'You shall teach them to your children, and speak about them when you sit down at home, when you are walking along the road, when you go to bed and when you get up' (11.19).

Indeed, this brings home a major emphasis in Deuteronomy. It is not just the king, or the priests, who are responsible for the religious and ethical life of the people. All Israelites are addressed by the law; all Israel has been 'chosen' by God. The classic expression of this is in 7.6–8, in which the verb which indicates that Yahweh has 'chosen' all Israel as his own people is the same as that which is used in the choice of David in contexts which deal with the divine choice of David and his line. All Israelites are brought within the scope of the law in this book, both in responsibility to obey it and by being included within its protection, including women, for example (e.g. 17.2ff.; 22.5; 13–30, a passage which severely limits men's absolute rights over women). By making all members of the community responsible for hearing and obeying the law they are elevating ordinary Israelites to a level which considerably limits the dominant place of both king and priest. It can be said in passing that one is almost tempted to make use of another anachronistic term from later Christian theology and describe it as a doctrine of the priesthood of all believers!

Indeed, it is in this matter that Deuteronomy introduces another of its 'subversive' elements. We have seen how strong is its propaganda about the right of Israel to the land of Canaan. But, just as the Deuteronomists make the Davidic covenant a conditional one, so the Deuteronomists emphasize that the Sinaitic covenant, made with the whole community of Israel, is a conditional one. In another real sense, the land is not theirs by right. It is God's land and it is his gift to his people. But the gift has conditions attached to it. If they fail to observe his laws, those laws which make every man and woman among them responsible and all members of the community, especially the poor and the weak, the responsibility of all, they will not find the land the prosperous place they expected and, ultimately, might even lose it. This is expressed most clearly in the blessings and curses which form the sanctions in chapter 28 for their behaviour in the land. The threats of loss of fertility of the land and of defeat by invaders lead up to the ultimate climax threatening that the miracle of the Exodus from Egypt will be reversed: 'Yahweh will bring you back to Egypt in ships, by that very way which I promised you would not see again, and there you will offer to sell yourselves to your enemies as male and female slaves, but no one will want to own you' (28.68).

Thus there is an element of subversion even about the main plank of Deuteronomy's propaganda. Yet, as was said earlier, there is no real inconsistency here. To explain why it was that both king and people had lost their national inheritance the Deuteronomists have offered their powerful critique of the society which proved to have failed. It is a point which has been powerfully expressed by E. W. Nicholson:

> Deuteronomy's vision of Israel is of a united and strikingly egalitarian society, one in which there are no centres of power but in which all participate as 'brethren' living together like an extended family upon its 'plot' of land given to it by Yahweh. Such a vision requires a rejection of the Israel that was, a nation divided politically for centuries past and whose social and communal bonds had increasingly been eroded under the impact of the economic system which emerged in the monarchical period.[16]

Throughout this discussion I have kept strictly to an examination of what is in the books of Deuteronomy and Joshua—2 Kings. I have not at any point raised the question, 'Who were these Deuteronomists?' It is not an easy question to answer. Some have argued that they were Levites, because of the strong place they give to the role and rights of the Levites.[17] Others have argued from the very strong parallels between Deuteronomy and the teaching of especially the northern prophets, that they were prophets.[18] Some have argued for links between Deuteronomy and the Wisdom teachers of Israel.[19] The idea that the movement they represent started in the northern kingdom of Israel under the influence of the prophets and then, on the fall of that kingdom, moved to the south and set about reforming traditional southern royal and temple theology, is an attractive one. These days when we recognize the functioning of 'cultic prophets' alongside priests in the sanctuaries, it hardly seems necessary to argue for long over whether they were prophets or Levites. On the other hand, they are much more steeped in the sacral traditions of Israel than most of the Wisdom writers show themselves to be in the literature we can trace to them.

Whoever they were, they draw on Israel's sacral traditions to claim Israel's uniqueness and divine right to the land of Canaan. The stridency with which they do this, particularly in their rejection of all other peoples and every trace of their religion, seems to argue for a time of uncertainty and threat, times when old certainties become more important and are urged without compromise. However, they have seen the failure of monarchy and even of the priestly religion of the temple to keep Israel in possession of what they see as its birthright. They therefore begin to put an emphasis on Israel as a religious community bound together mainly by the sacred law given to them from the time of their beginning as a nation by Moses. It is the duty of all members of the community to understand that law, keep it and teach it to successive generations. The idea of a community of all members of the society, equal from the smallest to the greatest, is a subversive element at work in the kind of unequal society which had grown up under the monarchy, a society where political, religious and economic power had succeeded in alienating whole sections of the people. Thus their call for compassion and equality for all under the law. Of course, while extolling the responsibility of all members of society, they are at the same time putting their own spin on Yahwism, working towards a situation in which it is the experts in Torah – they themselves – who will have a dominant role which neither king nor priest should have, they believe, without severe limitation and checks on their power. One can see how strong an appeal such an interpretation of Yahwism would make in the time of chaos and confusion after the collapse of the kingdom during the time of the Babylonian exile. When there is no longer either king or priest able to exercise their traditional and powerful mediatorial role, the law, which can be observed anywhere and by anyone, can be a cement to bind the splintered fragments of the community together, and those who reveal just what the law is and how it is to be kept in practice become the new force to be reckoned with. That is why the Deuteronomists must be credited with both propaganda and subversion.

CHAPTER FIVE

The Subversion of the Prophets

In the first chapter we looked at some examples of propaganda in the ancient Near East, the world of the Hebrews and the Old Testament. We saw it used as a tool for building up and buttressing the claims of those in power, those of the religious and political establishment. It could be seen to go a long way towards justifying the description of religion by sociologists such as Peter Berger, 'Religion legitimates social institutions by bestowing upon them an ultimately valid ontological status, that is by *locating* them within a sacred and cosmic frame of reference.'[1] The spirits of faithful believers, taught to believe that every word of 'Scripture' is of equal divine authority, may have sunk when faced with the many parallels to such propaganda in the Old Testament. Here also, it is all too plain, propaganda is being used as a tool to maintain and buttress the claims of political and religious authorities. Inevitably this posed the question, 'Is that all the Old Testament scriptures are?' At that point we merely raised one or two points which remain to be considered more fully now. I said that not every order which uses propaganda to justify its claims is necessarily bad. Only a few extremely radical people would believe that there has never been, or can never be, a good monarch or government, or that all the priests or other ecclesiastical authority figures who exercise power in religious structures are corrupt and self-seeking by nature. And, if there has seldom, or never, been a completely good governor, government or ecclesiastical authority (whatever we may mean by 'good' in such a context) there have often been beneficent ones whose achievements and the effects of whose rule, while they may have been mixed, might be said to have produced some good result for somebody. We have argued that the priests of Old Testament times achieved a very great deal in producing a Judaism which could survive the loss of political independence and 'secular' institutions. We have seen how the Deuteronomists, fierce critics of much to do with monarchy, nevertheless saw that in some hands, and under certain conditions, it could produce some good, or as they would put it, 'be used by God'.

At the same time, however, we cannot read the Old Testament, (let alone any other set of religious and historical documents), without realizing that the power structures are prone to abuse and injustice. Power comes all too easily to be seen as an end in itself, a tool to serve those who wield it rather than a means of serving the good of those for whose sake they have ostensibly been entrusted with it. And it is often those who themselves have least power, who are least able to challenge the selfishness, greed, corruption and neglect of those who dwell in palaces defended by the ramparts of a hierarchy of power structures, who suffer the effects of that abuse most. The wars of the great powers are mostly fought by those who control and manipulate different, but competing, power structures. They are usually paid for out of the produce and by the lives of the weak, for whom a change of power structure may well mean only a different taskmaster and a different postal address for their local tax office. The official religion of those authorities, as we have seen, tells the common people that the present order is the 'will of God' and serves to maintain the divine 'order' against all forms of intrusive chaos. How can those who have no wealth and no power, the victims so often of the privileges and abuses of those who profit from this 'divine order', bring about any change? Who will listen to them? Who speak for them?

The remarkable thing is that, in the same Old Testament which mirrors the claims of the official orders, voices do speak for them. The 'poor' and 'needy' (Hb. *'ebyôn, dal*), the 'humble' (Hb. *'ānî, 'ānau*), and all those whom society and circumstances leave without support – the widow, the orphan, the foreign immigrant – find their champions in its pages. Those whose complaints and cries for justice are so often expressed in the psalms of lament, are assured that God is on their side. And the prophets who, among others, bring this assurance so insistently, also assure the powers of the establishment, when they abuse their powers, that God is the champion, not of them and their orders, but of the powerless and the oppressed. This remarkable 'prophetic subversion' is a striking demonstration of what was said earlier, that religion can turn out to be an awkward servant. Those who think they can call on it for their own self-interest, just as Aladdin could call up the genie by rubbing the lamp the right way, get a shock. The genie sometimes comes when he has not been bidden, and it is not his supposed master's interests he comes to serve. In calling in religion as a servant of the state and the ecclesiastical structures, kings, priests and other authority figures find they have cast a boomerang with an awkward cutting edge. Instead of always decapitating their enemies, however, it may rebound on them. This 'prophetic subversion' is the subject of this chapter. A story often told it may be, but it remains one of the great legacies of the Old Testament for all time.

The origins of the prophetic movement remain shrouded in mystery for us. Of its beginnings in Israel we know only what the Deuteronomistic Historians have chosen to give us, mainly in the books of Judges, Samuel and Kings. There can be no doubt that their picture of its early figures is coloured both by their experience of the later prophets and by a strong 'theology of prophecy' which sees it not only as a means, by which God warns and instructs his people, but as a way in which God exercises his control over history. Just as he created the world 'by his word', so he brings events about in predicting them 'by his word', a word spoken through the 'true prophets'.[2]

Probably prophecy began in Israel as it did among many of their neighbouring peoples. Bands of charismatic figures like those described in 1 Samuel 10.5–13 and 19.18–24 were associated with religious sanctuaries and acted in the interests of the deity whose cult was observed at that particular centre. Gradually leaders would emerge of the type pictured in the Old Testament in the figures of Samuel, Elijah and Elisha. Early on such figures operated at quite a primitive level, as can be seen in the story of Saul and his servant going to Samuel to get an 'oracle', for the payment of a fee, concerning the whereabouts of some lost cattle (1 Sam. 9.5–27). They were remembered not only for what they said on certain occasions but for their legendary powers of miracle working. The 'miraculous' element plays a particularly prominent part in the Elisha cycle of stories. In addition, once the kingdom was established, court or 'mantic' prophets (the term relates to the giving of oracles obtained by divination), whose task was to advise, and sometimes to admonish, the king and the government, appeared. Prophets like Gad and Nathan seem to have played such a role. All of these phenomena were by no means peculiar to Israel. They are widely observed throughout the ancient world. So, also, are what are often referred to as 'cultic prophets', prophets who served alongside the priests in the sanctuaries, giving instruction and generally maintaining the relation between the deity and the people. The presence of such figures in Israel, especially at the Jerusalem temple, is now widely assumed in Old Testament scholarship, and it is generally believed they played a significant role in the composition and use of the psalms.[3] In the Deuteronomistic History a great variety of all such types of figures, many of them probably imperfectly remembered or understood, tend to be lumped together under the umbrella term 'prophet' and all treated as part of the divine provision of 'prophecy' to later Israel.

Just how, in fact, the 'classic', named prophets of the Old Testament relate to all these different types of prophecy, how far they may, or may not have been associated with worship at official cultic centres, and in what relationship, if any, they stood to the official institutions of palace and temple, are all matters which have been vigorously debated for a long time. There are those who think that with the so-called 'writing' prophets of the 8th century BCE (starting with Amos) a quite new phenomenon appeared.[4] Others have taken a more gradualist, evolutionary view of the development of prophecy.[5] Neither the exact development of prophecy, its nature, or the Old Testament theology (or theologies) of prophecy is our subject here. I am concerned with the words attributed to the prophets in the books which bear their names. Just how they got there, and what precisely was the role of any historical figure who has given his name to the book, is of secondary concern. For what it is worth, I lean towards the 'gradualist' view of the development of prophecy, and I suspect that many different types of activity and phenomena, mostly now labelled 'prophecy' by the Deuteronomistic Historians because of their theological concerns with prophecy, continued for a long time alongside each other in historic Israel. Although the prophets fiercely condemn those whom they described as 'false prophets', that should not be taken to allude exclusively to any particular type of prophet, such as 'ecstatic' or 'cultic' prophets. It was not the 'type' a prophet was which made him or her true or false. Amos, certainly, could look back on the prophets who had been before him as a gift from God to Israel (Amos 2.11). We do not know whether the prophets whose names the books bear functioned at the court or the temple or whether they were lone individualists. The answer to such questions may not by any means be the same for all of them. All we can say is that with some prophets, their words were remembered and committed to writing, probably because, in the passage of time, they were believed to have 'come to pass'. The experience of the fall of Jerusalem and the exile must have hastened the process by which those prophets who had warned of serious judgement to come were seen to have spoken truly. Further, we owe the prophetic books by no means just to them, but to those who over succeeding generations found in their words that which was relevant and applicable to their own day. Each prophetic book has gone through a long process of growth and redaction as the 'original' words were expounded afresh to later generations. It is easier to spot that such a process has been at work than always to be precise about just what any particular historical prophet said and how his words have been added to, adapted, placed in new contexts and given new emphases by later editors. There is so much about prophecy in ancient Israel that we do not know that a certain humble agnosticism about some of these questions is not entirely out of place.

Our concern here is with the books of the 'writing' prophets. I put the term 'writing' in inverted commas because we do not know just how much any particular prophet wrote himself or how much of his preaching was given orally, remembered, and then written down by others. There are very few references to writing in our prophetic books. Isaiah was told to write a certain message so that it might be a 'witness' to future generations that it had been spoken (Isa. 30.8). He also wrote down the symbolic name of his second child (8.1). It is possible that he is also referring to the practice of writing a message in 8.16, where he says, 'Bind up the testimony, seal the teaching among my disciples' (or, 'those whom I have taught'). Equally, however, that might refer to oral teaching. Jeremiah was told to write down his oracles, and he dictated them to his scribe Baruch (Jer. 36.1–4). When the king had the written scroll from which Baruch read the prophet's words torn up and burned (36.20–24), Jeremiah was commanded again to dictate his words on another scroll, which he did adding 'many similar words to them' for good measure, which only goes to show one should be careful about trying to stop a prophet from speaking (36.27–32). Habakkuk was another prophet told by God to write an oracle down to assure those who had to wait for its fulfilment that it had been promised and therefore would come to pass (Hab. 2.1–3).

All that, however, gives us only a very sketchy picture of the process by which the words from a prophet's mouth got on to the written scroll and by which such writings developed into our present books. It shows, what we have to suspect anyway, that both prophets and others had a hand in them and that the 'others' probably continued the interpretative and exegetical process for many generations after the life of the historic prophet whose name is associated with a particular book. It is, as I have indicated already, a difficult and probably forlorn task to attempt to separate the 'original' message of a given prophet from the tradition process to which it has been subject. Those who produced the final forms of the books were more interested in the contemporary relevance of that message than they were in preserving some 'original' form of it out of antiquarian or historical concerns. In the same way they did not usually think it important to concentrate much on the 'biography' of the prophet in the way people today like biographers to give them more intimate knowledge of a figure from the past. Not the messenger but the message, not the past but the present, were what mattered to the final editors of the prophetic books.

Before we turn our attention to the first of these 'writing' prophets, Amos, however, there are two incidents at least from the accounts of earlier prophetic activity recorded in the Deuteronomistic History which have sometimes been claimed to show the 'subversive' tendencies of the later prophets. The first is the confrontation of David by the prophet Nathan following the Bathsheba incident. This episode is recorded in 2 Samuel 11f. On any count it was a discreditable example of the abuse of royal power by David even if one may not think it entirely unparalleled in either the ancient or more modern world. David's army was at war against the Ammonites, besieging the town of Rabbah. On this occasion, David, the commander-in-chief of Israel's armies, stayed at home, delegating the campaign to others. While there, he saw Bathsheba bathing on a rooftop (the Hebrew narrator does not speculate on whether this was an entirely unpremeditated location for a bath) and lusted for her. She was married to a foreigner, Uriah, a Hittite, who was conveniently away on active service at the front. When their liaison made her pregnant, David hit on a ruse to divert suspicion. He had Uriah recalled on leave, ostensibly to get news of the campaign, and then sent him home with an invitation of sufficient ambiguity (literally, 'wash your feet': sometimes 'feet' is a term used euphemistically of the genitalia, e.g. Isa. 6.2) and even the wherewithal for a celebratory meal with Bathsheba, to arouse Uriah's suspicions ('Shall I go to my house to eat and drink *and sleep with my wife?*' verse 11). Ostensibly because his companions in arms are still in all the danger and discomfort of the battlefield he stays away from his home. That strategy baulked, David is forced into another, far more extreme. He sends written instructions under cover, carried by Uriah himself, to Joab, the commander, to 'arrange' for Uriah's death by exposing him in an impossibly hazardous situation in the battle. When news of his death came back to Jerusalem, Bathsheba, once the formal period of mourning was over, married David and had another son by him. The later story shows that Bathsheba was just as calculating as David. One senses that neither of them wasted too much useless remorse over Uriah.

It was at this point that Nathan confronted David. Cleverly, rather than rebuke him with the kind of moralistic lecture against which we are all proof, he begins by telling him a story – a parable, in fact, and it is remarkable testimony to the power of the parable. He tells David that there were two men in the same city. One was very poor, owning only one lamb, and the other very rich with large flocks and herds. When someone dropped in as he was passing the house of the rich man and needed feeding, the rich man took the one lamb of the poor man for the feast rather than one of his own.

David, used as king to having 'cases' brought to him as the ultimate arbiter of 'justice' for judgement in legal disputes, was up in righteous anger in a moment. That rich man deserved to die. At the very least he must make reparation of four times the amount he stole.

There follow some of the most famous words in the Old Testament: '*You* are that man,' says Nathan. Cleverly, the prophet has used the parable to get David to pass judgement on himself. It is a noteworthy example of a prophet standing up to the abuse of power and privilege by a king.

The other incident features a later prophet, Elijah, and a later king of the northern realm of Israel, Ahab, and is recounted in 1 Kings 21. One of the freemen of Israel, Naboth, had a vineyard which had been in his family for generations. It jutted into Ahab's royal domains, who made Naboth a bid for it, offering to resettle him on the ancient equivalent of a modern council estate on the edge of town. Naboth refused on the ground that the family ownership of land was a sacred inheritance. So, in Israel, even a small freeman could refuse the king a request, since, in Yahwism, all Israelites, royal and commoner, were kinsmen in the covenant relationship with God, having equal rights. Ahab knew this well enough, and so he goes home, lies down on his bed, turns his face to the wall, refuses all food and has a good old royal sulk. It is enough to attract the attention of his vigorous wife Jezebel, of a Phoenician royal family, whom Ahab had married to secure diplomatic and defence treaties with his powerful neighbours. She knows none of Ahab's inhibitions and berates him for his feebleness. '*You* are the one who exercises royal power in Israel,' she says shrilly. With her more absolute view of monarchy she cannot understand anyone being so weak as to let a mere commoner have his way when it is inconvenient to those in power. She instigates the bringing of a false charge against Naboth so that he receives the death penalty. Now Ahab can get his land without even paying for it!

The story is full of irony (remember that the king was meant to be the ultimate arbiter of 'justice'). But, again, he is confronted by a prophet, Elijah, who wastes no time on the literary niceties of a parable, but bluntly issues a warning of judgement of death on him and his wife.

These are, of course, fine stories, but it is doubtful if we can claim the adjective 'subversive' for them. To begin with, whatever historical background there may or may not be to them, they are used by the Deuteronomic Historians to illustrate their theology both of kingship and of prophecy. They are meant to show that only if the king is obedient to the laws of God will he be successful and know the blessings promised to David and his successors (no northern king even begins to qualify for these in their eyes anyway). Kings are not 'above the law' when it comes to God's laws. The terms in which Elijah rebukes Ahab are pure Deuteronomic language. Elijah speaks in verses 20–23 the very words which the historians use again and again in passing judgement on the various kings (e.g. 1 Kings 16.12f., etc.). Further, it shows the Deuteronomists' theology of prophecy, whereby God exercises his sovereign control over the events of history by first announcing through a prophet what he will do, and then bringing that word to pass.

But, further, neither prophet is recorded as using the incident to reject the institution of monarchy altogether, nor the continued existence of the state. They function in some ways as 'court prophets', whose role is to keep the word of the deity before the king and ensure that his rule is seen to be on a just basis. There are plenty of instances of the function of such prophets in the ancient Near East. For example, at Mari a prophet wrote to the king:

At the [inspection of] the omens Adad the Lord of Kallasu spoke as follows: 'Am I not Adad the Lord of Kallasu who reared him between my thighs and restored him to the throne of his father's house? After restoring him to the throne of his father's house, I again gave him a dwelling-place. Now, since I restored him to the throne of his father's house, I should receive from him an hereditary property. If he does not give it, I am the lord of the throne, territory, and city, and what I gave I will take away. If on the other hand he grants my request, I will give him throne upon throne, house upon house, territory upon territory, city upon city; even the land from east to west will I give him.'[6]

The demand that the king gives the god the obedience and reverence which is his due and that failure to do so will result in judgement against him while obedience will bring untold prosperity, is exactly the view of court prophecy the Deuteronomists hold. They challenge the king on what might certainly be called more ethical notes (at least in the two examples we have looked at – often, however, the demands are wholly cultic, worship at the central sanctuary and the toleration of no other gods) but the function of the prophet is the same. Rather than prophesying the end of the whole system, these prophets are like pilots on a ship. They show the course to steer by which the ship of state may be saved. They function within the system, and their aim is to preserve it.

It is somewhat different with Amos, for he was ejected from the royal sanctuary of Bethel by its high priest on the ground that he had been preaching sedition (Amos 7.10–17), a fairly well-grounded charge in the light of Amos's words recorded in 7.9, where he predicted the downfall of the ruling dynasty. Indeed, Amos is one of those rare churchmen in history who could not claim that his teaching had been distorted by his critics – Amaziah's paraphrase in 7.10f. being a fairly accurate summary of what he said.

We know as little about Amos as we do about most of the prophets. It is said he came from Tekoa, which is actually in the southern kingdom, about ten miles south of Jerusalem. His ministry appears mainly to have been carried out in the northern kingdom, however, for it is the ruling dynasty of Jeroboam II of Israel and the northern sanctuaries of Bethel and Gilgal which he attacks, while he speaks much about Samaria. References to Jerusalem and Judah probably belong to a later stage of the book's development in Judah after the fall of the northern kingdom, when editors expressed their sense of the relevance of what he had had to say about the north to the Judah of their own time. The evidence about his social status is somewhat ambiguous. The heading of the book (1.1, the work of editors) says that he came from the 'shepherds' of Tekoa. That might suggest someone rather humble, an impression strengthened by his own words about his background when he tells Amaziah that he had been a herdsman and a dresser of sycamores (7.14). That might indicate almost an itinerant worker, the kind of casual worker who goes hop picking in Britain in the summer or moved from job to job in the way described by John Steinbeck in his novel *The Grapes of Wrath*. Many have felt it strange, however, that such a man could have had so wide a knowledge of international affairs and such a grasp of the religious traditions of Israel. They have pointed out that the word used for 'herdsmen' in 1.1 (Hb. *nôqᵉdîm*, not the word which appears in the Hebrew text of 7.14, although the LXX suggests that it was originally the word which lies behind a present corruption, a suggestion followed by many commentators) can be used of someone like the king of Moab (2 Kings 3.4). This would suggest something like a 'sheep breeder' or even 'sheep trader', and it has been suggested that this would involve extensive travelling, which would account for Amos's wide knowledge and experience. We simply do not know. What he does tell us is that he was not a 'professional' prophet, employed in the service of the sanctuary (7.14). Nevertheless, he believed God called him to prophesy, and it was from something of a detached position that he launched his fierce criticisms of the royal house, the exponents of the official religion of the state, all leaders indeed, and the wealthy and powerful.

While we cannot be sure of the exact dates of Amos's activity it is clear that he prophesied during the reign of Jeroboam II. It is often said that the first half of the 8th century BCE (800 – c.750) was one of considerable security and prosperity for Israel. In 803/2 BCE a strong and powerful king in Assyria, Adad-nirari III, captured Damascus and broke the power of Syria, Israel's northern neighbour, by exacting crippling tribute. Israel no doubt had to pay up as well but does not seem to have been as heavily involved. But then a period of internal crisis kept Assyria busy at home and delayed her plans of imperial expansion westwards. Jeroboam came to the throne in 786 BCE at a time, therefore, when no great threat from outside menaced his kingdom. He was able to indulge in a little military expansion of his own. 2 Kings 14.25 speaks of his establishing Israel's borders across the Jordan even as far south as the Arabah, while Amos (6.13) alludes to the boasting of his contemporaries about their military victories, especially the capture of Lo-dabar and Karnaim, the first being a town east of Jordan (2 Sam. 17.27). Resulting control of lucrative trade routes and the absence of the need for paying tribute to any foreign power brought considerable prosperity to the kingdom, at least for some. A moneyed 'capitalist' class seems to have emerged whose members were able to lend money at rates favourable to themselves and who, by mercilessly foreclosing on the mortgages of any unable to pay, built up considerable estates (5.11). They are able to indulge in an extravagant lifestyle, owning summer and winter houses (3.15), costly interior decor with carved inlaid panels of ivory on furniture and walls (3.15; 6.4, examples of which have been discovered in archaeological excavations at the site of Samaria), enjoy rich banquets of meat and wine while, then as now, one sign of prosperity was the financial success of the cosmetics industry (6.4–6). Rather unkindly Amos depicts the craving for more money which money always produces as affecting also the wives of the landowners and merchants, 'cows of Bashan' he calls them, for which a modern British equivalent might be 'sleek Jersey cows', who urge their husbands to earn even more to keep up their standard of living (4.1). Once the purpose of life is found in economic growth, people, then also as now, become impatient with any enforced interruption of profit-making. In their case it seemed a shame to stop even for sabbath and religious observances (8.5f.), and Amos even suggests in the same verse that they 'fiddled the accounts' to their own advantage. This might have been all right had it not been at the expense of the poor whom they drove off their land and forced to sell out to them on scandalously unfair terms (2.6–8; 4.1; 5.11; 8.4–6). If ever the poor tried to bring a legal action 'at the gate' (the local equivalent of the court where the elders heard legal disputes), their wealthy oppressors were well able to buy a favourable verdict with suitable hand-outs (5.12).

All of this must have been condoned by the king (the ultimate champion of justice in the realm) and the priests, who must have winked at such practices as the bringing into the sanctuary for use as prayer mats clothes taken illegally from the poor as pledge of a debt (2.8, cf. Exod. 22.25–7). Indeed, the very people who are breaking the law of Israel in their financial transactions and by their treatment of the poor, are great supporters of the royal sanctuaries, of the whole religious cult which, as we have seen, promotes and maintains the royal rule and the power of the king's court. They keep its cultic requirements 'religiously' (4.4f.; 5.21–4), but they conveniently forget its demands for justice (5.15, 24).

In reaction to all this, the book of Amos shows literary techniques not dissimilar to that used by Nathan in his condemnation of David. Nathan employed the literary device of the parable to lead David on to moral condemnation which, only too late, he realized was self-condemnation (see above, pp. 96f.). The book of Amos uses a different literary *genre* but one that is directed to the same end. He uses the form of the 'Oracles against the Nations'. The book opens with a series of six oracles against nations which bordered Israel: Syria, Philistia, Phoenicia, Edom, Ammon and Moab.[7] Oracles against foreign nations figure in most of the prophetic collections of the Old Testament. In the major books, separate sections are devoted to them: Isaiah 13—23; Jeremiah 46—51; Ezekiel 25—32. Nahum is an oracle against a foreign nation, Assyria, in itself, and several other prophetic books divide into three main groups of oracles, warnings of judgement against Israel, promises of future deliverance for Israel, threats against foreign nations. Even in a small book like Zephaniah, one section (2.4–15) contains threats directed towards other peoples.

There has been a great deal of discussion about the origin and function of such prophetic oracles (the issues are discussed briefly by Barton in *Amos's Oracles*, pp. 8–15). Whatever their origin, whether that was in times of war or in the official cult, they seem to have acted as salvation oracles for Israel. We may see something of the thinking behind them in the strange story of Balaam in Numbers 22f. He was hired by the king of Moab, who was fighting with Israel, in order to utter a solemn 'curse' against Israel. 'And now go, curse this people for me because they are stronger than I am. Perhaps I shall prevail and we shall defeat them and I will drive them out of the land, for I know that anyone you bless is blessed and anyone you curse is cursed' (22.6). In other words he is calling up the ancient equivalent of a guided missile. The whole episode reminds us that the prophetic 'word', just like the symbolic deed of the prophet, was considered to be far more than merely declarative. The word or the deed released power and energy which were effective. The clearest expression of this in the prophetic literature is the well-known Isaiah 55.10f.

'Just as rain and snow descend from the sky,
and do not return there but water the earth,
making it fruitful and abundant,
providing seed for the sower and food for the eater,
so shall my word be which proceeds from my mouth,
it shall not return to me fruitless
but it will do what I want it to
and promote the purpose for which I sent it.'

The roots of this may well lie in sympathetic and mimetic magic. A prophet like the author of Isaiah 55.10f., however, would have argued for a powerful difference between magic and prophecy. Those who practise magic are trying to harness mysterious powers to their own ends (just as the king of Moab was in hiring Balaam). In prophecy, they believed, the power was God's and so was not under their control for the service merely of their own interests.

It is not possible to say just what had been the practice of such oracles against the nations and how their function was regarded before the time of Amos, because his is the first written collection of prophecy we have. We cannot put too much weight on the Balaam story for hard historical evidence since, as it stands, the story is a strong piece of pro-Israelite propaganda. Balaam refuses the office initially because Yahweh tells him not to undertake it. He persists in this refusal even when the cash incentive is raised considerably, until Yahweh himself tells him to go with them. However, when the prophet is riding on his ass to discharge the task, God becomes angry with him for doing so and sends an angel to block the road. Only the ass sees the angel and is whipped by Balaam because she stops and finally lies down in protest. Little wonder that God 'opened the mouth of the ass' which has an indignant (and very amusing) interchange of words with Balaam. At that moment, and none too soon one might think, God 'opens Balaam's eyes' as well, and he saw the angel roadblock and was told not to curse Israelites but to bless them instead.

It is an enjoyable story and one, perhaps, not without its comfort for teachers, preachers, lecturers, for almost everyone indeed apart from authors, in assuring us that occasionally God can speak through the mouth of an ass. But it is on a somewhat primitive level as a reliable historical source and is, of course, a piece of pro-Israelite propaganda. Nevertheless, we may assume that normally the oracle against a foreign nation was seen as a powerful support for the people of God, a means of showing them and their enemies just whose side 'He' is on.

We may assume, then, that Amos's hearers would have welcomed and been assured by a series of oracles denouncing their feared and hated neighbours. The formula of the oracles varies a little, but in general they open with a threat of judgement against each nation 'for three transgressions and for four', a literary technique suggesting sins of ever-increasing number and enormity. Then the specific charge is made against them. Each is condemned for some act of inhuman cruelty, for what we would now call war crimes. We have seen quite enough of them in our time to have been able to think up a suitable name for them. It is noteworthy that these are not by any means acts only against Israel. They include unnecessary savagery by the Syrians when they invaded Gilead, selling prisoners of war as slaves, breaking alliances, ripping open pregnant women. Because they have acted so unnaturally, so much against any basic 'natural' law of justice (see Barton, *Amos's Oracles*, pp. 39–50), God is about to judge them. This judgement will take the form of military invasion by an enemy and will be directed principally against the strongholds of the established state and their kings (1.5, 15; 2.3).

All that would doubtless have been most welcome to Amos's audience. It would have assured them that God was on their side (since he was against their enemies) and that they could relax safe in their unique relationship with him as his special people. There is no pleasure quite like that of hearing other people's sins denounced nor of learning that those one does not like are destined for a sticky end. Just like David when he heard Nathan's parable, they would have agreed that such sins were terrible, well deserving of all the thunderbolts in God's armoury of justice.

Imagine, then, with what a shock they must have heard the prophet continue with exactly the same formula of denunciation and threat of God's action against the Israelites themselves (2.6):

> This is what Yahweh is saying:
> 'For three rebellions of Israel and for four
> I will not call him back.'[8]

Then their 'crimes of cruelty' are spelled out. The differences are two. The charge against them is far longer than any against their foreign neighbours. And whereas the other nations have been charged with cruelty against foreigners, Israel is charged with cruelty against her own people. It is the ruthless and merciless exploitation and oppression of the poor by the strong and wealthy which is exposed and denounced. The special relationship between Israel and God is not denied. They are reminded of what they must so often have celebrated in their liturgy, that God had delivered them from slavery in Egypt, kept them in the years of wandering in the wilderness, given them the military victories by which they had entered Canaan (the land of the 'Amorites'), and had sent them prophets to teach them, and the Nazirites, with their special vows of dedication, to inspire them. Yet they had refused to listen to the prophets and sought to bring the Nazirites down to their own level. They had not *acted* in any way as a special people (2.9–12). So they also are threatened with military disaster. The prophecy which should have been a tool for maintaining their security and status and helping to secure the defeat of their enemies has here been turned against them. It has become an instrument destructive of the establishment rather than a title deed of the validity of its claims to divine appointment.

These shock tactics, whereby the usual function of prophecy is stood on its head, and the establishment's power claims are turned against the whole apparatus of religion and state, are repeated in the book. In the opening of chapter 3 Amos takes words again familiar to and loved by a people assured of their special status as God's own people:

'Only you have I known among all the families of the earth.' (3.2)

But what a corollary is drawn:

'*Therefore* I will punish you for all your evils.'

Amos does not deny their special status. He turns it against them. Their special position placed upon them special responsibilities, especially of an ethical and moral kind. In one way Amos anticipated the words, 'To whom much is given, from him much is expected' (Luke 12.48). By their unbrotherly treatment of each other (there is a real irony in Amos's words, 'You only have I know of all the *families* of the earth') they have rejected their status as God's family. (We might say, by their 'uncovenant-like' treatment of each other they have forfeited their 'covenant' relationship with God, but we need to be careful because Amos does not use the term 'covenant' of Israel's relationship with God. Whether that was because it was not yet used, being an invention of the Deuteronomists later, or whether because, though known by this time, it seemed to Amos to have the wrong connotations, is much disputed among scholars.) Salt is rubbed in the wounds of their national pride by another outrageous statement (as it would have seemed to them) in Amos in 9.7:

> 'Did I not bring Israel up from the land of Egypt? – *and* the Philistines from Caphtor *and* the Syrians from Kir?'

Again, their traditions are not denied. They are right to think that God had delivered their ancestors from slavery in Egypt. But God has been in the movement of *all* peoples in history, in those of their traditional enemies as well as in their own. It would be difficult to think of a firmer rejection of their claim to 'special' status.

So Amos 'subverts' the religious claims of the nation state of Israel. Whatever may have been the position in the past, God now views them in no way differently from all other nations. He judges them all on the same moral and ethical basis of action.

But Amos subverts those claims also in another way. God intends to dispense with the whole political and religious establishment of Israel. He has passed sentence on it. The wealthy will not live in the stone houses they have built or the great estates they have wrested from their rightful owners (5.11). The nation will be defeated in battle (2.13–16; 3.11; 6.1–7). In particular, the royal house of Jeroboam will be destroyed (7.9) together with the official sanctuaries whose cult supported that royal power (3.13f.; 5.4f.; 7.8f.). Indeed, it seems that in the fifth and last vision of Amos in 9.1f., direct action is threatened especially against the sanctuary (presumably Bethel, but the fact that it is unnamed may suggest any sanctuary or all of them):

> I saw Yahweh stationed upon the altar
> and he said, 'Strike the capitals so that the thresholds shake:
> break them on the heads of all of them.'

Whether what is envisioned is a command to the prophet to perform a symbolic act in striking the altar or a direct action of God himself, the scandalous, even blasphemous effect must have been the same. The very sanctuary which ensures God's presence in the community, a bastion of the royal power, sacred in every respect, is to become the object of God's rejection and judgement.

It is no wonder that the sanctuary's official priesthood thought enough was enough. For, in attacking the sanctuary and its worship, Amos was threatening the whole foundation of the power and position of God's royal representative on earth, the 'sacral' king. He is told to leave Bethel and the kingdom once and for all (7.10–13) just because it is 'the king's sanctuary and a temple of the royal kingdom'.

So Amos subverts the whole power base of the royal and priestly establishment in Israel. This is something new, as far as we have any records. As we saw earlier, neither Nathan nor Elijah are credited with having gone so far. Amos believes there is no place for a 'first aid' kind of tinkering with the practices of the establishment in order to improve things and so *save* it from disaster. He simply announces that it is too late. Disaster will be sure and swift – and total (9.2–4, where we seem to have an ironic parody of the comfort offered by Psalm 139.7–12). The question of whether Amos, in spite of this, saw any hope beyond judgement is not one which need concern us here. In chapter 9, verses 9–15 do express hope for a future beyond judgement, but their originality to Amos has been much debated. It is difficult to think he would have tried to bring comfort to the people of the north by assuring them that they would one day return loyally to a Davidic king (9.11f.). The north had rejected that line with some thankfulness. And Amos's charges against the north are certainly not those of the Deuteronomists later, who believed their true evil was that they had abandoned both the Davidic line and the Jerusalem temple. Not where or how they worship but how they act is his criterion. It is just possible that the picture of some escaping the judgement like stones not falling through the holes in a sieve (9.9f.) might have been his, in line with earlier calls for repentance (5.6f., 14f.). But if there is to be a future for the oppressed 'poor' and 'righteous', there is certainly to be none for the political and ecclesiastical establishment. Amos is wholly subversive of the claims of those in power.

At this point it is hard for the writer and the reader to avoid catching each other's eye. Strictly speaking, it is the Old Testament scholar's brief to try to explain as well as he or she can just what he thinks the biblical author is saying. When that is done he or she can bow off the stage in thankful anonymity, concealed in a smokescreen of objectivity. If we go on to ask, 'Does what the biblical writer is saying here make any sense?', or 'Is there any way it can possibly be relevant or even "true" for later times?', the scholar is no more equipped than anyone else to answer. When Amos says (as he appears to) that, because a great divide has opened up between the 'haves' and the 'have nots' in eighth-century Israelite society, and because that divide is perpetuated by the crooked dealing of the wealthy and powerful with the connivance of those in power, God will now 'judge' the kingdom by sending enemies among them who will destroy the state, can we take him seriously? The problem is exacerbated for us by something Amos himself says: 'Does disaster (the Hebrew word can mean moral evil but also 'trouble' of any kind) overtake a city when Yahweh has not caused it?' (3.6). That appears to mean that God looks down, sees what is happening, and immediately 'sends' his judgement, if not in the shape of a thunderbolt from heaven, then at least in the form of an enemy from somewhere handy on earth. So we ask with some incredulity, 'Does God (always providing we believe the term means anything real and objective) still do the same?' If our politics not only tolerate but actively encourage real injustices in our modern society is he likely to do something similar?

As Amos's saying just quoted shows, the Hebrew prophets saw God as the immediate and direct cause of everything. Our modern way of thinking would need a few intermediate steps in the argument. We might put it something like this. Amos shows that any society is in danger which has a growing number of people who feel no self-interest in it whatsoever. Society has so isolated and alienated them that they no longer identify themselves with it. 'They' have become the enemy, and 'they' are not external foes but the privileged members of the political and religious establishment who are manipulating the system in their own interest. To use a term much in use in contemporary British political debate, when many people no longer feel they are 'stakeholders' in their society, then that society is in danger. If it is subjected to some real crisis from outside or within, it is likely to crumble because there will be no united home front to meet that crisis. We do not have to go as far back as Amos for illustrations of the truth of this. The French Revolution and the Marxist revolution in Russia are only two of a long series of instances of its truth in political history. But political establishments, run by those in power for those in power and manipulated by the wealthy in the interests of their wealth, have often shown themselves slow to learn such lessons from history. If there ever does emerge a political system run on the principle that 'there is no such thing as society', probably the safest thing that can be said about it is that its days are numbered. In such a sense Amos's diagnosis and warning do not seem entirely antiquated, whether we use his language of 'the judgement of God' or content ourselves with a more empirical phrase such as 'an inner political, economic and social dynamic' or 'the outworking of the processes of history'.

Having broken off the main argument for this brief chat with the reader, it is time to get back to stern duty. Amos was an out-and-out subversive with regard to the official state of his day, the state of king and priest, the state where temple and palace were conveniently about the same business.

As I said earlier, however, we must always be careful about lumping together all the phenomena described as 'prophecy' in the Old Testament and treating them as all examples of a single, homogeneous whole. Not even all the prophets who have left us the books named after them can be described in such blanket terms as 'cultic' or 'anti-cultic'; not all necessarily acted as isolated individuals rather than in groups or on the staff of a sanctuary; not all were either 'ecstatic' or 'rational' (whatever either of those terms may mean). And not all were necessarily 'subversive' in the sense in which I am using it here, concerned, like Amos, to see an end to, rather than merely a reform of, the major political and religious institutions of their day.

Amos and Hosea afford a powerful instance of such differences between prophets, all the more remarkable when it seems that they must have been at least near contemporaries in the northern kingdom of Israel (although Hosea, unlike Amos, was himself a northerner). As we read the two prophets, however, we get very different pictures of the state of society there. Amos is full of the social injustices which were being tolerated and perpetrated. Hosea concentrates much more on religious apostasy, what is often referred to as their joining the worship of Yahweh with that of Canaanite deities (religious 'syncretism' as it is called). The difference is by no means absolute. Amos does challenge some of their religious practices.[9] Hosea offers also a powerful criticism of society's leaders, including king, nobles and priests. He uses the literary form of a legal dispute (Hebrew *rîb*) in which God brings a charge against his people as though he were counsel for the prosecution in a law court. This is found in chapter 4. First there is the summons:

Hear the word of Yahweh, people of Israel,
for Yahweh has a charge against those who live in the land.

That is followed by the reading of the charge sheet:

There is no faithfulness or loyalty,
no knowledge of God in the land;
there are cursing, lying, killing, theft and adultery,
the breaking of all moral barriers, and bloodshed upon
bloodshed.

This is all fairly general and seems to be based upon some form of
the Ten Commandments (Exod. 20.3–17; Deut. 5.7–21). Those
dealt both with Israel's relationship with God and their relationship with each other as members of God's covenant 'family', and
that seems to be very much the emphasis in Hosea. He is concerned
about the breakdown in relationships, above all in their relationship with God but also in their own personal relationship with
each other which he sees as consequential. His charges about
their worship of Canaanite gods (which he compares with marital
infidelity) and of seeking defensive military alliances with other
powers (rather than trusting in God), both of which he sees as a
result of the break in their relationship with him, need not concern
us here. But he certainly charges the leaders of the people – king,
nobles and priests – with dereliction in their duty since they should
have been giving the people a proper example and establishing
and maintaining justice. He sees parties within Israel plotting,
full of devious intrigue, each trying to forward their own sectional
interests at whatever cost to society as a whole. They hang round
dark corners of the court, plotting and hatching schemes:

Their hearts burn with intrigue like an oven,
all night their anger is smouldering;
in the morning it blazes up like a flaming fire;
They are all as hot as an oven;
they devour their rulers.
All their kings have fallen,
not one of them calls on me. (7.6f.)

Small wonder that like attracts like, and when they have got their
party man on the throne, he and they together terrorize all others:

> With their wickedness they delight the king,
> the princes with their schemings. (7.3)

Hosea thus seems to feel that monarchy itself is rotten. It is a moot (and probably not very important) point whether he is denouncing the institution itself or merely expressing his distaste for those particular kings who hoisted themselves on to the throne by their plotting and that of their henchmen. The result was that Israel had kings who were not of God's appointment:

> They made kings – but they were not from me –
> They elevated princes – but I knew nothing of it. (8.4)

Something of the feeling of the 'anti-monarchic source' of 1 Kings 8 (see above, pp. 82f.) seems to show through, however, in this:

> Now where is your king so that he may deliver you in all
>   your cities?
> or your rulers concerning whom you said,
> 'Give me a king and leaders.'
> I gave you a king – in my anger –
> and I removed him – in my wrath. (13.10)

Nor is Hosea any more flattering about the priests and the prophets:

> With you is my dispute, O priest [the line needs a little emendation
>   to make sense]
> By day you shall stumble, and the prophet with you at night: . . .
> My people are destroyed from lack of knowledge.
> Because you have rejected knowledge,
> I reject you from being my priest.
> Because you have forgotten the instruction of your God,
> I too will forget [you and] your descendants. (4.4–6)

It is not clear what Hosea saw would be the future of the kingdom. Strong threats of destruction from God (11.5–7; 13.9) alternate with hints that God, because of his enduring compassion, cannot let that be the last word (esp. 11.8f., cf. the call for repentance in 14.1–8). Indeed, there are much clearer calls to repentance in Hosea than there are in Amos, although he also seems to see that the only hope is with God acting in grace. Some have thought that the calls for repentance come from an early stage in his ministry but that he came later to see that Israel was so hopeless a case that only by an act of grace could they be saved.[10] Others suggest that the calls for repentance belong to a later, Deuteronomic editing of the book in the south.[11] A more theological writer argues that the book of Hosea makes the point that God, in acting to save people, does not bypass their own wills and their own response but rather works through them by renewing them.[12] As I have already said, it simply is not possible for us to know in any prophetic book just what came from the historic figure of the named prophet himself and what has to be attributed to the development of his teaching in the course of the tradition.

Perhaps all we can say, in summary, is that Hosea's concept of the leadership of the northern kingdom was 'subversive' in that, even if he believed God had originally appointed them to their office, they had shown themselves quite unworthy of the office and neither they nor their office were any longer to be considered as 'sacral'. What he envisaged to be the future of the kingdom is not clear to us now. He does not seem, from the evidence of the book as we have it, to have gone as far as Amos in saying that God had finished with it nor that the covenant relationship was over.

A similar guardedness seems to characterize the message of Isaiah of Jerusalem, a prophet who was active in the southern kingdom of Judah later in the 8th century BCE. We have to use words like 'seems' and 'possibly' and 'maybe' when we are talking about Isaiah's teaching since the usual problems about just what he said and how the message has been adapted in the course of the book's growth and transmission, problems which confront us in all the prophetic collections, meet us here tenfold. Interpreters differ widely, almost wildly, in their understanding of just what Isaiah said, in the light of how much of the present book they attribute to him and how much to later hands.

What we can be fairly sure about is that Isaiah attacks the political, social and economic ills of the society of the south in much the same way as Amos, and to some extent Hosea, did in the north. He attacks the rich and powerful members of the community for their oppression of the poor and weak. God is not impressed by all their scrupulous religious observances when they act as they do:

'When you spread out your hands [i.e. in prayer]
I will avert my eyes from you;
when you add prayer to prayer
I am not listening.
Your hands are full of blood.
Wash yourselves, purify yourselves,
remove the evil of your actions from my sight.
Stop doing evil, study how to act well;
Seek out justice, straighten out your ruthlessness;
secure justice for the orphan and defend the widow.' (1.15–17)

In his famous 'Song of the Vineyard' (5.1–7) Isaiah employs something of the same ruse as Nathan in his parable to David, enlisting his hearers' sympathy for the owner of a vineyard who finds it offers no sweet grapes in spite of all his hard work in it, before delivering the sting in the tail by showing them that he is talking about God and his 'vineyard', Judah. In a masterly play on words he brings the song to its conclusion:

'I expected justice [*mishpāt*),
but behold, bloodshed [*mishpāḥ*],
righteousness [*ṣᵉdāqah*],
but behold, the cry of the oppressed [*ṣᵉdāqah*].'

In Judah also the rich secure favourable verdicts in the courts by the liberal use of bribes, they secure 'the vindication of the wicked for a bribe and they frustrate the clearing of the innocent' (5.23). Again, whole estates are built up as the wealthy drive the poor off their own land when they are unable to meet their debts:

Woe to those who reach out for house after house,
who join field to field, until there is room for no more,
and they live in [splendid] isolation amid all the land.' (5.8)

Their lives too are marked by all the blunted sensitivities of over-indulgence and excessive wealth (e.g. 3.16—4.1; 5.11f.).

You cannot get much more direct than that, and there was much more in the same vein. Yet, when all is said and done, the final impression Isaiah gives is not of a great radical. It has sometimes been argued that he appears to have come from aristocratic stock, or even that he had some position in the 'official' temple cult.[13] Whatever the truth of that (and all details of his life can be only matters for speculation) he does appear to have had an instinctive feeling for a 'correct' social order. Among the troubles he predicts for the community if it persists on its present course is the breakdown of that order. In 3.1–8 he speaks of the chaos which can only ensue when the proper leaders at every level of society are taken away by God. They include military men, judges, prophets, city 'elders', counsellors, as well as those well versed in more arcane mysteries. Mere youths will be thrust into positions of responsibility, every faction of society will be set against the other, and – surely the worst of all – youths will be offensively insulting to their elders. Things will have broken down so far that they will be pleading with anyone to take over government who can be talked into it. Even women may have positions of authority! All this appears to offend susceptibilities in Isaiah which never seem to have cost Amos a moment's sleep.[14]

For all this Judah will know judgement, and Isaiah's picture of that judgement, like that of Amos and Hosea, is of invasion and destruction by an enemy. And yet, that judgement never seems to be quite final, or, at least, the future is open and can be vitally influenced by the community's repentance if it will only return to God and his ways. Three passages may be referred to. The first is found in Isaiah 1.21–6. Up to a point this is a typical oracle of judgement. It begins with the charge to be brought against the city of Jerusalem (vv. 21–3). Whereas it had been meant to be (and once was, apparently) the centre of justice and 'righteousness', now it has become a scene of murders, of leaders ('princes') rebelling against authority and making allies of thieves, where the search for bribes and payments for representing certain interests at the heart of government is unashamed, while the rights of those who cannot afford the price are frustrated. This charge is followed by the announcement of judgement beginning as it so often does with the word 'Therefore'. And this begins in traditional fashion with the threat that God will take vengeance on those who have proved themselves by their conduct to be his 'enemies' and he will direct his power (symbolized by the term 'hand') against his own city. But, abruptly, this conventional oracle of judgement switches to become a promise of deliverance. The whole process of judgement will be like a smelting of metal, with the aim of restoring the leaders to what had been from the first their call, to be establishers of justice. Then the whole nature of the city under their charge will change to one of righteousness and faithfulness. A second passage (17.12–14) portrays judgement against Jerusalem rather in terms of some psalms which picture the enemies of God and Jerusalem attacking the city like the flooding in of the waters of chaos. Psalm 93, for example, reads:

> The floods have lifted up, O Yahweh,
> the floods have lifted up their voice,
> the floods have lifted up their uproar. (v. 3)

But, suddenly, God asserts his power in quelling them as he did at creation:

> Mightier than the sound of many waters,
> than the sea's breakers,
> Mighty is Yahweh in exaltation. (v. 4)

And this power is exercised from his throne in the sanctuary at the heart of the city:

> Your decrees are entirely trustworthy;
> holiness becomes your sanctuary
> Yahweh, throughout the length of days. (v. 5)

In just the same way the Isaiah passage tells of the threat from the surrounding nations as the roaring of flood waters. But, at a moment, God intervenes and, by morning, the threat has passed away. The difference between the threat of the night and deliverance in the 'morning' recalls another psalm celebrating God's presence in his holy city where, even if 'the waters roar and foam', God, in the midst of his city, will help her 'at the break of morning' (Ps. 46.6).

One more Isaiah passage to be considered is 29.1–8. Again the city, apostrophized as 'Ariel' (= 'altar of God'), is surrounded by an enemy. This time God speaking in the first person says it is he who will be laying siege to it, which means, presumably, that he will have brought the opposing army to its walls. But, at the moment of their deepest and direst distress, God will suddenly 'visit' his city and will interpose, defeating the city's enemies and delivering Jerusalem.

We have to stress again that we just cannot know how much of this 'dual' note of both threat and promise goes back to Isaiah himself. It may be that he saw only threat and others have added the note of hope later. It may be that he did see a deliverance from God, but only the other side of judgement and disaster. Or it may be that he saw that either could happen, but that everything depended on how the people responded to God's call. He does not seem to show much optimism about this in the chapter which describes his 'call' in 6.1–13 (where the last line foretelling the surviving of 'the holy seed' as a remnant is undoubtedly a later addition). The conviction that his preaching would only harden, blind and deafen his hearers, may have been written later in his ministry when he had become disillusioned with the people's failure to listen. But he is credited persistently in the book with challenging those who were threatened with judgement to have 'faith'. He called on even a ruling member of the Davidic dynasty, Ahaz, to have faith, with a play on words in 7.9 which might be rendered, 'If you don't lean on God, how can he support you?' He called on rulers and people to have faith in God rather than seek military alliances with other powers (e.g. 30.15). All the time 'Yahweh waits to show grace to you' and 'exalts himself to show compassion to you' (30.18).

There are such conflicting signals from the present form of Isaiah 1—39 that any conclusion must be tentative (and needs much more justification than there has been room to give here). I venture the conclusion, however, that Isaiah, like Hosea, fiercely attacked the abuse of power by king and leaders, denounced the whole apparatus of the state religious cult which was being used to defend those in power while cloaking their misdeeds, and threatened devastating judgement on the state. However, he stood more in the line of figures from the past like Nathan and Elijah, and to some extent, Hosea. He saw himself as sent to warn the 'powers that be' but longed, if at all possible, to save the order of society. To that extent he cannot be labelled as 'subversive' in the same way that Amos could be, and was.

It is quite a different matter with one who must have been his contemporary in Judah in the later part of the 8th century BCE, Micah. Neither prophet mentions the other, which might seem strange when two prophets were supposed to be saying very similar things in the same city at the same time. In fact, with one exception, no prophetic collection mentions one of the other prophets by name, even when they must have been contemporaries (e.g. Haggai and Zechariah). The exception is Micah himself, who is recalled in the book of Jeremiah where one of his oracles is actually cited (Jer. 26.18f., cf. Mic. 3.12). The words of Micah and Isaiah are often very close to each other. In one case (Isa. 2.2–4, cf. Mic. 4.1–4) the books have very nearly the same oracle, but that is much more likely to be the result of the incorporation later into each book of a familiar oracle than a case of one prophet actually borrowing from the other. Nevertheless, in his critique of Judah's social and political life Micah sounds just the notes that Isaiah does. Isaiah said that some people couldn't get up early enough to start another day of their profligate lifestyle (Isa. 5.11f.) and Micah depicts them lying awake at night planning their next piece of infamy (Mic. 2.1). That, when they set about it next morning, turns out to be exactly the same kind of greedy acquisition of land and property at the expense of the 'poor' which Isaiah described.

> They desire fields and snatch them,
> houses, and take them;
> they oppress a man and his household,
> a man and his inheritance. (2.2, cf. Isa. 5.8)

They treat their fellow-Israelites just as a foreign conqueror does in time of war:

> You act against my people
> rising up like an enemy;
> you seize the cloak off the back of the peaceable,
> from those who go about their business in trust.
> You dispossess the women among my people
> from the homes they enjoy;
> from their infants you remove their shelter for ever. (2.8f.)[15]

Micah is forthright in his denunciation of those described as the 'heads' and 'rulers' of Israel.

> Listen, you heads of Jacob, and rulers of the house of Israel;
> should not you know what justice is,
> you who hate good and love evil?
> You strip the skin from people's backs,
> and the flesh from their bones;
> you devour the flesh of my people . . . (3.1–3)

In other words, those who were charged with leadership of the community and with the responsibility of ensuring fairness and justice for all have abused their power. They make themselves rich by exploiting the very people who relied on them, those whom, ominously for the leaders, God describes as '*my* people'. Such a description of them was not only ominous for the leaders, but is highly significant for our understanding of the enormity of the prophetic subversion. The God who had been called in as the God of the rulers, of the whole political and ecclesiastical establishment – who claimed to rule by his appointment and to be the chosen instruments for effecting the order of his rule, who claimed in their propaganda 'God is with us' – is said by the prophets like Micah to be quite other. Not of the rulers, the powerful, the wealthy, but of the poor, the weak and the oppressed does God say 'they are "*my* people"'. The God of the prophets identifies himself with all who are wronged and denied justice.

On the other hand there were prophets who avoided such awkward conclusions which might have affronted their paymasters. They who, according to Micah, should have been warning of the consequences of such actions by the powerful, had been silenced. They too had joined in the general greed and rush for wealth. They give favourable oracles to those who are in a position to pay them and reserve their threats for those who are without influence (3.5).

So the religious leaders, both priests and prophets, have become puppets of the ruling classes. Apparently all of them are lumped together under the general title of 'heads' and 'rulers' for it this whole group which is indicted with 'not being able to stand justice' and 'twisting' all that should be 'straight' (3.9), and Micah then continues:

> Its [i.e. Jerusalem's] heads give judgements for bribes;
> its priests deliver instruction for hire,
> its prophets offer divination for money. (3.11)

Yet it is just these people who are propping up the whole apparatus of the state, giving it just that cloak of religious legitimacy we have seen to be the aim of royal and ecclesiastical propaganda. So they solemnly repeat the assurances of the official temple cult:

> Yet they depend on Yahweh as they claim:
> 'Is not Yahweh in our midst?
> No trouble shall befall us.' (3.11)

This is not far from the confident claims of that liturgy as expressed in some psalms:

> God is in her midst – she shall not be moved;
> God will deliver her at the break of dawn . . .
> Yahweh of hosts is with us,
> The God of Jacob is our refuge. (Ps. 46.5, 7, Hb. 6, 8)

But it is at this point that Micah goes farther than Isaiah. Perhaps he was more detached, because he is said to have come from outside Jerusalem. Perhaps, as some have suggested, he was angrier because he came from lower down the social scale, and knew about oppression from the bottom of the pile. I have sometimes thought of him as the 'Piers Plowman' of the Old Testament. Whatever the truth of all that, he is as certain as Amos that God intends to bring down the whole present 'establishment'. Jerusalem, claimed as the holy city, the city of God's choice, of his dwelling, of his chosen king from the Davidic dynasty, is going to be utterly destroyed:

> So *on your account* [i.e. on account of the leaders and rulers]
> Zion will be ploughed up like a field;
> Jerusalem shall become a heap of ruins,
> and the mountain of the sanctuary an elevated thicket. (3.12)

That is the devastating verse which, unsurprisingly, seems to have etched itself into the memories of later generations, for it is the one cited in Jeremiah 26.18f. It is significant that Micah was remembered there as a prophet of judgement. Although that is the dominant theme in the first three chapters of the book, it is by no means, however, the only emphasis in the book as a whole. In chapters 4—5, particularly, notes of hope are sounded, some of which are the exact 'mirror image' of the threats which have preceded them. Many of these must be classed as 'post-exilic' additions.[16] It is, nevertheless, by no means impossible that Micah himself saw some future for the 'little people' of the nation after the collapse of the kingdom. The passage at 4.6f., which speaks of God gathering 'the lame', while it appears to suggest a return from the later exile, might well echo a note of his which has not otherwise been recorded for us. However, this material need not concern us here, for, whatever Micah may, or may not, have said about the future, it would only follow the end of the whole present order. Even the picture of another ruler to come from Bethlehem (5.2–4) presupposes the end of the present Davidic dynasty. With regard to the power and truth claims of the political and religious establishment of his day, Micah was wholly a subversive.

He is closely followed in this by another prophet of Judah from the next century, Zephaniah. The book of Zephaniah says that he prophesied in the reign of king Josiah (640–609 BCE). If that is so (there are some who have felt that what he has to say would fit much better the time of Josiah's successor, Jehoiakim) then it might seem as though he must have said most of what he had to say before the time of the religious reform assigned to king Josiah in 621 BCE. At least, that is the date of the reform given by the Deuteronomistic Historians in their account of the affair (2 Kings 22f.), and they show the vital importance to that reform of a 'book of the law' which was 'discovered' in the temple, usually taken by scholars to have been some form of the book of Deuteronomy itself. As we have seen, however, the Chronicler suggests that Josiah had begun his campaign of religious reform from very early in his reign (2 Chron. 34f., esp. 34.3–7), although it is quite feasible that the Chronicler had theological axes of his own to grind. The whole question of the timing, the nature, the motive, and the extent of Josiah's reform is a most complex one.[17] One would not gather from reading Zephaniah, to some extent Jeremiah, or Ezekiel, that such a religious transformation had taken place in Judah. That means, as I have said, that either the accounts of its effects were exaggerated or, in Zephaniah's case at least, he marked something of the general disquiet among faithful religious people following the reign of Manasseh, in the early days of Josiah, which showed that a climate was being prepared in which some religious reform could be undertaken and command wide support.[18]

In fact he attacks many forms of religious and cultic abuse and apostasy which he says were current in Judah at the time, while offering a scathing criticism of just the kind of social ills which had been the target of the eighth century prophets before him. The religious abuses only concern us in that, as we have seen, there can be no separating of the religious and the secular, the political and the cultic, in a society like that of Judah and Israel during the time of the monarchy. It reveals the view of some, at least, in that community, that those charged with administering affairs in conformity with the laws of God were being careless and indifferent in the way they carried out their charge. So he can speak of priests who have cheerfully married the worship of Ba'al and other deities with the worship of Yahweh as 'idolatrous', and who do not really consult Yahweh in the directions and instruction they give (1.4–6). Perhaps it was one of those times of some luxury and extravagance when only what was foreign was considered '*chic*'. Certainly members of the royal court, the nobles and members of the royal family, were among the many 'who dress themselves up in foreign attire' (1.8). As so often, extreme wealth for some was obtained by ruthless exploitation and oppression of others:

> 'I will visit in judgement all who leap out of the doorway,
> filling their masters' houses with [the loot of] violence and
>   dishonesty.' (1.9)

It is not exactly clear whether these hired thugs leap out of the doorway in surprise attacks on passers-by or whether they leap into the houses of their victims to rob them, but there is no doubt what the results of their actions are.

The description of 'the city' in 3.1–4 (the city is unnamed but verse 5 suggests it must be Jerusalem, even if she typifies all cities, rather as Nineveh does in 2.13–15) is as a city of 'oppression' (v. 1). Then Zephaniah goes on to specify various groups as the target of his attacks:

> Her leaders within her are roaring lions;
> her judges are evening wolves
> who leave nothing for the morning;
> her prophets are reckless,
> men of treachery;
> her priests profane all that is sacred,
> they violate the law. (3.3f.)

In a clever parody the prophet goes on to contrast them with the God whose representatives they are supposed to be:

> Yahweh in her midst is righteous,
> he does no evil;
> morning by morning he brings his justice to light;
> he never fails. (3.5)

Of course the daily administration of Yahweh's justice can only be effected through the very leaders who have shown themselves so to disregard it. They are 'wolves of the evening', unable to wait for morning to achieve their greedy ends, in painful contrast to Yahweh, who seeks every morning to bring his justice 'to light'.

So Zephaniah's scorn is directed always towards the members of 'the establishment': the rich, the priests, prophets, palace officials, members of the royal family, the foppish and effete rich, the traders whose only aim is to amass 'silver and gold' (cf. 1.18). Their extravagance and materialism have had a deadening effect on any spiritual or religious sensibilities. They are like wine 'thickening upon the lees', that is, wine which deteriorates in quality when it is left undisturbed (1.12, cf. Jer. 48.11). Whatever their notional beliefs, they do not let thoughts of any possible actions of God trouble their complacent way of life (1.12).

In the same way as Amos and Isaiah did, Zephaniah predicts a 'Day of Yahweh', a day when God will come to judge the whole system. (There are a considerable number of parallels between Amos, Isaiah and Zephaniah to a point which suggests that Zephaniah, or, at least, whoever compiled the book, was somehow aware of the tradition of their preaching.) It will be a day when the whole *status quo* will be inverted. It will be those who can be labelled as 'the mighty' (1.14), representing the 'city', that is, the whole religious and political system, who will be distressed. Those most affected will be those who suddenly discover all their wealth is no longer able to shelter them from life's blasts (1.18). It will be the 'proud' who were contemptuous of the weaker (2.8, 10, an oracle directed against foreigners, but foreigners who show exactly the same attitude as Israel's own native oppressors). Yahweh will go through the whole city as though with powerful lamps, flushing them all out from their hiding places (1.12). Indeed, 'on that day', the whole order which was brought out of chaos at creation, the very order these representatives of the deity claim to embody, will be reversed (1.2f.). Those who saw themselves as continuing Adam's role in the divinely given administration of the earth (Gen. 1.26–8) will find themselves, like Adam, driven out. For the end of 1.3 reads, 'I will cut off "Adam" from the face of the ground' (*ʾᵃdāmah*). This is all a rejection of the whole 'system' in the name of God, as total as anything we found in Amos or Micah.

But, like Micah, Zephaniah speaks of a group of people who are described in the same words as those used in the psalms, the 'humble', the 'poor', the 'lowly'. They are addressed in 2.3 and summoned to faith through all they are now suffering. On the 'Day of Yahweh' which will bring down all the great and mighty, Yahweh will leave 'in the midst of you' (the very place where now the corrupt officials are, 3.3a) 'a people humble and poor' (3.12). These are the people who, unlike the present establishment, will be found 'not to do wrong', the very words which describe Yahweh himself in 3.5: they will not 'utter lies' and 'there shall not be found in their mouths a deceitful tongue' (3.13). These are the people who will be preserved through the cataclysm of the 'Day of Yahweh' and preserved by God as a 'remnant' (2.3; 3.12f.)

This is a thoroughly radical reversal of fortunes. Its rejection of the apparatus of 'sacral kingship' and the temple/palace hierarchy is total. Yahweh himself will act directly. There is no mention even of some 'messianic' figure in the future. God himself is the only one depicted as 'king' in this book (2.11; 3.15). Zephaniah, and the group who extended his preaching into the present form of the book, had learned not 'to put their trust in princes', and so the whole book is full of the language and imagery of the psalms which celebrate the universal kingship of Yahweh. It is this which brings hope for the little people. His subjects will be 'the lame and the outcast' (3.19). Subversion could hardly go farther while stopping short of any call to arms against the present powers. There is no need for that, just as there would be no chance of its success. Like Micah, they are full of the faith that God is the God who comes to the rescue of 'my people' (2.9b).

There was a contemporary of Zephaniah, namely Jeremiah, and we can hardly end our survey of the 'prophetic subversion' of the pre-exilic monarchic period without at least mentioning him. But the book of Jeremiah presents us with enormous problems. The reader who considers him or herself a non-specialist in the minutiae of contemporary biblical scholarship must get thoroughly tired of people like me saying all the time, 'We cannot tell what in the book came from the prophet himself and what came from later hands.' But nowhere is this truer than in the book of Jeremiah. The whole book has been thoroughly edited in 'Deuteronomic' circles from the time of the exile (and, perhaps, even beyond). The object of that editing was to relate whatever the original teaching of Jeremiah may have been to the situation after the fall of Jerusalem. There are three types of material in the present book: poetic oracles, prose sermons and prose biographical sections. It has widely been thought that the prose sermons, at least, represent a 'Deuteronomistic' preaching of the prophet's words to the exiles in Babylon, explaining why the national disaster befell them and what they needed to do to have any hope for the future. But some, also, believe that the Deuteronomists have had a big part to play in the picture of Jeremiah that is presented in the biographical sections. It is believed they used these to draw out theological lessons on the nature of the word of God and its effect when it is accepted or rejected.[19] Some believe that different hands have had such a large – and often conflicting – part in every section of the book, including the poetic oracles, that they virtually despair of being able to discover 'the Jeremiah of history'.[20] Others have felt this to be unnecessarily pessimistic.[21]

I do not intend to embroil myself or the reader in all the niceties of these endless (and ultimately unanswerable) questions at the end of what is already a formidably long chapter. I think it is important, however, to pick out two aspects of what the book of Jeremiah has to say, whoever is responsible for the present form of the sayings, and however consistent they may or may not be with other notes to be heard in the book. The first is the so-called 'Temple Sermon' in Jeremiah 7.1–15. Jeremiah was told to stand at the entrance to the temple in Jerusalem and proclaim a message to all who came to its doors to worship there. The message consisted of a call for repentance, a change of actions, so that God might continue to let them live in 'this place' (presumably both the city and the temple are meant). Then follows the well-known saying: 'Do not put your trust in lying words saying, "Yahweh's temple, Yahweh's temple, Yahweh's temple"' (v. 4). That parodies the repeated claim that God has chosen Jerusalem and the temple as the place where he lives (the same rationale of the temple we find among many nations of the ancient Near East, as we have seen). They are called upon to change their way of life in fairly traditional terms:

'... if you secure justice between one another;
if you do not oppress the immigrant, the orphan or the widow,
and do not spill innocent blood in this place,
and do not follow after other gods to your own harm,
then I will let you live in this place which I gave to your ancestor
for ever and ever.' (vv. 5–7)

Like many of the prose sermons in the book, that is expressed in very 'Deuteronomic' language. But it is reinforced with an unusual warning:

> 'Go to my place which was in Shiloh, where I first caused my name to dwell, and see what I did to that because of the evil of my people, Israel.' (v. 12)

Again, pure Deuteronomic language. Now it is perfectly possible that behind this was an original word of Jeremiah to the worshippers of his day. It is equally possible that the Deuteronomists during the exile took his words and used them and elaborated on them to explain to the despondent Jewish exiles in Babylon just why it was that the temple, which Yahweh had promised would be his dwelling place 'for ever', had, in fact, been destroyed. Or, again, it may have been only they who had any part in it. However, as it stands, it represents a bold assertion. There was nothing eternally sacrosanct about the city of Jerusalem or its sanctuary. God had dispensed with such things before, and he could do so again.

The other peculiarity about the book of Jeremiah as it stands, is that it actually names some of the Davidic kings in terms of bitter criticism and biting sarcasm. At least, one should qualify that by saying that in 22.13–17 there is a bitter attack on a king who is named in a prose addition to the oracle in verse 18 as Jehoiakim. However, the scathing contrast between the king being pilloried and his father suggests that the identification is a reasonable one. The oracle criticizes the king for indulging in vast and extravagant building projects (we have seen how grandiose building schemes were themselves a form of royal propaganda) but for doing so at the cost of injustice to and extortion from his people.

> 'Are you a king because you excel with cedar?' (v. 15)

His father (Josiah) had enough to eat and drink yet he dispensed 'justice and righteousness' and 'judged the cases of the humble and needy', but, as for Jehoiakim,

> 'You have no insight or feeling
> except for your profit;
> for spilling the blood of the innocent,
> for doing violence and feathering your own nest.' (v. 17)

The result will be a violent death and burial outside Jerusalem, a grave fate for a king, who would thus have no memorial or lasting tribute to his name.

That is followed by a similar threat to his brother Jehoiachin who followed him. He will be rejected by God as the one bearing the insignia of office (the 'signet ring', a seal of authority). He and his children will be exiled (which turned out to be true enough) and that will mark the end of the dynastic line:

> Thus says Yahweh:
> 'Record this man as stripped of posterity;
> one who will not prosper in his lifetime.
> For no man will prosper by sitting on the throne of David,
> no one will rule again in Judah.' (v. 30)

It is strange that the office of king is hardly mentioned in the first part of the book (chs. 1—20). In the biographical sections Jeremiah is depicted as having conversations with Zedekiah, who succeeded Jehoiachin as the puppet king of the Babylonians in 597 BCE. Such oracles as those we have looked at in chapter 22 might also, therefore, be the work of the Deuteronomists, bringing the same kind of critical theological judgement to bear on individual kings as they do in the books of Kings. On the other hand, they seem to have held out some kind of hope for Jehoiachin, as the end of their work in 2 Kings 25.27–30 shows, a passage echoed in Jeremiah 52.31–4. Further, the tradition of the book does record that Jeremiah aroused real hostility by predicting that it was useless to defend Jerusalem against the besieging Babylonians, since God had decreed that it would fall. Better, indeed, for people to leave the city and go over to the other side. Not surprisingly, he is said to have been put in custody for this 'lowering of morale in time of war' (32.1–5). Foreseeing the fall of the city, the destruction of the temple and the exile of the king with the end of the Davidic dynasty did not mean he had no hope for the future, however. The same chapter records the tradition that he bought a piece of land at this time symbolizing his conviction that 'houses and fields and vineyards shall be bought in this land again' (32.15). But whoever is responsible for all this, the announcement of the destruction of the temple, the capture and destruction of the city, the attack on specific kings and the threat of the end of the Davidic line in the book of Jeremiah is the work of a true subversive.

We have seen enough in this chapter to show that, when political and religious power figures harness the power of religion to buttress and validate their claims, they are playing with fire. In the hands of many of the prophets of Israel that very religion became a stick with which to beat those who, they believed, had betrayed the high calling of their office. How easily those in power, in all ages, have come to forget the circumscriptions of that power. The Israelite prophets maintain that power is given as a trust for the sake of others. When that trust is betrayed, God becomes the God, not of the betrayers, but of the betrayed.

I had got that far in this chapter when it was read by a friend who made one of those trenchant comments which have so often put friends, readers and generations of students in his debt. He asked whether we should not assume that the prophets often had 'propaganda assumptions of their own' and he pointed me in particular to the work of two scholars, Robert Carroll and David Clines, who have argued strongly for this.[22]

It is clear that the prophetic books as we have them do engage in propaganda. To take just one example, the final form of the book of Jeremiah makes powerful propaganda on behalf of the claims of those Jews who were in exile in Babylon to be the legitimate representatives of the 'true Israel', the true people of God. So, in Jeremiah's vision of the two baskets of figs (ch. 24), it is the Babylonian exiles who are the 'good figs' while those who remained in Judah were the 'bad figs'. It is the Babylonian exiles on whom God will 'set his eyes for good' by bringing them back to the land and who will be 'my people' (vv. 6f.). By contrast, those who remained in Judah under Zedekiah will come under the divine curse, pursued by sword, famine and plague so that they become an object of horror in the eyes of 'all the kingdoms of the earth'. For good measure, it is not only the Jews in Judah who are so contemptuously dismissed but the Jewish diaspora in Egypt (vv. 8–10), who are also accused later in the book of all kinds of cultic and moral irregularities (chs. 43f.).

It is difficult to believe that Jeremiah himself uttered such words. Indeed, when he was offered the choice by the Babylonians of going with the other exiles to Babylon or staying in Judah he is recorded as choosing to stay (40.1–6). The anti-Judean and anti-Egyptian elements in the book must be due to Deuteronomists who themselves came from the exile in Babylon and used the figure of

Jeremiah to assert divine authority for their claim to post-exilic dominance.

It is the burden of Carroll's work on the prophets that in every case, not just in the book of Jeremiah, we cannot know what the original historic prophets did or said or why they did it, since the books that bear their names are really the products of later editors who had their own political and religious axes to grind, just like those who introduced that anti-Judean and anti-Egyptian propaganda into the book of Jeremiah. '... these written collections of material *now* in written form may have been weapons in ideological conflicts within society and between communities and were therefore profoundly political in nature, intent, and publication' (Carroll, 'Prophecy and Society', p. 214).

Well, of course, they may, and I have been quite open in this chapter in admitting that we do not really know just what in our prophetic books stems originally from a particular prophet and what from those who later produced the books which bear his name. It would be surprising if later generations did not find in the prophets' attacks on the political and religious 'establishments' of *their* day material which was relevant to the political and religious cross-currents of later times, and our examination of the material of the visionaries in the next chapter will show that this could well be so. Nevertheless, I find Carroll's pessimism too negative. It is one thing to say that the image and message of a prophet has been shaped by those who followed him. It is quite another to say that nothing is left but the shaping. There are significant differences between the accounts of the prophets' activities and words in the books which have come to us, which suggests that something individual in each case came to the tradition and has remained in the tradition. If all was due to the tradition, all would have been honed down to a standard 'identikit' picture of a prophet, and that has not happened. Amos, for example, attacked the worship going on at Bethel. But his were not the reasons later Deuteronomistic editors had for rejecting it. They rejected it because of their belief that all along only worship offered at Jerusalem was valid. Amos attacked the worship there because of the disparity between words professed in worship and deeds committed in life (e.g. Amos 5.10–14). There *is* what many have regarded as an alternative 'Amos tradition' recorded in 1 Kings 13, where an unnamed prophet from the south comes to the north to denounce the altar at Bethel. There the reason for the divine judgement against it is exactly that of the Deuteronomists (1 Kings 13.1f.) and he has undoubtedly become a mouthpiece for their theology and propaganda. Yet a different Amos tradition has been preserved in the book which bears his name.

But I return to the point I have made throughout this chapter. The prophetic books as we have them do contain the words we have examined, and the words we have examined show powerful attacks on those who have wielded political, economic and religious power oppressively. As such they may be seen legitimately as examples of those who, in the name of religion, counter the claims of those in power, despite the fact that those claims were also buttressed in the name of religion.

Clines's article is an attack on those who, in commentating on the text of the Old Testament (he takes Amos as an example, but his strictures apply to similar treatment of any text), import into the text ideas and preconceptions of their own which they bring in from 'outside' or 'above' the text (hence '*meta*commentating'). He suggests that Amos's attacks on the wealthy are often interpreted from the somewhat 'liberal' stance of modern commentators with their own mildly radical political programme. 'Would it not be just as true to say, Amos hates the rich because he is not one of them?' (Clines, 'Metacommentating Amos', p. 146). '... we need to recognize that the prophet's is only one voice in his community. The prophet, and the text, have a corner to fight, a position to uphold ...' (p. 147).

I think that approaches the point my friend wanted to make. Perhaps the prophets whose work we have examined were just propagandists for other groups and, therefore, their words must be seen as the counter-claims of those who, for whatever reason, were denied power.

These are proper warnings. We all tend to bring a great deal of mental furniture to stock what we imagine are the empty rooms of our attitude to the text before us. Carroll himself likens the biblical text to a 'dark glass in which we see our own reflections more often than the social reality which produced the text' ('Prophecy and Society', p. 220). We have to admit we do not know what inner tensions and conflicts lie behind any given biblical text before us.

But we do have the text and, again, I would want to stress, those texts contain the words we have examined, however they got there, from however many hands, and with whatever hidden and mixed motives they were finally penned. And the text does not give me the impression that Amos attacks the riches of the wealthy just because he regards wealth in itself as wrong, so expressing a kind of 'sour grapes' attitude. He attacks the luxury of the rich and powerful because they have gained that power at the expense of the poor and use it to oppress those whose poverty gives them no voice in society. I must leave it to readers to decide whether this is an example of 'metacommentating' the text or seeing something which is actually there. For, at the end of the day, these prophetic texts do offer one unmistakable note of 'propaganda', whatever other concealed purposes we may think we may, or may not, detect in them. They engage in propaganda on behalf of the poor and the oppressed and this 'counter-propaganda' is subversive of those who claim, not only power by divine right, but divine right to exercise that power in any way which suits them. When all allowances have been made, I still believe we can speak of an Old Testament 'prophetic subversion' and that this subversion has proved to have a powerful and lasting relevance for later times.

CHAPTER SIX

The Subversion of the Visionaries

In times of great distress when people can only despair of the present, the tendency has always been to create either a golden past or a dream of a golden future. One thinks of the negro spirituals when a people, denied their own home and the reality of human dignity, dreamed much of the joys and splendours of heaven. Similar tendencies can be seen in the popular hymnology of the nineteenth century. To us in a more affluent and 'sophisticated' age it can seem strange that 'heaven', often crudely and literally pictured, could figure so prominently in collections of hymns such as those of Sankey and Moody, the American evangelists. Had we been among the urban slum dwellers of the nineteenth century, however, among all the squalor depicted by Dickens in his novels, with little money to purchase food, health care, or education by which to work our way up and out of our place in the system, we might have sung them with a great deal more enthusiasm than we can now imagine. In other words, those who have no real stake in the present order often dream of a different one in some ideal future. And such hopes may often themselves be subversive of that present order. Whether or not they lead to some kind of action to secure a change, or whether they lead to patient resignation waiting for God, or some other, to bring it about, they are hardly likely to be conducive to more than at best passive support of the present establishment. Sometimes, therefore, such hopes may be said to be sectarian, in the sense that they represent the hopes and ideals of certain underprivileged groups, and their hopes may be actively discouraged by those in power.[1] But the literature expressing such hopes may not necessarily or by any means always be sectarian. There may be periods when whole communities are suffering, under a foreign invader and occupier for example, and such an experience can lead to a united front of 'protest literature' among people who are divided along many other lines. Or, even, leading members of a community, who feel themselves excluded from power by others whom they think less worthy than themselves, may express their hopes for a coming reversal of fortunes.

The purpose of this chapter is to consider just such a strain of radical hope for the future in the literature of the Old Testament. To some extent it has already been sounded in the prophetic books we considered in the last chapter. Even from the 8th century BCE prophets were looking for a 'Day of Yahweh' when he would act to reverse the present state of things and restore liberty and rights to the weak and underprivileged members of society. But, more especially after the exile, such hopes for the future began to sharpen, at least among some in the post-exilic Jewish community, and prophetic literature tended more towards what has often been called the 'apocalyptic'.

It is a question-begging term which is still endlessly debated among biblical scholars. The name comes from a Greek word which means 'an unveiling' or even 'a disclosure' or 'revelation'. The only time it occurs as a title in the Bible is in the book of 'Revelation' where the title of 'the Apocalypse (revelation) of John' has been given to the book, after its opening words, 'The Apocalypse of Jesus Christ' (in other instances of its use in the New Testament it bears only its more general meaning of 'revelation'). Nevertheless, the book of Revelation has many links to the book of Daniel in the Old Testament and to other Jewish works of a similar nature at the time.

Several issues have concerned scholars in their discussion of 'apocalyptic'. One of the most difficult has been to find an exact meaning of the term. This has been bedevilled to some extent by failure to agree on whether we are talking about a certain literary type or genre, so involving a description of the main characteristics of such literature, or a particular theological outlook, or even 'mindset', as we would say. Another topic of concern has been the origins of the movement. Are these to be found in earlier Old Testament prophecy, among the 'Wisdom' circles in Judah, or are they due to Persian influence, or a mixture of any or all of these? Finally, what kind of circles produced the literature? Was it the work of dissidents, or those who saw themselves as descendants of the prophets, from priestly circles, or representatives of mainstream Judaism (if there was such a thing at that, or any time)?

Following the method I have used already to keep this book to the kind of length where even one or two people might read it right through, I am going to bypass this scholarly debate as I have done with others, because in the end it is what this literature has to say that matters, especially where it touches on the kind of issues we are discussing. It is only when we have seen what it has to say that we can hope fruitfully to start the theorizing.

I will content myself with one or two very general observations. Whatever we call this later literature in the Old Testament, and whatever we think about who wrote it and why, there does seem to be a shift in the nature of the way it regards God's action in history. The prophets tended to think of God as active in this world's history now. He may be working to a final goal of the whole historical process, but he does so through the actors and events of history. If Assyria marches against Israel, God has sent her. If God decides to teach his people lessons, he sends them into exile. In due course he uses someone like Cyrus to enable them to return. In some of this later literature, the writers appear to be despairing of this world's history. The times are so evil, the suffering of his people so intense, that it can only be explained by saying that God has allowed powers of evil to have their way – for a time. History can only be seen as getting worse and worse, until suddenly, at an appointed time, God will break into this world's history from outside and above it, and bring about what can only be described as 'a new heaven and a new earth'. So whereas the prophets usually call their hearers to 'repent', for so, they believe, the course of history may be changed, these later writers call people to 'hold the faith' in spite of all appearances that their faith seems unjustified. It is too late for 'repentance'. The course of history is now fixed, the lines between good and evil are drawn. For the moment, the powers of evil are having their day. But that day is ticking towards midnight and the break of God's new day, the ushering in of his new kingdom. The break between the 'now' and the 'then' is complete.

Two factors lead to such a change of emphasis, I believe. The first is that, to those who produce this literature, the times do seem to be getting worse and worse. False leaders oppress those who believe they are God's faithful, righteous remnant. At the time of the writing of the book of Daniel, in the 2nd century BCE, faithful Jews are being actually persecuted for their faith, while they see 'renegades', ('quislings' is the term of our time) betraying the faith by place-seeking and by selling out to the Greek culture of their time, 'going native' as it were. The only hope for those who see themselves as 'the faithful' is an act of God, but the only act of God possible to meet the gravity of the situation is to overturn this whole, evil world order and bring in a new one. This should not seem strange to us. We have seen in our time a kind of secular apocalyptic in Marxism. For those who saw themselves as utterly betrayed and alienated by the economic, political and social order, there was no hope but revolution. Not for them the reforming tinkering with the system by enlightened liberals who believed it could be touched up a bit for the better here and there. For them, the axe of revolution had to be laid to the root of the tree to bring the whole thing down. That is something of the outlook of Jewish apocalyptic. It is the product of times of despair, of the weak who seem to have nowhere to turn and who exercise none of the levers of power and influence.

Another factor in this sharpening sense of a great conflict going on is the development of an out-and-out monotheism. Often what seem like monotheistic statements earlier in the Old Testament turn out on close inspection to be only a strong statement that Yahweh is the only God *for Israel*. Other gods may exist, but their power is insignificant compared with the universal sway of Yahweh as king. But when the belief has emerged (at least among some) that there *are* no other gods at all, the problem of evil becomes ever more acute. And so begins to develop an idea that there are malevolent spirits also at work in the universe, trying (vainly ultimately but only too effectively at the moment) to oppose God's good plans for his world. So later Jewish apocalyptic traces the fall back, not to Genesis 3 with the eating of the fruit in the garden, but to Genesis 6, with its strange story of an intermarriage between 'the sons of God' and 'the daughters of men'. There was an earlier fall of angelic beings who are the source of evil in God's world. We see this tendency already at work in the Chronicler, who makes the story of the tempting of David by God to take a census (2 Sam. 24.1) into a tempting by 'Satan' (1 Chron. 21.1). We see it in the account of battles between angels in heaven in the book of Daniel, battles which are being projected on earth in the conflict between evil powers and the faithful (Dan. 10.13f., 20f.; 12.1). Of course, such a view offers no theological or philosophical answer to the problem of evil, it merely pushes it one stage further back, but it is an understandable one in extreme circumstances.

Having said all this, however, it is important to stress that these are tendencies only. Prophecy merges into apocalyptic, and apocalyptic retains many of the insights of prophecy. Most of our Old Testament books appear as though somewhere on a gradated dial, where a needle swings to all points between the extreme limits. That is why scholars can so much enjoy themselves arguing over just which books are and which are not 'apocalyptic'. I particularly enjoy the scholarly term 'proto-apocalyptic' which is used of some of them, a sure giveaway that we are talking about varying degrees of emphasis rather than absolutes of black or white.[2] In this chapter I shall be dealing with material drawn from the post-exilic prophetic literature, and shall leave on one side the exact 'label' each properly should have. I have lumped them all together under the title of 'visionaries', a label of cowardly, but convenient ambiguity.

One matter of great interest to do with the subject of this book is how the post-exilic writers treated the whole matter of kingship after they had seen the Davidic dynasty toppled from the throne, its last representative Jehoiachin exiled and the line apparently running into a terminus. There certainly must have been, and were, those who longed for its resumption after the exile. Scattered through the main prophetic collections of the Old Testament are a number of 'messianic' passages looking forward to the renewal of the Davidic dynasty at some point in the future. The most important of such passages are, Isaiah 11.1–9; Micah 5.2–4 (Hb. 1–3); Jeremiah 23.5f. = 33.15f.; 30.9, 21; Ezekiel 17.22–4; 37.22–5. I do not propose to examine these. We have no means of knowing what were their dates of origin and at what stages in the development of the books which contain them they were introduced into their present context. It is worth observing, however, that none of them is necessarily uncritical of the earlier historical succession of Davidic kings in Jerusalem. As we saw when we were discussing Micah, the emphasis in such passages on the righteousness of the *future* king, on his being placed in office by Yahweh himself, and on the way he will exercise a just rule for all, may offer its own kind of critical subversion of the historical line which had known so abrupt a break in its continuity. But in Judah, around 520 BCE, there was a prophet, Haggai, who apparently held out hopes of a resumption of the Davidic line in the person of Zerubbabel, the Persian appointee as governor of the small territory around Jerusalem. We know very little about him. The Chronicler tells us he was a grandson of Jehoiachin and so a descendant of the Davidic line (1 Chron. 3.17–19). Haggai encouraged him and Joshua the high priest to lead the people in rebuilding the ruined temple, promising the return of Yahweh to it to reign there as universal king. There he would receive tribute from the nations and secure conditions of prosperity and peace throughout the kingdom. Zerubbabel appears to have a significant role in this, for God says of him: 'On that day, oracle of Yahweh of hosts, I will take you, Zerubbabel, son of Shealtiel and my servant, and I will set you like a signet ring, because I have chosen you' (Hag. 2.23). This does not make a royal role for Zerubbabel fully explicit, yet it is often pointed out that the term 'signet ring' is used of Jehoiachin in Jeremiah 22.24, although there in a context of threat of removal from office. This does suggest that someone, probably the prophet, saw a restoration of the Davidic line lying within the purpose of God for Zerubbabel. Coming amid the strongly eschatological notes in the little book of Haggai, it does seem as though something more exciting than merely a continuing governorship under Persian domination is envisaged for him.

However, such a note of hope does not continue. Even in the book of Haggai there has been a movement in the editorial framework, within which the oracles of the prophet are set, to strengthen the role of Joshua, as high priest.[3] The same tendency is even more strongly marked in Zechariah 1—8, especially in the stern warning to Zerubbabel in Zechariah 4.6b—10a that his role is not one of military power, but merely that of 'temple builder' and of joint rule with the high priest (see also the words which give almost the greater part to the priest in 3.6–8; 6.9–14, where the priests are guarantors of a coming of one described as 'Branch' – a messianic term – at some unspecified time in the future. No immediate candidate for the vacancy in the royal line seems to be envisaged.) Thus the evidence, such as it is, from the prophets immediately following the Babylonian exile, that is, from Haggai and Zechariah 1—8, does not suggest that hopes for a restoration of the Davidic line lasted very long or had much influence.

Against the tendency of the 'messianic' passages cited above and the hopes of Haggai, there are a number of powerful voices to be heard. The first is that of the prophet of the Babylonian exile whose work is found in Isaiah 40—55 who, because his name is unknown, has had to suffer under the title of 'Second Isaiah'. Great hopes are expressed in those chapters for a dramatic renewal of God's purpose for Israel in which he will bring them back from exile, come among them to reign as universal king, restore the land to a paradisaical fertility and plenty, and bring all the nations into subjection to him as they are forced to see by his actions on behalf of Israel that he is the only God. Yet in all this there is not one mention of a restoration of the Davidic dynasty or the installing of any human king at all. On the contrary, the institution of monarchy is to be 'democratized'. The covenant with David is to be renewed, certainly, but not with any human king. It is to be renewed in a new relationship between God and the whole community of Israel. What David was to the nation of Israel, all the people of Israel are now to be to the nations of the world:

> 'I will make with you an eternal covenant,
> my faithful covenant love for David.
> See how I made him a witness to the peoples,
> a leader and commander for the peoples.
> See, you shall summon nations you do not know,
> and nations which do not know you shall run to you,
> in order that Yahweh, your God,
> and the holy one of Israel, may make you glorious.' (Isa. 55.3–5)

The impact of this has been summarized by one commentator: '. . . these verses contain no promise of the restoration of the Davidic monarchy in the person of one of David's descendants; rather what is stated here is that the covenant promises, originally made to David as leader of the nation, are now transferred directly to the whole people.'[4]

After that the silence is deafening. Isaiah chapters 56—66 are usually thought to have achieved their present form some time after the exile, even if they incorporate some material of earlier origin. There is no mention in them of any human king. There is much hope for future action of God on behalf of his people (of very varied kinds) but it is God who acts directly and immediately without the agency of any royal figure. Malachi, usually dated somewhere in the first half of the 5th century BCE, has plenty to say about the priests, as we shall shortly see. But a king finds no place in his hopes for the future. Another post-exilic prophet, Joel, is also silent on the matter. The book of Daniel has nothing to say about a king. It is just possible that some 'royal' elements may be found in his picture of 'one like a son of man' who appears 'on the clouds of heaven' and is presented to God ('the Ancient of Days'). To this figure 'dominion', 'glory' and 'kingdom' are given, and it is promised that all nations will serve him (Dan. 7.13f.).

Whoever is meant, the figure clearly represents the ideal Israel, and all the emphasis is on the eternal rule of God, whose Kingdom can be depicted in human terms in contrast to the 'bestial' kingdoms of human might and oppression which have preceded the breaking in of God's rule. The one 'like a son of man' is not a messianic, deliverer figure. He comes *to* God (not from him) and receives *from* him the Kingdom. Later in the chapter (e.g. vv. 18, 27),he is seen as a symbol for 'the saints of the Most High' and it is they (collectively) who receive the Kingdom.

And that is that. It is meagre fare for those who believe that, after the exile, the great majority of Jews were longing for the return of a Davidic king, a powerful 'Messiah' (the Hebrew term means 'anointed one') who would deliver them from the oppression of all their enemies and restore the ancient glories of the kingdom. There is little evidence to support such a theory.[5]

There are, however, allusions to a king and the line of David in Zechariah 9—14. It is universally agreed that these chapters come from (a) different and later hand(s) from Zechariah 1—8. The reasons are given in all the commentaries.[6] All agree that they are post-exilic and later than Zechariah 1—8. There is little agreement on much else about them. Many believe there is a break between chapters 9—11 and 12—14 pointing to separate headings (Hb. *mass'ā*) at 9.1 and 12.1 and to a change in 'tone' in these two sections. Some have argued for a closely structured unity throughout while others see the chapters as now forming some kind of developing unity, although doubtless utilizing much material of diverse origin.[7] The chapters contain much material of a strongly eschatological nature, that is, looking forward to future action and intervention by God on behalf of his people. In these one may detect a sharpening 'apocalyptic' note in chapters 12—14. Scattered throughout both sections of the book are a number of passages strongly critical of the leaders of the community and which I have described as 'controversy passages'. To these we shall turn shortly. It is very difficult to 'date' all the material in Zechariah 9—14 (in spite of the fact that some recent commentators claim to be able to). All we can really say is that they seem to witness to growing eschatological hopes over a period of time after the exile, hopes which become ever more hostile to the official leadership of the community and more sharply 'apocalyptic' as those hopes are disappointed and deferred.

For the moment, we need to consider two passages which have a bearing on the subject of kingship. The first is the very well known prediction of the coming of a future king which occurs in 9.9f. which I will cite from the REB version:

> Daughter of Zion, rejoice with all your heart;
> shout in triumph, daughter of Jerusalem!
> See, your king is coming to you,
> his cause won, his victory gained,
> humble, and mounted on a donkey.
> He will banish the chariot from Ephraim,
> the war-horse from Jerusalem;
> the warrior's bow will be banished,
> and he will proclaim peace to the nations.
> His rule will extend from sea to sea,
> from the River to the ends of the earth.

This will be well known to many readers because of its link with the story of Palm Sunday, of the entry by Jesus into Jerusalem, an incident clearly inspired by this passage from which Matthew's Gospel quotes (Matt. 21.1–9, cf. Mark 11.1–10; Luke 19.28–38). Our task, however, is to try to understand what is its thrust in Zechariah 9. The immediate context is little help since the chapter is clearly comprised of a great deal of varied material the individual parts of which have only loose connections with each other.[8] We have to fall back on the contents of the passage itself. Who the king is is left unspecified. It cannot be Yahweh himself, since when he speaks in the first person he speaks of the king in the third person (v. 11) and the idea of Yahweh riding on a donkey is a somewhat fanciful one. How is he described? Each of the epithets is of significance. The first one, which REB renders as 'his cause won' (Hb. *ṣaddîq*) is used of the Davidic king in Psalm 72.1, where the worshippers ask that God will give the king 'your righteousness' (Hb. *ṣedeq*) so that he may judge the people in righteousness. It is also used of the 'Servant' in Second Isaiah, where in one of the so-called 'Servant Songs' (the four usually so described are found at Isaiah 42.1–4; 49.1–6; 50.4–9; 52.13—53.12) the Servant says 'he who pronounces me righteous [Hb. *maṣdîqî*] is near'. The word not only means 'righteous' but carries the idea of legal acquittal as of one who is declared 'innocent' in a court, and also one who is thus 'vindicated' as God is shown to act on his behalf. That is why REB can render it 'his victory won' and why some other versions rendered it as 'just' (e.g. AV). The second adjective consists of a passive participle from the root of a Hebrew verb which means 'to deliver' or 'to save' (Hb. *nôshāʿ*) and so can be rendered as either 'saved', 'delivered' or even 'bearing salvation'. He is both the recipient of and the bearer of God's deliverance. The same passive participle is used of the Davidic king in the psalms, where Psalm 33.16 reminds the king that he is not 'saved' by the might of his great army but by God, an idea taken up in Zechariah 9.10. Further, there was the widespread idea that the Davidic king was the instrument by which God's salvation was mediated to the people, most explicitly stated in the so-called 'last words of David' in 2 Samuel 23.1–7, where verse 5 reads, 'Will he [i.e. God] not prosper all my salvation [*yishʿî*] and every wish?' Again, however, the same thing is said of the 'Servant' in Isaiah 49.6, where God says to him, 'I will give you as a light for the nations that my salvation (*yᵉshûʿāthî*) may extend to the ends of the earth.' Finally, the king is said to be either 'humble' or, as it might be rendered, 'afflicted' (Hb. *ʿānî*). For the moment we must leave aside suggestions that the Davidic king, like the Babylonian king, took part in an annual cultic ritual of renewal in which he was symbolically afflicted on behalf of all the people.[9] We may, however, note that Psalm 18.27 (Hb. 28), where the speaker must surely be the king, says, 'For you deliver (*tôshîaʿ*) a humble (*ʿānî*) people'. But this is still another term which is used of the Servant when, in the last song, the speakers say, 'we considered him stricken, smitten by God and afflicted' (a passive participle of the same verb used in Zechariah 9.9).

We must not make too much of the fact that he comes riding on a donkey (only one animal is meant, the repetition being due merely to parallelism, a feature of Hebrew poetry, even although Matthew misunderstood it (Matt. 21.2f.)). Although in Christian tradition this has come to symbolize great humility, the original does not necessarily intend any such association to be made. Genesis 49.8–12 sees the donkey as a mount fit for a king (as it was regarded throughout the ancient Near East) and it is quite possible that the Genesis passage, the so-called 'Blessing of Jacob', was one source of inspiration for the Zechariah picture here. Nevertheless, the passage does have one more surprise for us, for it goes on in verse 11 to quote one of the 'royal' psalms, Psalm 72, to which we have already alluded. That has a verse about the Davidic king which runs,

> He will rule from sea to sea,
> from the River to the ends of the earth.
> Before him his foes[10] will bend the knee,
> and his enemies shall lick the dust.' (vv. 8f.)

Zechariah 9.10 accurately cites the first two of those lines but makes a significant alteration, avoiding the bloodthirstiness and chauvinism of the second two:

> He shall speak peace [Hb. *shālôm*] to the nations.

Conclusions about just what is going on here have to be tentative (as they so often have to be with the material in these difficult and obscure chapters). We cannot immediately deduce that the 'speaking peace' to the nations implies a quite different type of monarchy from that of the pre-monarchical period. It may simply mean that when he exercises universal and undivided sway, not only over Israel but over all nations, there will be peace because all will be subject to his ruling. Nevertheless, we do note certain points. There is no mention of a 'Davidic' pedigree. The oracle is silent on everything about the king except his character and the nature of his rule. Further, is it entirely coincidental that each of the 'royal' attributes is matched by qualities assigned in Isaiah 40—55 to the 'Suffering Servant'? Could it be that the nature of earlier kingship is being sharply redefined so as to indicate that a future king, when he does come, will truly be the 'servant', not the master and oppressor of his subjects? One thing is sure, he is intended as a direct counterbalance to those who are so fiercely attacked in these chapters as false 'shepherds', passages which will occupy us shortly.

However, although there is no mention of the Davidic line here, there is elsewhere in Zechariah 9—14, in 12.7—13.1. This occurs in the second section, which some have assigned to a different author and which I have described as being more sharply 'apocalyptic'. In its heightened hopes for a radically new future, the context of these immediate verses depicts God using his people to overcome the 'nations' who have come to besiege Jerusalem. It is promised that God will intervene to deliver Jerusalem, and, from the way God supports those in the city, the people of Judah generally will take heart. Indeed, it is they who will be delivered first, 'so that the glory of the house of David and of the inhabitants of Jerusalem may not be magnified over Judah' (v. 7). At the least that seems to suggest a certain amount of provincial suspicion of the capital city (not unknown in later times), but it may also seem to imply a determination not to go back to the kind of centralized power and wealth which so angered the people of the north in the reign of Solomon that they refused the rule of his son after his death (1 Kings 12). Notice also that the line of David is by no means the *means* or *agent* of the deliverance. Its representatives, with everyone else, are the passive recipients of God's deliverance. It is true that in a very strange and difficult verse (v. 8) it is said that 'on that day Yahweh will act as a shield around the inhabitants of Jerusalem so that the weakest among them will become like David and the house of David will become like God', a comment so strange indeed that a pious glossator, shocked at what seemed the blasphemy of this, added the words, 'like the angel of Yahweh in front of them'. What it may be suggesting is that the house of David will be restored to its right relationship with God (just as God had once told Moses that Aaron would be his mouthpiece and he would be 'like God' to Aaron, that is, he would direct what Aaron was to say just as God directed the way the prophets spoke (Exod. 4.16)). That the house of David *needs* such restoration is made abundantly clear by what follows. It has to take its place alongside every other section of the community and the whole people, who, 'on that day', will together mourn and lament for their sins, which they see have 'pierced' God (or, perhaps, God's faithful representative, the prophet, whom they have rejected), and on whom God will pour out a new spirit and for whom he will open a fountain of purifying waters for their cleansing (12.10—13.1). This is far from a triumphant 'messianic' hope for a future Davidic king. Only as that house is utterly renewed alongside the whole community will it be fit for any divinely given role in the future.

We have seen enough to show that there is little evidence for a widespread hope for a restoration of the old royal line after the exile. Either the 'royals' are ignored altogether, or their role is envisaged as being sharply redefined, or it is expressly said that only a radically new kind of monarchy can have any place in God's future kingdom. The visionaries are indeed subversive of the historic monarchy.

How did the priests who largely took over control of the post-exilic theocratic community (alongside governors of whom we hear so little) fare? In the eyes of at least some, they also were seen to be too often abusing their power and their privileged position, and they too come in for strong criticism.

No one is more critical of them than Malachi, the last of the prophets to have given his name to a book. We cannot be sure of his exact dates but it is often said that he must have been active in the first half of the 5th century BCE, for he shows just the kind of abuses in society which Nehemiah set about reforming when he came to Jerusalem (in 445 BCE). He expresses his teaching in a series of 'disputes' with his hearers, using a kind of question and answer format in which he makes his own statements, takes up rhetorically his hearers' objections and then expands his own assertion as he answers them. One of these (1.6—2.9) consists of a fierce denunciation of the priests for the way they are discharging their sacred office, sacred because it was based on a covenant between God and Levi (2.4, 8). They are like sons dishonouring their father or servants their master (1.6) in that they have offered any old animal in sacrifice to God where the law stipulates that the sacrificial animal should always be a perfect specimen (1.7f.). No doubt they were pocketing the difference between the cost of the sound animals they insisted the worshippers should present to them and those they actually did offer. They treat God in a way they would not even do to the governor (1.8). Better than such a travesty of worship if the doors of the temple were closed for good (1.10, something which must have seemed an outrageously scandalous suggestion). Indeed, they are shamed by those even of other nations who express real thankfulness to their creator when they offer their thank-offerings (1.11). It is small wonder that such a thought appeared outrageous to the priests of Malachi's day. It has been too much for the conservative theological sensibilities of scholars even in our own time. Suggestions for muting such a dangerously liberal note abound – Malachi was referring to the grain offerings of Jews in the Dispersion (i.e. those who were living in countries other than Judah); or this is an 'eschatological' picture of some future reign of God when people of all nations will worship him. It seems that few of the prophets would be invited to preach from many of our pulpits today. Stripped of the cotton wool insulation in which conventional piety has wrapped them, they are far too radical.

It might seem that all these are merely technical, 'cultic' matters of proper ecclesiastical procedure. Not so, says Malachi. Milton once said, 'New presbyter is but old priest writ large' (from his sonnet, *On the New Forcers of Conscience under the Long Parliament,*

1646). Malachi might well have said, 'New priest is but old king writ large.' For they, also, were oppressive, he maintains. 'You bring what has been taken in robbery' (1.13). According to Malachi, one of the major functions of a priest was to teach, to give true instruction in all matters to do with the law, both cultic and ethical. How could those who conducted their own lives in such a way give any kind of true instruction? 'You have turned aside from [my] way' and so, 'you have caused many to stumble in the law' (2.8). Forthrightly, Malachi announces God's rejection of such priests if they do not change. He will judge them by making them ritually unfit for their office and 'you will be carried away' (2.3).[11]

Just as disillusion with the historic monarchy led to the kind of future hopes we have been following in this chapter, it is no surprise that Malachi sees the need for a radical change of the priesthood in the future. The passage which announces this, 3.2b–4, is actually out of place where it occurs, interrupting the announcement of Yahweh's coming in answer to the weary cries of those who long for his action in order to bring justice against evildoers and act on behalf of the oppressed (2.17—3.2a, 5). The passage which announces a 'refining' and 'purifying' of Levi probably originally belonged to the oracle denouncing the priests we have already considered. But, wherever it should be placed, there can be no doubt that it is another of the hopes of the visionaries which is subversive of the present order.

We have already seen that there are three passages of a strongly polemical tone in Zechariah 9—14: 10.1–3a; 11.4–17; and 13.7–9. They are directed against those described as 'shepherds'. Like much else in these chapters they present considerable problems for our understanding, and there is no space (or need) here to involve ourselves in lengthy and detailed discussion of them all. There is a great deal of echo of earlier scriptural books and passages in these chapters, and these passages are no exception. The very description of the leaders of the community as 'shepherds' echoes especially Jeremiah and Ezekiel, who attack the leaders of their time in just such terms (indeed, one word in Zechariah 10.3, 'he-goats', rendered as 'leaders' in RSV, is used only by Ezekiel in such a context, Ezekiel 34.17). While for the earlier prophets 'shepherds' must often have denoted kings (and is used explicitly of them in metaphor in Psalm 78.70–72, where there is play on the idea that David was literally a 'shepherd' and then became 'shepherd' of Judah), there is no doubt that, in context, the term often covered a wider range of officials, including priests and prophets. In these post-exilic chapters it must be the priests who are the main targets, although those seen as false prophets are also attacked here (13.2–6).

In Zechariah 10.1–3a it is suggested that people are turning in times of extremity, such as drought, to diviners and exponents of magic rather than to God, and this is directly attributed to lack of proper direction from their 'shepherds', very much in line with the way Malachi attacked the priests. There is such strong echo of Jeremiah 14.1—15.4 that the actual details may be a little stylized, but there is no doubt that the prophet mourns the lack of clear leadership in matters of religion. Chapter 11 verses 4–17 contain so many difficulties that it can hardly be discussed briefly.[12] Here we must content ourselves with one or two observations. The passage seems to contain at least two, if not three acts of 'prophetic symbolism' in which the prophet declares his growing alienation from the 'shepherds' who are supposed to be leading the flock. These stand condemned of exploiting their people by selling them to those who apparently work them to death (11.4). They are interested only in their own wealth and without pity for any who stand in their way. For this the prophet breaks two staves, an act which seems to indicate God's intention of severing his covenant ties with the religious community such leaders represent, while the prophet dissociates himself from any connection with the official temple (11.7–14). The passage ends with the threat that Yahweh will raise up a worthless shepherd who will exploit the weak and poor of the community shamelessly. In other words, they will be judged by getting the kind of leadership they deserve. It is very difficult to say exactly what lies behind this and what the precise charges are, especially as this also is full of themes from an earlier prophet, in this case Ezekiel (esp. ch. 34). To that extent this also may be described as 'stylized'. The same is true of the last passage, Zechariah 13.7–9, in which God announces that he will reject the 'shepherd' by judging the community. He will, however, preserve a remnant through the ordeal (which is likened to a smelting process), who will respond to God directly. Of this community, spoken of as a single being, so great will be its unity, it is said,

> 'He will call on my name and I will answer him;
> I will say, "He is my people";
> and he shall say, "Yahweh is my God".'

Intermediaries like priests, who have so manifestly failed in their responsibilities, are now dispensed with. The old covenant relationship is renewed directly between God and his people.

The same note is heard in the book of Joel, the last of the visionaries to concern us in this chapter. Again with this book as with others there are many difficult questions to be answered concerning its date, its unity or lack of it, and, in particular, the literary *genre* of the book.[13] The first two chapters[14] provide a kind of 'prophetic liturgy' in the face of some disaster or series of disasters. The troubles seem to cover a plague of locusts (some have thought these might be a symbol for the invasion of a foreign army), drought or fire. How far these relate to actual disasters or how far, being liturgy, their language is kept vague and general so that they could be used in all kinds of situations, is not clear. What is clear is that the prophet interprets them in the same way as earlier prophets did, as a sign of God's judgement on 'the Day of Yahweh' (1.15; 2.11). In each case the priests are exhorted to lead the people in an act of penitence and mourning, calling on God to intervene on their behalf (e.g. 1.13f.; 2.12–17). We should note here particularly the call to the priests to lead the people in such worship in 1.13 and 2.17. This is followed by the assurance that God would hear such calls and intervene so that the whole situation will change to one of joy and prosperity (2.18–27). To this have been added two sections of hope for a more distant future of a more 'apocalyptic' nature. Chapter 3 now sees the 'Day of Yahweh', not as a day of judgement against Israel to be averted by penitence and prayer, but as a day when Israel's enemies will be shattered and they themselves delivered (3.9–21, an obviously composite passage which, like so much else in the book, is full of echoes of earlier prophecy). But it is the addition of 2.28–32 which is of special interest to us here. It is not altogether clear whether the calls to the priests to do something about the situation in the first two chapters indicate impatience with their present idleness and indifference. They do sound a little like members of an opposition party calling on the government of the day to start doing something about some problem or other! In view of the many parallels between the book of Joel and Zechariah 9—14 it would not be surprising if this note were there. Certainly, what is heard in 2.28–32 is very similar to the note that was sounded in Zechariah 13.9 announcing the renewal of the *whole* community:

'And it shall happen after this
that I will pour out my spirit on all flesh;
and your sons and daughters will prophesy;
your old men will dream dreams
and your young men shall see visions.
Even on your male and female servants
in those days I will pour out my spirit.' (Joel 2.28, Hb. 3.1)

P. L. Redditt, in an important article, argued that this can only be read as radical or, in my words, subversive.[15] God is going to be in direct, unmediated contact with every member of the community, from the highest to the lowest. They will all be anointed by the Spirit of God in the way that, earlier, kings, priests and prophets were held to be. They will not need those who hold themselves to be specially qualified and specifically appointed to tell them what God thinks and what he is saying. There will be a kind of universal 'priesthood of all believers', to coin a phrase from the Protestant Reformation. In fact, in the course of post-Reformation church history, it has been a phrase and a concept far too radical and revolutionary for most Protestant churches to take on board. Only the most extreme radical and political groups have dared to believe in Joel's vision of a time when God is directly available to all. Indeed, there have been enough instances of the dangers of such radicalism to make died-in-the-wool conservatives of many an erstwhile reformer, as it did with Luther. We can tame it with safety only by consigning it to a distant future, meanwhile guarding closely the approaches to the corridors of political and ecclesiastical power. Joel's is a 'vision' which is shockingly subversive of the present order. And it shows what we have been seeing in this chapter, that the old prophetic spirit did not die out after the exile. The visionaries carried the torch and shone it both on the hopes they formed (or did not form) about any future monarch and in the way some of them at least were prepared to attack abuses of power wherever they saw them, whether such abuses were perpetrated by king or by priest.

CHAPTER SEVEN

The Subversion of the 'Universalists'

One of the dire consequences of teaching for many years is that one's mind gets twisted into thinking in questions. As I begin this chapter I find myself toying – with the greatest pleasure – with a possible question to set a class of theology students, especially those interested in the history of religion: 'Is there ever such a thing as a *national* God?', that is, 'Has there ever been an ethnic or national group who have envisaged a god all to themselves, one who was concerned with them and with them alone?'

As with many of the questions I have set students over the years, I am by no means sure of the answer myself. But in the area I do know about there are certainly suggestions in the Old Testament that some Israelites did sometimes so think of Yahweh. They did not deny that there were other gods. Chemosh was the god of the Moabites, as we learn from the 'Moabite Stone' and from such passages as Judges 11.24. No doubt the Moabites, and other people, thought similarly. The various different titles given to Ba'al, such as Ba'al Pe'or, etc., suggest that various localities and regions believed they had their own particular manifestation of Ba'al. A strange verse in the so-called 'Song of Moses' in Deuteronomy 32.8f. reads as follows:

> 'When God Most High [Hb. *'Elyôn*] gave the nations their
>   inheritance,
> when he divided up human beings,
> he established national boundaries
> according to the number of divine beings;
> but Yahweh's own inheritance is his people,
> Jacob is the portion of his inheritance.'[1]

That seems to express the idea that every nation has its own tutelary deity, although, of course, it leaves no doubt that Yahweh is the supreme God who has overseen the allocation and kept the best for himself, namely, the people of Israel. So for Israel, the view that Yahweh was Israel's *national* God could coexist with a polytheistic outlook, and, no doubt, the same applied for many other peoples. There can be no doubt, in fact, that the many various groups who made up early Israel were polytheists and that many of them combined worship of Yahweh with worship of other gods. We have the evidence of the early prophets to this effect – especially, but not exclusively, of Hosea – together with the fierce calls of the Deuteronomists to the people to worship only Yahweh. Preachers do not denounce things which are not happening. Then as now you can learn a lot about both preachers and their congregations by listening to sermons.[2]

As our first chapter showed, however, gods as well as kings and emperors tend to get swollen heads. For reasons we have seen, the size of head of gods and kings tends to correspond exactly. For gods are extremely convenient when it comes to establishing the 'divine right' of one person or one dynasty to rule within a particular territory. They are also extremely useful when a particular ruler wants to extend his territory. They not only offer a bit of divine help to the national armies when it comes to fighting, but they sanction the whole imperialistic enterprise by giving it the nature of a holy crusade. It was firmly believed that the aim of the Roman gods was to extend the rule of the Caesars (and so their own) so that the benefits of Roman law and justice (*mos* and *ius*) could be known throughout the world and all nations be united under the blessings of a *pax Romana*. A very similar outlook was seen to be behind Assyrian imperialistic expansion as Liverani showed in his analysis (see above, pp. 18–21). The light and order of the 'centre' is being imposed on the benighted and uncivilized 'outer' reaches of the world; unity is being imposed on the chaotic strife of warring and competing nations and the wealth of the world is being brought to its proper centre, where king and gods rule jointly.

How did Yahweh fare in this competitive world? We have seen that a good deal which looks at first blush like universalism among his devotees turns out on closer inspection to be nothing different from the mindset of the surrounding nations of the ancient world. The promise to Abraham that through him and his descendants 'all the nations of the earth would bless themselves' (Gen. 12.3) is seen to justify the extension of David's empire in which other nations find peace and prosperity under his control and that of his successors (see above, pp. 30–32). There is plenty of evidence to suggest that wars of defence and expansion fought by the Israelites were also 'holy wars' in which Yahweh was imposing his order on the 'chaos' of the surrounding nations. Yahweh thus establishes his credentials as the 'supreme god'. In the ancient world, either conqueror nations took the images of the gods of the captured people away back to their own land as a sign of the triumph of their 'national' gods, or the victorious gods subsumed into themselves the being and nature of the gods they had 'defeated'. There is plenty of evidence from the Old Testament, well demonstrated by Smith (see n. 2), that Yahweh assumed the titles and qualities of other gods, especially the gods of the Canaanites. So his titles come to include those which originally designated other gods, *'El 'Elyôn* (originally the god of the Jebusites in Jerusalem); *'El 'Olām*, *'El Bethel* and so on. He takes over many of the characteristics of Ba'al, like him being depicted as 'the rider of the clouds', as lord of all storm phenomena, as the divine warrior, as the one who overcomes the dark waters of chaos. A psalm like Psalm 29 could almost be a Canaanite hymn in that nearly all the qualities ascribed to Yahweh are found in the Ugaritic literature as characterizing Ba'al, while a hymn celebrating victory in battle and ascribing it to the victorious march of Yahweh against Israel's enemies is equally full of Canaanite parallels. (See Judges 5.1–31, the 'Song of Deborah' and compare it with Habakkuk 3.2–15). To such evidence we must add the *ba'al* compounds in the names of Israelites especially in the earlier periods, such as Jerubba'al, another name for Gideon (Judg. 7.1), while even one of Saul's sons was called Ishba'al (2 Samuel 2.8. The name actually means 'man of Ba'al'. An editor of the books of Samuel, expressing the sensitivities of later times, has altered all the names with *ba'al* compounds to *bōsheth* – the Hebrew word meaning 'shame'. The result gives us impossible names like 'Ishbōsheth', meaning 'man of shame').

So as Yahweh proved powerful in battle he could be seen to be showing his supremacy over the gods of other nations, just as, in the story, the image of Dagon, the Philistine god, fell flat on its face before the ark of Yahweh (1 Sam. 5.1–5). Of course, if ever the Israelites were defeated it could only be because Yahweh was angry with his people for some reason, just as in the story of the defeat of Israelite forces at Ai which proved to be due to the sin of

Achan (Jos. 7.1–26). Exactly the same idea occurred to others. When Mesha, the king of Moab, was defeated by the Israelites headed by Omri, it was recorded on the Moabite Stone that it was because 'Chemosh was angry at his land'.[3]

Thus the concept grew of Yahweh as so much the supreme God that other deities became demoted to merely god-like beings, angelic beings almost, who served under his direction in a kind of heavenly 'court', or 'the Council of Heaven' as it is often called. Such beings existed to go on Yahweh's errands and do his bidding. We see such a 'Council' at work in the story of Micaiah and the 'false prophets' in 1 Kings 22 where God discusses with its members how to lure the Judean and Israelite kings to their judgement. We see it in the Prologue to the book of Job where 'the Satan' is one of such beings who comes to report on his activity to Yahweh along with all the others (Job chs. 1f.). It is hinted at in a most mysterious way in Psalm 82 where the lesser divine beings are reprimanded for failing to secure justice in the realms under their jurisdiction. After the exile the idea reappears, as we saw in our last chapter. The terrible things which are happening on earth can only be explained as a projection of an internecine war in heaven between Yahweh and his angels and those who have rebelled against him, the representatives of oppressor nations like Persia and Greece, as they are depicted in the book of Daniel.[4]

As we might expect, the strongest notes of Yahweh's subjection of other gods and so of other nations are sounded in the royal psalms. Psalm 2 depicts the futile rebellion of the nations against Yahweh and 'his anointed'. Yahweh has set his king in Zion, 'my holy hill'. This king has only to invoke Yahweh's aid and he will make the nations his king's inheritance. His king 'will break them with a rod of iron'. So let the kings of the other nations be careful. They had better 'serve Yahweh', that is, acknowledge his overlordship. Psalm 72 speaks of the king having dominion from 'sea to sea' and predicts that his enemies will bow down to him and lick the dust, while tribute will come from nations everywhere, brought in subjection by their submissive kings. This means that 'peace' (*shālôm*) will extend everywhere because all nations will have been defeated by the king of Israel and will be subject to his rule. As the victorious king imposes his rule of justice on all his subject peoples there will be peace between them, just as a strong king by his rule imposes peace on the various warring factions within his own kingdom. Psalm 110, for good measure, tells how Yahweh's 'priest king' will shatter kings and will arbitrate between them.

Perhaps as time went on it was inevitable that some more searching questions were asked about Yahweh's relationship with other nations. Various factors may have played a part in deepening theological speculation about this. The experience of devastating defeat at the hand of other powers must have challenged the superficial traditional beliefs of what might be called 'royal Yahwism'. Again, the experience of exile when many influential thinkers among the Jews actually got used to living among foreigners must have set their minds to work. The situation would have been just a little similar to the experience of many Western nations as an ever-increasing number of ethnic immigrants have come to live among them. If I am not mistaken, issues concerned with 'comparative religion' have come to loom much larger on the theological horizons of many Westerners as they have got used to seeing a Hindu temple or an Islamic mosque just down the road. And in Israel, a growing sense, at least among some, that there was only one God, must inexorably have raised the question about the ultimate relation between that one God and *all* peoples.

Did any or all of this combine to raise profound questions about the *exclusivity* of Israel's relations with God? Did ideas arise which were subversive of Israel's claim to be in a special and unique way 'the people of Yahweh' and so 'superior' to all others? Is there anything approaching what might be called universalism in the Old Testament?

It has to be freely admitted that a good deal of what appears at first to be universalism, and has often been claimed as such, turns out on closer inspection to be, at best, only a rather modified form of it. If other peoples are seen as one day coming to share the worship of Yahweh with Israel it will be as those who have been forced into admitting Yahweh's overlordship and have seen that Israel was all along his favoured people. We might consider an oracle common (with a few variations) to Isaiah and Micah.

> It shall come to pass in the last days
> that the mountain of Yahweh's sanctuary
> shall be founded as head of [all] the mountains
> and shall be exalted above the hills.
> Many nations shall go and say,
> 'Come, let us go up to the mountain of Yahweh,
> to the sanctuary of the God of Jacob;

so that he may instruct us in his ways
and we may walk in his paths.'
For from Zion Torah shall proceed
and the oracle of Yahweh from Jerusalem.
He will arbitrate between many nations
and give judgement between strong nations from far away.
They will forge their swords into ploughs
and their spears into pruning tools.
Nation shall not raise sword against nation
and they will not study warfare any more.
Everyone shall sit under his vine and fig tree,
with none to terrify them. (Mic. 4.1–4 = Isa. 2.1–4)[5]

The fact that virtually the same oracle appears in two prophetic books does not mean that one prophet copied from another. It must have been inserted at a later stage of the editing of both books. Most scholars believe it is of post-exilic date, and this is quite likely. There is no mention of the king's role in all this. The emphasis on 'Torah' suggests a later time and may even hint at the role of the priests, since they were the experts in teaching the niceties of the law and their role in this receives greatest prominence after the exile, especially in the work of the Chronicler and in such a passage as Malachi 2.6f. The oracle presents an idyllic picture which, naturally enough, has been much quoted in later times. It still implies, however, the supremacy of Jerusalem and of Israel. It is a peace based on the submission of the mightiest and furthest nations to Yahweh and to Israel as the mediators and dispensers of his rule of law. The most we might say is that it envisages a transition of the role of Israel from a military supremacy to a *religious* supremacy. But the submission of the nations remains a precondition of this idealized future. That is why the final editor of the book of Malachi has not found it inconsistent to add a little later an oracle which threatens 'many nations' with the fierce judgement of Yahweh, a judgement in which he will use his people Israel like a fierce animal to 'pulverize' them with iron horns and bronze hooves so that they bring their wealth as tribute to Yahweh (Mic. 4.13).

Very close in content and tone to this (probably post-exilic) oracle are some to be found in Zechariah, a post-exilic prophet whose activity is dated around 520 BCE. In a series of 'visions of the night' with accompanying oracles, he announces that God intends to reverse the fortunes of his people after the exile, removing the threat from foreign nations who have defeated, plundered and exiled them, seeing that the temple is rebuilt, that the community is cleansed from sin and that conditions of peace and fertility are ushered in. In the oracle following the third vision which promises the rebuilding and divine defence of Jerusalem (2.1–5, Hb. 2.5–9) God promises vengeance on those nations who have ravaged Judah, because anyone who touches them touches 'the apple of his eye' (v. 8, Hb. 12). By contrast when Yahweh 'waves his hand' over them 'the plunderers will become the plundered', and plundered by those who had formerly been their servants. Yahweh will return to live among his people in Zion, and then we read, 'And many nations will join themselves to Yahweh on that day and shall be my people' (v. 11, Hb. 15). Then 'Yahweh will inherit Judah as his share in the holy land and will again choose Jerusalem' (v. 12, Hb. 16). This certainly could be read as an extension of the covenant relationship between Yahweh and Israel to all the nations.[6] It is perhaps a little discouraging to find that the same Hebrew verb, 'to join', is used in Isaiah 14.1, which also speaks of Yahweh's choosing Israel and of 'aliens *joining* themselves to the house of Jacob'. The next verse, however, makes it clear that their role will be as slaves, as a judgement for their having enslaved the Israelites. There are some uncomfortable parallels between this and Zechariah, who also announces the turning of the tables on Israel's oppressors. However, whatever it means precisely that these foreigners will become 'my people', there can be no doubt that Israel retains the favoured position.

The passage most reminiscent of the Isaiah/Micah oracle, however, occurs in Zechariah 8.20–23. This announces that 'Many peoples and strong nations shall come to enquire of Yahweh of Hosts and to entreat the favour of Yahweh.' To this is added a verse which seems to hold out the promise of some purpose to the exile of Jews who have been dispersed from their homeland. They will prove to have a mediating role in bringing other nations to a knowledge of Yahweh. 'In those days ten men from all the languages of the nations shall seize hold of the sleeve of a Judean, saying, "Let us go with you for we have heard that God is with you."' This certainly appears to be opening the idea of a universalistic extension of the relations of Yahweh with all people. It is rather in the spirit of Genesis 12.3. Jews will appear to do so remarkably well from their relationship with Yahweh that others will decide to seek the same God. This in no way challenges the unique and supreme place of Israel, but it does tend to show a more generous spirit to others. The last verse, particularly, is probably an addition to Zechariah 8, which itself, with chapter 7, both echoes and reinforces with later admonitions the teaching of both Zechariah and Haggai. But, if Zechariah 2.11 can be traced back to the prophet, whoever has added this may well argue that he has kept within the spirit of the prophet himself.

The biggest conundrum is posed by the prophet of the exile from whom Isaiah 40—55 derive, often called 'Second Isaiah', since his words have been joined to the words of Isaiah of Jerusalem.[7] So apparently contradictory are the signals we pick up from these chapters that the views of commentators have ranged all the way from seeing Second Isaiah as an out-and-out universalist to those who have argued that he was an almost xenophobic particularist! His message is that God is about to intervene in a powerful and dramatic way to reverse the fortunes of his exiled people who have now suffered enough for their earlier sins. He is going to bring them back to their own land in a repeat of the miracle by which originally he brought their fathers back through the desert from bondage in Egypt. So great will be the demonstration of his power as the supreme creator and redeeming God that other nations will come to concede that their gods have no comparable power, hardly indeed any independent existence, and so will acknowledge Yahweh as God. It is in this way, and not in any sense by being 'missionaries', that Israel will prove 'a light to the nations' (42.6). Indeed, Israel will be a 'suffering servant', by the cost of whose sufferings the nations' 'kings' and 'rulers' will come to see that God is God. This is the burden of the last of the so-called 'servant songs' in these chapters.[8] It opens in 52.13–15 with a statement in first person divine speech in which God speaks about his servant. After an initial humiliation (v. 14) he will eventually so prosper (v. 13) that kings will be amazed as they see what they have never seen before and hear what they have never understood before (v. 15). The song then switches to first person plural speech, but the connection with 52.15 makes it clear that the speakers are in fact the gentile kings, representatives of the gentile nations who have plundered Israel, for their opening words take up the theme of 52.15:

> Who has believed what we have heard?
> and to whom has Yahweh's strength been revealed?

What they have now seen is the weak, defeated 'servant' vindicated by God, and so have come themselves to realize the power and strength of this God. The servant's sufferings have thus proved 'vicarious'. He has borne the cost of the divine revelation to others. It is sometimes argued against this interpretation of the song that the servant is said here to have suffered innocently (53.9) whereas elsewhere Israel is said to have suffered exile because of her sins (e.g. 40.2). However, that difficulty disappears when we recall that the speakers are the very kings who have invaded and exiled Israel. *Vis-à-vis* them Israel had done no wrong. She had not invaded Babylon – Babylon had invaded Israel. The Babylonians could not know that, according to the prophet, they were the unconscious instruments of divine judgement against his own people.

Now all this acknowledgement of God by the nations might well make it seem that Second Isaiah was a universalist and that his dream was of all nations acknowledging Yahweh as the only God alongside Israel. And there are other passages which might reinforce such an impression. Isaiah 45.22f. sounds a ringing cry which has been the text for many a missionary sermon in the history of Christendom:

> 'Turn to me and be saved,
> all the ends of the earth.
> For I am God – there is no other.
> I have sworn by my own Being
> from my mouth has gone forth right judgement,
> a word which shall not return.
> To me every knee shall bow
> every tongue shall swear [allegiance].'

That sounds fine, especially when as a text it is followed by an eloquent and forceful sermon. But there are several ways of understanding it. Is it a call to all peoples to turn to Yahweh and find deliverance or is it a call to all exiled Israelites to return and join in the triumphal procession back to Jerusalem of Yahweh's redeemed people? That is certainly the note which sounds elsewhere in these chapters, e.g. 41.17–20; 43.14–21; 48.20f.; 49.8–13; 52.11f. And if every knee is to bow to Yahweh, is it the willing worship of the convert or the forced submission of the conquered? For there are plenty of other passages which speak of the defeat by Yahweh of those nations who have humiliated his people. In

49.22 it is said that the oppressor kings and queens will be the very ones who bring the Israelites back to their homeland and there

> 'with their faces to the ground they will bow down to you;
> they will lick the very dust of your feet.'

It is a somewhat less than generous welcome to the nations now 'enlightened' by what God has done for Israel. Indeed, apparently God even finds other nations expendable in his special favour towards Israel.

> 'I have given Egypt as your ransom
> Ethiopia and Seba as your substitutes.' (43.3)

Small wonder, then,

> 'The produce of Egypt and the merchandise of Ethiopia
> and of the Sabaeans, those powerful men,
> shall pass to you and be yours
> and they will come after you, travelling in chains;
> before you they will prostrate themselves,
> to you they will pray,
> "God is only with you;
> there is no other God apart from him."' (45.14)

This seems to be the universalism of this prophet. The nations will come to know God through Israel and be forced into submission to him and to them. There is little subversive here! It is one of the most powerful assertions of Israelite supremacy in the purposes of God to be found anywhere in the Old Testament.[9]

It is somewhat different in Isaiah 56—66, often referred to as 'Trito-Isaiah'.[10] The opening section in 56.1–8 seems to reflect something of a priestly concern for right observance of Torah, especially over keeping the sabbath. This, it seems, is the touchstone of acceptability to God rather than birth, nationality or even physical disability such as being a eunuch. Elsewhere the eunuch is forbidden to enter the sanctuary (Deut. 23.1, and later, v. 3, the same passage forbids such foreigners as Ammonites or Moabites). In Leviticus 22.24f. neither animals whose testicles were crushed nor the animals of foreigners were to be permitted as sacrifices. So it looks as though this passage is a deliberate reversal of the earlier law. Here both the foreigner and the eunuch

157

are explicitly admitted providing they keep the law on such matters as sabbath observance and all that is involved in 'the covenant' (vv. 3f.). And foreigners who 'join themselves' to Yahweh (the same Hebrew verb as we found in Zechariah 2.11, Hb. 15) will be brought by Yahweh himself to the sanctuary to offer prayer and sacrifices:

> 'for my sanctuary shall be called a sanctuary of prayer for all peoples.' (v. 7)

That probably means only that those foreigners who actually embraced Judaism as a faith would be welcome, and so may only make explicit a much older practice towards those known as *gērîm*, that is sojourners, such as Ruth the Moabitess was. Nevertheless, it represents a widening concept and shows how Israel's supremacy could be seen in religious rather than purely military terms. It is a view perhaps extended a little in the remarkable ending to Zechariah 14 (a late text), in which it is envisaged that Yahweh's rule from the temple in Zion will mark it as a place of religious pilgrimage and worship for people of all nations (Zech. 14.16). Even Egyptians, their erstwhile oppressors, will come to the high point of Israel's worship at the Feast of Tabernacles. Indeed, only by so doing can foreigners, including the Egyptians, ensure the blessings of Yahweh's fertility on their land (vv. 16–19). Again, we are moving along a road which is seeing Israel's special position in relation to Yahweh as implying religious rather than mainly military consequences for the gentile world. However, it has to be admitted that the same passage follows a bloodthirsty picture of Yahweh's judgement against the nations (14.12–15) with the inevitable plunder coming as tribute, a section which means that an editor has had to limit his promises for the future gentile worshippers to 'every one who is left among all the nations...' (v. 16).

The same alternation of threat of divine judgement against the nations and concern for their ultimate salvation appears to be found elsewhere in Isaiah 56—66. I say 'appears' because, once again, a certain ambiguity characterizes an apparently universalist passage. In Isaiah 66.18, God says,

> 'I know their deeds and their plans, and I am coming to gather all the nations and those of all languages, and they shall come and see

my glory. And I will set a sign among them. And I will send some of them as survivors among the nations, Tarshish, Put, Lud, those who draw the bow, Tubal, Jawan, the distant coastlands, those who have not heard of my renown and have not seen my glory, and they shall reveal my glory to the nations. And they shall bring all your kinsmen from all the nations as an offering to Yahweh, with horses, chariots, in wagons and on mules and dromedaries to my holy mountain, to Jerusalem,' says Yahweh, 'even as Israelites bring their offerings in clean vessels to Yahweh's sanctuary. Indeed, some of them I will take as priests and Levites', says Yahweh.

Deathless prose it is not, but it is theologically surprising. This really does suggest a missionary enterprise to all the world for those Israelites who have survived – the names are meant not to be exclusive, designating just certain peoples, but symbolic of all. They are, in fact, based on passages in Ezekiel (such as 27.10–24). These will come themselves and bring all the Jewish people dispersed throughout the world to Jerusalem and so they will see and hear of the glory of Yahweh for themselves. Indeed, one reading of the final verse even suggests that some of these foreigners will be admitted to the service of the priesthood, something by no means all Jews were entitled to, of course, since, as we have seen, priestly prerogatives were strictly limited after the exile to the Aaronites chiefly and, to a more limited extent, to Levites. Indeed, one tradition records that those who could not prove their priestly pedigree after the exile were not readmitted to their priestly status (Ezra 2.61–3). The ambiguity lies in the fact that those referred to in verse 21 could be the returned Jews of the Diaspora. But since verses 18–20 clearly refer to foreigners, it is at least possible that verse 21 does also. This is still a variation on the 'foreigners coming in subjection to Jerusalem to worship Yahweh bringing their wealth as tribute' theme, together with the 'Israel as sole means of revelation' theme. But it is advancing down a road towards a much greater equality of all peoples in the service and worship of Yahweh.

Further still along that road is the truly amazing fragment found in Isaiah 19.24f. which reads:

In that day Israel will be a third with Egypt and Assyria, a blessing in the midst of the earth whom Yahweh of hosts has blessed saying,

'Blessed be my people Egypt, and the work of my hands Assyria, and Israel my inheritance.'

In the larger context this occurs in the section of the book of Isaiah devoted to oracles concerning foreign nations. More immediately it is one of a number of addenda to an oracle denouncing Egypt (vv. 1–15) all of which begin 'In that day' and which foretell various fates for Egypt. The relation of these segments to each other is not our concern here. Our passage is usually (and surely rightly) regarded as a very late addition to the book, an addition which is aimed at showing that God has a more positive purpose beyond judgement for other nations as well as for Israel. Again we may assume that the names are meant to be stereotypical: both Egypt and Assyria had been oppressors of Israel in her history. Someone believes that the cure for this will lie not merely in a subjugation by brute force of such hostile powers but in their being treated by Yahweh just as he had treated Israel. The covenant phrase 'my people' will apply equally to Egypt, and Assyria is as much the result of his creation as Israel. Israel may have been the sole means of revelation and may have held a unique relationship to Yahweh (they are his 'inheritance'), but the end result of that will be a peace between nations who are eventually all to be equally God's 'special' people.

Which brings us finally to the book of Jonah. There is much discussion about the exact nature and genre of this book and, indeed, of how it is to be interpreted. Its punch line in the final verse, however, speaks of God's great compassion for the people of Nineveh – of all places.[11] Read one way, the little book of Jonah is a devastating attack upon not only the substance of much national political and religious propaganda but also its spirit. In my view the book is best read as a kind of 'homiletical exegesis' of earlier biblical material. Jonah, for example, was a prophet mentioned in 2 Kings 14.25, significantly just the kind of nationalist, 'propaganda' prophet who predicted victory for Jeroboam II in his wars of expansion. However, the name 'Jonah' is also the Hebrew word for 'dove', and we see it used as a synonym for Israel by the prophet Hosea, for example. In 7.11, Ephraim is likened to a *yônah*, senselessly calling on foreign powers for help rather than trusting in Yahweh, while in 11.11 their return from exile is promised and likened to a flight of 'doves'. A different but similar picture of the nations bringing back the Israelites from captivity is found in

Isaiah 60.8, where they are depicted as flying like a cloud and like 'doves'. Indeed, interestingly, they are said to be brought by ships from Tarshish, the very place to which Jonah escaped when he was called by God to go and preach to Nineveh. We are not told at first why Jonah resisted God's 'prophetic' call, but he took ship in exactly the opposite direction, to the western Mediterranean. The storm which blows up has the heathen sailors in great fear and devoutly calling on their gods while Jonah, ironically, is asleep on his bunk. Indeed, these heathen sailors are generously portrayed as over against the surly Jonah. Not only are they full of greater religious zeal but, when it becomes clear that it is he who has brought the disaster upon them all by way of divine judgement, they do all they can rather than lighten ship by throwing this unfortunate passenger overboard. Again, the irony is heavy when, asked who he is, Jonah replies, 'I am a Hebrew, and I worship Yahweh, the God of heaven, who created the sea and the dry land' (1.9), for how then did he expect to escape from him by flight to another part of his created world?

The incident of the rescue in the 'big fish' is well known but, again, this is an echo of other biblical themes. For in Jeremiah 51.34 and 44 we have exactly this image of the exile in Babylon and God's deliverance of his people from it:

> 'He has eaten me, he has discomforted me,
> the king of Babylon . . .
> he has swallowed me like a sea-monster . . .
> he has filled his body with me for a delicacy;
> he has rinsed me out.'

That is followed in verse 44 by God saying

> 'I will mete out punishment on Bel in Babylon,
> and bring out from his mouth what he swallowed.'

The imagery of the story therefore is that of earlier biblical themes. 'Jonah/Israel' was called by God for the sake of the nations. She refused this destiny and, as a result, was punished with exile in Babylon. Now, however, God has rescued her and given her a second chance just as he called Jonah again to the same task which he had earlier refused after the fish had – very understandably – disgorged him.

This time Jonah goes. The fact that 'Nineveh' here is meant to symbolize the gentile world (and perhaps particularly that part of it which had oppressed Israel) rather than indicate a particular city is shown by its fantastic size (3.3 tells us that it took three days to get across it, something it has taken modern traffic jams to make a near reality in our cities) and, improbably, when they heard the message of God's threatened judgement against them because of their sin, they all repented, from the king to the lowliest of his subjects – even the animals joined in the fast of repentance!

One would imagine that this would please a prophet, much like a modern evangelist seeing the whole congregation getting up out of their seats and coming forward to the penitent bench. But Jonah is furious and vents his indignation on God. It is, in fact, only now that, with the consummate skill of the narrator, we learn why Jonah did not want to go to Nineveh in the first place. He feared not failure, but success. He says,

'I knew that you are gracious and compassionate, slow to anger, of great mercy and that you repent of harsh judgement.' (4.2)

This is a strikingly significant saying because it is a direct quotation of one of the great 'covenant' texts of the Old Testament, Exodus 34.6. The difference here, however, is that, whereas in the Exodus context it was the covenant relationship between God and Israel which was the subject, the promise that God would forgive Israel her sins and remain constant to her, now exactly the same promise is being held out to the heathen.

In an amusing but moving conclusion to the story Jonah goes off to have a good sulk and watch the city, perhaps hoping against hope that God might yet burn the hated Ninevites with fire and brimstone. But when his sulk is fuelled by the disappearance of a shrub which gave him shelter from the heat of the sun, God gently rebukes him saying, 'You had pity for the shrub which you did not create and which grew in a night and died in a night. And I, shall I not pity Nineveh, that great city, in which there are above one hundred and twenty thousand people who do not know their right hand from their left, as well as many cattle?' It is such a splendid ending that prosaic comment could only detract from it.

In this chapter we have not found a very great deal of what might be called genuine universalism. Usually texts which speak of the future relations between God and other nations turn out on close inspection to be propaganda claims for the special status of Israel. The other nations will know *mos* and *ius* as they subject themselves to the overlordship of Yahweh, and so of his people. There will be a *pax Judaica*, to coin a phrase. Certainly, before the exile, this was usually thought to involve subjection to Israel's king. Israel would grow rich by the tribute other nations brought and as a result of the peace imposed on those who formerly had endangered them.

After the exile the more military aspects of this may have faded a little. Not surprisingly in a period when the priests held sway in a hierocracy which was still subordinate to a great world power, there begins to be a swing to the idea of Israel being the dispenser of religious truth. Israel's unique and superior position would be shown by the intervention of Yahweh on their behalf, attacking and breaking those gentile powers who refused to submit to him. Yet, for survivors among those nations, and for all who would listen, there would be those who would come to see that Yahweh was the only effective God and would come to worship and acknowledge him. No doubt they would bring their tribute as well and they would bring back those Israelites who had been taken away into dispersion after defeat, but Israel's hegemony is seen more and more in religious terms.

But we have seen throughout this book that religion, even when it is used as an instrument of propaganda, is a dangerous ally. There were some, possibly only a very few, who seem to have caught something of a new vision of what it really meant to say that Yahweh was the one and only God and was, therefore, the God of all nations. They caught the subversive vision of a God who would bring peace and unity on earth, not by force of arms and imposing submission on others, but by claiming them as truly his own people as much as the Israelites themselves. The 'special' covenant love was to be lavished upon all, and all were to be included in the special covenant relationship. No doubt, as the book of Jonah shows, such universalist subversion would have been far from popular among all. For some would have seen all too clearly that, once allow this awkward theological insight, and the claims of their propaganda to a unique and superior relationship would lie dead in the ashes, burnt in the fire of the love of a God who is a Father, not just of one specially favoured group, but of all people everywhere.

Conclusion

It is time to round up some of the results of this enquiry. I have been trying to show the relevance of each new stage of the investigation as we have gone along, and so there is no need for great length here. But certain things have emerged for me as I followed up the leads suggested by my rereading of the *Aeneid* and spotted some parallels between that and the stories of the early heroes of Israel's prehistory.

The first is that the Old Testament documents turn out to be children of their time and of their social, political and religious context. They are driven, at least partly, by the same kind of need to justify and promulgate the authority claims of those in power as all the other states and empires in the ancient Near East knew, whether the system of government they are seeking to defend is a monarchy or a hierocracy. For them, as for other nations, religion is the mortar which binds together the ramparts behind which they protect the authority and right order of their rule. We must recognize that among the driving power and motives which produced the writings of the Old Testament are the same sociological and political needs which gave birth to the literature of all their neighbours.

This means that to all the other evidence of the 'human' side to the Scriptures it has been the achievement of critical scholarship to uncover (limitations of the writer's knowledge, sociological and cultural conditioning and so on), we must add this real note of political and religious propaganda. Its presence is unmistakable and cannot be made to disappear by a wave of the magician's wand by the exegete or apologist for a particular point of view about the Bible's truth and authority.

However, it is most important to stress something I have emphasized throughout the book. To say that something is a piece of propaganda is not to dismiss it as necessarily 'false' or 'untrue' or, even more, religiously and theologically unworthy. Propaganda claims, like all other claims, can be true or false or, usually, a mixture of both. And it would be quite unnecessarily nihilistic to assert that all human power and authority systems are always and inevitably wholly evil. It would be, incidentally, a nihilism which no part of the Bible, Old or New Testament, sanctions, even where they are at their most critical. We have tried to show that both monarchy and hierocracy contributed vitally to the health and continuance of the people of Israel and the development of that religious genius which has been one of their major legacies to the world. The propaganda claims of the king as chosen and empowered by God to act as his representative in a nation which he had called, the attempts of both the Deuteronomists and the priests to reinterpret what it meant to be the people of God when Yahwism was no longer the official religion of a ruling monarchic dynasty, these all exhibited real religious and theological value as I have tried to show in discussing them.

However, if that were all we had in the Old Testament, it is doubtful if it would have proved to have the perennial appeal and challenge it has had. For one thing, all political systems are transient, and if we had nothing but the work of their apologists, that work would be of little other than historical relevance now that all their systems have crumbled into the dust of history. But further, it is a truism to say that all power corrupts. The loftiest ideals, the most noble of human social and political constructs, become tainted by self-interest. Power, from being a means for the service of the people, has a natural bias built into it by which it becomes an end in itself, or a means to achieving the ends of those who are fortunate enough to wield it. Royal courts in former times had their court jesters, those who used the tool of humour to keep some sense of proportion and realism before those rulers who otherwise would have taken themselves far more seriously and far more at the face value of their own self-assessment than was good for them − or for their subjects. But every court needs its prophets as well, its critics who from some point of detached objectivism, can watch for the bias and call for its correction.

And this Israel did produce, superbly and, as far as we have any evidence, uniquely in the ancient world. There were those, prophets and others, who exerted an influence which, in Peter Berger's words quoted in chapter 1, 'may be traced all through the Biblical tradition, directly related to its radical transcendalization of God, finding its classic expression in Israelite prophecy...' (see above, p. 5). These were the ones who proved subversive of the established orders when those orders were seen to be abusing their divinely appointed role. These were the people who demonstrated that, again in Berger's words, '. . . religion appears both as a world-maintaining and as a world-shaking force'.

Just as we have to remember that not all propaganda is 'bad', so we have to realize that not all subversion is necessarily good. Subversion may be as mixed in motive and as questionable in its results as the power claims of any established order. People may challenge the power of others because they themselves want their own hands on power in order to make it serve their ends. I quoted earlier Milton's disillusioned words at the time of the English Commonwealth, 'New Presbyter is but old Priest writ large' (see above, p. 143). One tyranny had been brought down only to be replaced by another. Many reformers at different times have wanted freedom of expression, but freedom only for the expression of their convictions. They have been quick enough to silence the views of others when they achieved power. Not many 'subversives' have had the courage of a Thomas Helwys, who wrote to King James I, '. . . for men's religion to God is betwixt God and themselves: the King shall not answere for it, neither may the King be judg betwene God and Man. Let them be heretikes, Turcks, Jewes, or whatsoever, it apperteynes not to the earthly power to punish them in the least measure' (*The Mistery of Iniquity*, 1612, p. 69). Even some of the Pilgrim Fathers who fled from oppression in England to the New World were not prepared to allow that kind of freedom to others when they got there.

The fact is that both power and protest, propaganda and subversion, can be both noble and tainted. Both can start with the loftiest ideals, but those ideals can become twisted and self-serving. The achievements of both usually turn out in the light of history to be at best compromised and incomplete. How shall we then judge them? By what criterion can we decide whether those in power or those giving voice to protest come nearest to the mind of God or, more empirically, achieve most in the service of men and women? There is, it seems to me, one startling verse which I have quoted in the chapter dealing with the subversion of the prophets, which might be said to encapsulate a principle of the Old Testament which is both fundamental and startlingly revolutionary. Attacking the powerful and wealthy who exploit the poor of the community, Micah addresses them:

Conclusion

> Listen, heads of Jacob
> and rulers of the house of Israel.
> Should you not understand justice?
> Yet you hate what is good and love evil:
> you strip the skin off *my people* ... (3.1f.)

The italics there are mine. How ominous those two words are for the rich and powerful. Not they, but the poor they are exploiting are Yahweh's people. Of course, the whole community claimed that special relationship with God by which it could be said, 'I am your God and you are my people' (cf. Exod. 6.7). Micah, like the other prophets and visionaries, subverts that by saying that when those God has placed in power abuse their privilege and status, using other people to serve their interests rather than making the welfare of others their main aim, then God abandons them and becomes the God of the underprivileged, the powerless and the oppressed.

We have to be careful even here. There is a theology of envy as well as a politics of envy. God is not against the rich and the powerful just because they are what and where they are. Few congregations now would sing very happily the hymn which included the words,

> The rich man in his castle,
> The poor man at his gate;
> God made them high and lowly,
> And ordered their estate.

Nevertheless, we cannot assume that God has no interest in the rich man and his family living in their privilege. The challenge of the Bible is, however, that if the poor man at the gate is there because of the abuse or neglect of the rich castle dweller, God is the God who lives outside the gate with the poor. It is all the 'little people' of society, without wealth or power to pull the levers of the state machine in their own interest, who are God's special concern, whom he will defend and for whom ultimately he will secure justice. That is the extraordinary upside-down world of values which the subversives of the Old Testament proclaim. And this should not be a total surprise to Christians whose New Testament testifies to an incarnational theology in which God comes to dwell among peasant people and is born in a stable.

Two points remain, the first of which has been made several times throughout this book. There are enormous dangers in a reading of the Scriptures in such a way as to ignore the human, conditional, one might even say the 'incarnational' element in them. If we fail to realize that not everything is a direct word from God, not every sentiment is equally authoritative and binding for all times under any possible combination of circumstances, then we are certainly heading for trouble. To fail to realize the human limitations of both the propaganda and subversive elements of the Old and New Testaments but to credit them with absolute and unquestioning divine authority, however they are put into practice, leads directly to a political and religious absolutism which consigns some human beings to second-class status in the Kingdom of God and so among the kingdoms of men. It leads to claims of absolute rights to certain territory and to the legitimacy of a dehumanizing treatment of others, all in the name of God, which is a denial of the deepest voices to be heard in those same Scriptures. And when two or more ethnic or political groups make the same claims about the same territory and the same privileges in the name of the same God, the results can well be catastrophic.

But, perhaps, there is another point to be made from this study about how we may read the Scriptures mistakenly. We may insulate them in a cosy wrapping of personal, devotional piety, and go to them only to draw from them reassuring words of personal and individual encouragement and enlightenment. Of course, there is a great deal of personal devotion and piety in the writings of the Old Testament. Individuals there have left moving and inspiring records of their own experience of God, experiences often forged in the white heat of suffering and persecution. But if we look *only* for such a private hotline to God in them we sanitize them. With the Bible wrapped away in a cupboard in our own home or in a church pew, there is little danger of any devastating fall-out from it in our world of social, economic and political realities. We shall have done the unthinkable – we shall have tamed and domesticated the Bible. We shall be deaf and blind to the white heat of social, political and economic forces which produced them. We shall never hear the explosion of their social and political dynamite.

It might not be a bad thing to give the last word to William Tyndale, who worked and struggled to bring the Bible to everyone in the land even, in his own famous term, to the 'ploughboy'. How difficult it is for us to think that anything as tame as we have made the Bible should ever be regarded as dangerous. Although, even now, many who have gone back to it in the name of 'liberation theology' have discovered to their cost that governments still do fear it when people start taking its political, social and economic message seriously. Listen, however, to Tyndale:

> A thousand books had they [rather] to be put forth against their abominable doings and doctrines than that the scripture should come to light.

I know the language of religious polemic was more robust in those times. But he was talking about – would you believe it? – *the Bible*.

The Terms 'Propaganda' and 'Subversion'

It seemed inevitable in a book entitled as this one is that some-where I should discuss exactly what I mean by the terms 'propa-ganda' and 'subversion'. Both because it might have seemed a bit forbidding at the outset and because it is probably best to consider the terms in the light of the way I have actually used them in prac-tice, I decided to consign them to an Appendix in the hope that any readers hardy enough to have read so far will not baulk at the final hurdle.

The trouble with a word like 'propaganda' is that we all use it and are quite happy about its meaning – until we have to define it. I can only say in what sense I have been using it without, I trust, being quite as subjective as Lewis Carroll's Humpty-Dumpty in *Through the Looking Glass*, 'When *I* use a word ... it means just what I choose it to mean, – neither more nor less.'

We can start with some sort of objectivity by noting that the word was first used in the seventeenth century of a group of car-dinals appointed to oversee the foreign missionary work of the Roman Catholic Church. In its original context, therefore, it had something to do with presenting a particular case in such a way as to gain assent to it and acceptance of it by others. The coward's way is always to turn to the dictionaries, and I see that *The Shorter Oxford English Dictionary* has extended this original function of the word to 'any association, systematic scheme, or concerted move-ment for the propagation of a particular doctrine or practice'.

I would want to say, therefore, that at its widest it is 'the presentation of material so as to express a particular belief or set of beliefs in such a way as to command assent to it from those to whom it is addressed'. This is not far from a briefer definition by M. Z. Brettler in the book referred to in note 6 to chapter 1: 'The word, in the sense of an attempt to persuade a group to follow a particular ideology, can be used profitably in relation to the Bible and other religious texts' (p. 14). He further quotes with approval J. Ellul, 'Propaganda as it is traditionally known implies an attempt to spread an ideology through the mass media of communication in order to lead the public to accept some political or economic structure or to participate in some action ...' (*Propaganda: The Formation of Men's Attitudes*, tr. K. Kellen and J. Lerner, New York, Knopf, 1965, p. 166).

Such definitions, including the one I have offered, are all very well, but they are probably too wide, since they could include, for instance, all history-writing, which, by its very nature of selection and presentation of events, is already offering an interpretation of that history. Indeed, the same could be said not only of the writing of history but of any writing. This book, in so far as it expresses my ideas, could equally be said to be a work of propaganda. So I would want to go on to say that propaganda is something more than merely the expression of a personal belief or opinion, but that it has an element of self-interest in it. Very often (although not always) it will be work which represents the interests and claims of some particular group, whether that grouping be of a political or religious nature or, as often happens, a mixture of both. This has been well expressed by F. C. Bartlett:

> Practically everybody agrees that propaganda must be defined by reference to its aims. These aims can, in fact, be stated simply. Propaganda is an attempt to influence opinion and conduct – in such a manner that the persons who adopt the opinion and behaviour indicated do so without themselves making any definite search for reasons.

That quotation may be found in 'The Aims of Political Propaganda', in D. Katz et al. (eds.), *Public Opinion and Propaganda: A Book of Readings*, New York, Holt, Rineheart and Winston, 1954, p. 464.

This stresses two elements involved in 'propaganda' as distinct merely from argument or attempt to convince. It stresses the aim of the propagandists, including what I have referred to as including some degree of 'self-interest', and speaks of its methods which tend to bypass, or at least powerfully to influence, the self-conscious reasoning powers of the individuals addressed. This is a most important aspect of propaganda, at least in the way I have understood it. For those who use it, propaganda is usually far more than a stimulating intellectual exchange of ideas in the objective, disinterested spirit of an Oxford tutorial (or, I am sure, a Cambridge supervision). Good teaching does not try to implant answers in the students' minds. It seeks to arouse and energize their own critical faculties, not least concerning what one is saying oneself, in the hope that they will be able to arrive at their own view. That is not so with propaganda. As that is usually used, it attempts what might be called a 'pre-programming' of the human mind so as to elicit the answer which suits the ends of those using it. In other words, as we have seen, it is a means by which those employing it seek to justify and maintain power, and it has often proved a weapon which could be the equivalent of many battalions.

I am indebted to K. W. Whitelam for learning about Bartlett's article, who also quotes the passage I have cited in his own work, 'The Defence of David', *JSOT*, 29, 1984, pp. 61–87. He goes on to make a further claim about propaganda being defined to some extent by its aims. He says, '. . . propaganda is an extremely subtle form of communication which cannot be divorced from the audience addressed' (p. 66). In that I am sure he is right, although I am less happy when he goes on to claim that it needs to be congruent with the 'fundamental beliefs and hopes of the society which the propagandist shares – but which strikes a chord with them' (p. 67). Sometimes that may be true, but I think we have also seen instances where the aim of the propagandists is to foster a new political or religious outlook on the part of others by which they may gain assent to the position and privileges they are claiming for themselves or their group.

I deliberately used the word 'material' in my own very general definition of propaganda because we have to recognize that not all propaganda is literary, or oral. Indeed, in a simple society in which many of the masses may not be able to read, the literary presentation of propaganda must be aimed primarily at select inner circles of those who wield power and hold positions of responsibility in the 'court', or at administrative officers in political or ecclesiastical hierarchies. For the masses, buildings and other visual means of communication are best suited, a point Whitelam also makes.

> Royal fortifications, temple-palace complexes, and public buildings would have displayed before a wide audience, both internal and external, the might, power and wealth of the king and his court. The sheer size of the structures would have denoted

assurance and power, and their visibility and simplicity would have communicated to all levels of society.' (p. 69)

He refers to the Egyptian pyramids and the architectural glories of Rome and its Caesars. To this could be added the great ecclesiastical buildings down the ages, buildings such as Solomon's temple and many Christian cathedrals. Pictures also would have had dramatic effect. To have seen bas-reliefs such as those depicting the fate the Assyrian king, Sennacherib, meted out to those who withstood him, in which being impaled alive on sharp stakes was only one feature, would have been a powerful object lesson to any others tempted to try their luck at rebellion.

For obvious reasons, I have limited myself to literary forms of propaganda in the ancient Near East and in the Old Testament. I hope enough has been cited to show that propaganda was one means by which political and religious dynasties and groups justified their hold on power and claimed validity and authority for their particular insights and beliefs. However, as I have said before, we cannot simply assume that all propaganda is bad. Whitelam, again, reminds us that it is a neutral term (pp. 65f). Not all the political power or religious truth claimed in propaganda was totally false or invalid or without benefit to anyone else. Nevertheless, while its claims may have contained truth, questions must arise about the manner in which it asserts those truths. Even if we give propaganda a conditional discharge, I do not think it leaves court quite without any stain on its character.

Perhaps one further point needs to be made. We have seen that most political powers in the ancient Near East (and the states of Israel and Judah were no exception) used religion to bolster their power claims. Thus 'political propaganda' makes use of 'religious propaganda' – indeed, so closely were these wedded at that time that they are virtually not distinguishable. But we should recognize that this is something a little different from 'religious propaganda', in which people try to claim authority for and assent to certain religious beliefs and interpretation of events. Obviously such propaganda also appears in the Scriptures. For our purposes, as I say, they are virtually indistinguishable, but we need to keep an eye open for occasions when the two do diverge. I have not felt it right in this book to venture opinions about the 'truth' or 'value' of the various religious and theological claims made in the Old Testament (let alone the New) but I have wanted to show something of the use of religious propaganda in the interests of those in power.

However, there is an obvious gradation of meaning here. It is not always easy to tell just at what point vigorous and forceful expression of opinion passes over into being 'propaganda'. That is why it is not easy to label all literature as either 'propaganda' or not. There is a kind of 'Richter scale' of propaganda techniques, and this will always leave the door open to a wide range of definitions as to just what each of us calls propaganda and what we do not.

'Subversion' is perhaps a more difficult term to justify since it often conjures up ideas of armed or violent protest and revolution. There is little, if any, call to armed resistance in the Old Testament. The tendency is to leave the overthrow of powers deemed evil to God, although there is a good deal of quiet satisfaction gained from contemplation of just what it is he will do to them, with, or without, the help of human agencies.

However, 'subversion' means literally 'overturning', from the Latin *subvertere*. I have used it to describe the criticism which seeks to deny the validity of the claims to power of those in power. The aim of the criticism of political and ecclesiastical propaganda which we have examined is to bring that power to an end, not merely to reform it, even if the methods this subversive criticism advocates are not those of armed revolution. Indeed, I have tried to distinguish between efforts aimed at reforming an existing system (as in the two cases of Naboth and Elijah I cited in chapter 5 and which I have not called 'subversion') and announcements and words which believe that those systems must be overthrown, so evil have they become. But I have to acknowledge this is walking something of a tightrope. It is often very difficult to work out exactly just what effect any particular prophet thought his words would have, whether it would bring about the doom of those condemned, or lead to their 'repentance'.

Just as we cannot assume that all propaganda is 'bad', nor can we assume that all subversion is 'good'. Sometimes it represents aims just as selfish by those out of office as the propaganda of those who currently walk the 'corridors of power'. But, sometimes also, as we have seen, its criticism of the way power is being exercised is based on deeper insights. With eyes not blurred by the haze of privilege, some can see much more clearly when power has become the means by which the rulers serve interests of their own rather than the interests of those for whose sake they have been entrusted with power.

NOTES

1 Propaganda in the Ancient Near East

1 I discuss briefly in the Appendix the way I understand the term 'propaganda' in this book.

2 *The Oxford History of the Classical World*, 1986, p. 632.

3 Peter Berger, *The Social Reality of Religion*, London, Penguin, 1973, p. 42.

4 The term 'Old Testament' is a Christian one expressing the view of the Church that it is to be admitted alongside the 'New Testament' as part of the Christian canon. It is not a term used by Jews and, to avoid implying imperialist religious claims, many Christian scholars now refer to 'the Hebrew Scriptures' rather than using the more traditional title. I have kept the term 'Old Testament' in this book only because its wider familiarity makes it more convenient. My use of it certainly does not imply any lack of respect for my Jewish colleagues or for the integrity of their understanding and interpretation of their sacred Scriptures.

5 Again, I discuss my use of this term in the Appendix.

6 There have been a number of studies which certainly raise the issue. Examples are R. P. Carroll, *Wolf in the Sheepfold: The Bible as a Problem for Christianity*, London, SPCK, 1991, a characteristically vigorous and challenging examination of some of the dangers of a 'literalist' use of the Bible. J. van Seters mentions the theme in his book *In Search of History*, New Haven and London, YUP, 1983, although he does not make it central. M. Z. Brettler gives attention to the topic in *The Creation of History in Ancient Israel*, London and New York, Routledge, 1995, see esp. pp. 13f., where he argues for a neutral understanding of the word 'propaganda'. He also helpfully provides a very full bibliography of general works on the nature of propaganda, see esp. Notes 61–73, pp. 155–7. R. B. and M. P. Coote, *Power, Politics and the Making of the Bible*, Minneapolis, Fortress Press, 1990, deal with it but tend towards somewhat exaggerated and insufficiently founded views. J. P. M. Walsh, SJ, dealt forcefully with the idea of Israelite subversion of established orders in the name of Yahweh in his book *The Mighty From Their Thrones: Power in the Biblical Tradition*, Philadelphia, Fortress Press, 1987. His study remains useful and moving even though many Old Testament scholars would now question his view that Israelite religion was from the first a 'covenant' religion, different in kind from that of all its neighbours. Many scholars note 'propaganda' elements in the course of their examination of biblical texts, especially in the history writing of the Old Testament, but as far as I am aware it has seldom been treated as a central issue in any major study. A good study of the use of propaganda in the ancient near east generally is to be found in M. Larsen, *Power and Propaganda: A Symposium on Ancient Empires*, Mesopotamia, Copenhagen Studies in Assyriology, 7, Copenhagen, Akademisk

Forlage, 1979. Other more detailed works which affect our study here will be noted as we go along.

7 There are plenty of instances of 'propaganda' in the New Testament, but the limitations of the competence of the writer and the demands of length mean that only the Old Testament writings are being considered in this book.

8 'Yahweh' is the nearest we can get to the name for the God of the Israelites. Hebrew was originally written without vowels, and the four consonants of the divine name, the 'tetragrammaton' as it is termed, were YHWH. The vowels were only added later by Jewish scholars. Since the name was by then regarded as too sacred to utter, they inserted the vowel signs for the Hebrew word *Adônai*, which means 'Lord', intending the word 'Lord' rather than the divine name to be spoken. The word 'Jehovah' which appeared in the earliest English versions was a hybrid made up of the consonants of the divine name YHWH and the vowels of the word 'Lord'. No Jew ever did say 'Jehovah'. In modern English versions the convention is that, where the name YHWH occurs in the original it is printed in capitals 'LORD'. Where the Hebrew word 'Lord' occurs, it is printed with only the first letter as a capital, 'Lord'.

9 Translations may be found in J. B. Pritchard (ed.), *Ancient Near Eastern Texts Relating to the Old Testament*, 3rd edn, Princeton, N. J., Princeton University Press, 1969; and Stephanie Dalley, *Myths from Mesopotamia: Creation, the Flood, Gilgamesh and Others*, Oxford, OUP, 1989.

10 These texts date from the 14th century BCE and were discovered at Ugarit, whose modern name is Ras Shamra. The site is situated near the Mediterranean coast in the extreme north west of Canaan in what is modern Syria and was then a region under the control of Phoenicia. A translation and commentary of the texts may be found in G. R. Driver, *Canaanite Myths and Legends*, Edinburgh, T & T Clark, 1956, and it is his translation from which I quote.

11 The best study of the nature of the Canaanite texts and their influence on the Old Testament is to be found in J. Day, *God's Conflict with the Dragon and the Sea: Echoes of a Canaanite Myth in the Old Testament*, Cambridge, CUP, 1985.

12 The phrase was that of A. Hoffman in an article entitled 'Propaganda and Political Justification in Hittite Historiography', in H. Goedicke and J. J. M. Roberts (eds.), *Unity and Diversity: Essays in the History, Literature and Religion of the Ancient Near East*, Baltimore and London, Johns Hopkins, 1975, pp. 49–62. There is a discussion of the document and its possible links to the story of 'David's rise to power' in the Old Testament by K. McCarter, 'The Apology of David', *JBL*, 99, 1980, pp. 489–504. The document was translated and published by E. H. Sturvant and G. Bechtel in *A Hittite Chrestomathy* (another word for a kind of anthology), Philadelphia, University of Pennsylvania, 1935, pp. 42–99, and quotations are from this.

13 J. A. Wilson, 'Egypt', *The Interpreter's Dictionary of the Bible*, vol. II, New

York and Nashville, Abingdon Press, pp. 39–66. The quotation occurs on p. 46, col. 2.

14 J. D. Ray, 'Egyptian Wisdom Literature', in J. Day, R. P. Gordon and H. G. M. Williamson (eds.), *Wisdom in Ancient Israel*, Cambridge, CUP, 1995, pp. 17–29. The quotation occurs on p. 20.

15 G. Posener, *Littérature et Politique dans l'Egypte de la XIIe Dynastie*, Bibliothèque de l'Ecole des Hautes Études, 307, Paris, 1956. The translations from his work are mine.

16 The translation is that to be found in Pritchard, *Ancient Near Eastern Texts*, p. 418.

17 Pritchard, *Ancient Near Eastern Texts*, pp. 378f.

18 'Egyptian Wisdom Literature', pp. 20f.

19 Mario Liverani, 'The Ideology of the Assyrian Empire', in M. T. Larsen (ed.), *Power and Propaganda: A Symposium on Ancient Empires*, Mesopotamia, Copenhagen Studies in Assyriology, 7, Akademisk Forlage, Copenhagen, 1979, pp. 297–317.

20 See A. R. Johnson, *Sacral Kingship in Ancient Israel*, 2nd edn, Cardiff, University of Wales Press, 1967, pp. 10f.

2   Royal Propaganda in the Old Testament

1 This is the view, for example, of J. van Seters, *Abraham in History and Tradition*, New Haven and London, YUP, 1975.

2 For example, Christoph Levin, *Der Jahwist*, Göttingen, Vandenhoeck und Ruprecht, 1993.

3 A vivid, almost swashbuckling, demolition job is done by R. N. Whybray, *The Making of the Pentateuch: A Methodological Study*, JSOT Supp., 53, Sheffield, Sheffield Academic Press, 1987.

4 One example of this, by a scholar who by no means denies all the findings of 'traditional' Pentateuchal study, is D. J. A. Clines, *The Theme of the Pentateuch*, JSOT Supp., 10, Sheffield, Department of Biblical Studies, University of Sheffield, 1978. It is also basic to the approach of B. S. Childs, *Introduction to the Old Testament as Scripture*, London, SCM Press, 1979. He stresses that, while methods which uncover the existence of various sources and strands in the present text and concentrate on the methods by which they came to be redacted are legitimate, attention must also be given to the final, canonical form of the text and the theological concerns of those who shaped it. The method is sometimes known as 'canon criticism'. Those who would like to see a clear and judicious summary of the various methods used by biblical scholars in their attempts to interpret the biblical text can do no better than consult J. Barton, *Reading the Old Testament: Method in Biblical Study*, London, Darton, Longman and Todd, 1984.

5 A full study of the process of reuse of earlier material in later exposition can be found in M. Fishbane, *Biblical Interpretation in Ancient Israel*, Oxford, OUP, 1985. Another interesting book, comprising a series of essays on the subject, is D. A. Carson and H. G. M. Williamson (eds.), *It is Written:*

Scripture Citing Scripture: Essays in Honour of Barnabas Lindars, Cambridge, CUP, 1988.

6 Commentators have long argued about the unity of Genesis 15 and the date of the origin of its various components. Some have argued that the separate 'Elohistic' source (E) begins here. Many believe it has achieved its present form by a long and complex process of growth. Fortunately, neither the question of its unity nor its date (or dates) need concern us here. We need only to observe the function it serves in its present context.

7 R. E. Clements, *Abraham and David: Genesis 15 and its Meaning for Israelite Tradition*, SBT, 2nd series, 5, London, SCM Press, 1967.

8 For an excellent translation and critical edition of the *Mabinogion*, see the 'Everyman' edition, translated by Gwyn Jones and Thomas Jones, London, J. M. Dent and Sons; Rutland, Vt., Charles E. Tuttle Co., Inc., 1989.

9 For example, F. M. Cross, 'The Themes of the Book of Kings and the Structure of the Deuteronomistic History', in *Canaanite Myth and Hebrew Epic*, Cambridge, Mass., HUP, 1973, pp. 274–89; R. D. Nelson, *The Double Redaction of the Deuteronomistic History*, JSOT Supp., 18, Sheffield, 1981.

10 Including the scholar who pioneered the idea of a 'Deuteronomistic History', M. Noth. For an English translation of his work see *The Deuteronomistic History*, JSOT Supp., 15, Sheffield, 1981.

11 For example, E. Würthwein, *Studien zum Deuteronomistischen Geschichtswerk*, *BZAW*, 227, Berlin and New York, De Gruyter, 1994.

12 Carol Meyers, 'Jochin and Boaz in Religious and Political Perspective', *CBQ*, 45, 1983, pp. 167–78. The vital importance to state propaganda of building and visual symbols in Israel and the middle Near East generally is also stressed by K. W. Whitelam, 'The Symbols of Power: Aspects of Royal Propaganda in the United Monarchy', *Biblical Archaeologist*, 49, 1986, pp. 166–72. He says, 'The sheer size of the structures would have denoted assurance and power, and their visibility and simplicity would have communicated to all levels of society' (p. 169). He mentions the excavations of powerful casemate walls dating from the reign of Solomon at Hazor, Megiddo, Gezer, Tel Beit Mirsim, Beth-Shemesh and Tel Qasile, as well as the temple in Jerusalem itself of course (though the date of some of these excavations has been questioned since the time of the writing of his article).

13 No one has stressed more the propaganda value of the story of David and Solomon than K. W. Whitelam, especially in his article 'The Defence of David', *JSOT*, 29, 1984, pp. 61–87. The whole account is, according to Whitelam, cast in favour of the Davidic dynasty. It is intended both to establish and defend the claims to power of that dynasty. By showing how David gains Yahweh's approval, so that even the second child of the illicit liaison with Bathsheba (Solomon) is Yahweh's choice as his successor, and in showing how all who oppose David are struck down, the courtly and aristocratic élite, the real target of the work, is discouraged from trying ever to rebel against the dynasty. The work is all the more effective be-

cause of its 'artistic genius'. Again, one is reminded of works such as Virgil's *Aeneid*.

14 Robert P. Gordon, *1 & 2 Samuel: A Commentary*, Exeter, The Paternoster Press, 1986, p. 235.

15 So T. N. D. Mettinger, *King and Messiah: The Civil and Sacral Legitimation of the Israelite Kings*, Coniectanea Biblica, OT Series, 8, Lund, Gleerup, 1976.

16 An English translation of this by M. D. Rutter and D. M. Gunn may be found, *The Succession to the Throne of David*, Historical Texts and Interpreters in Biblical Scholarship, 1, Sheffield, Almond Press, 1982.

17 In most forms of the Hebrew verb there is no difference between the ordinary indicative and the jussive. Thus all the verbs in this psalm could be rendered in English either as 'He *will* . . .' or as a prayer, '*May* he . . .', and both translations can be found in different English versions. It makes little difference, however, to the way the king's role was understood. Either he was, or was expected to be, the intermediary between God and the nation, the one through whom all God's purposes for them were to be fulfilled.

3 Priestly Propaganda in the Old Testament

1 The events outlined so baldly here may be read in more detail in 2 Kings 23.28—25.30, and throughout the book of Jeremiah, especially in chs. 37—44.

2 The phrase, used to describe a kind of theocratic/civic community based on rule by a temple hierarchy, was first employed by J. Weinberg, 'Die Agrarverhältnisse in der Bürger-Tempel-Gemeinde der Achämenidenzeit', *Acta Antiqua Academiae Scientarum Hungaricae*, 22, 1974, pp. 473–86. It is discussed by J. Blenkinsopp, 'Temple and Society in Achaemenid Judah', in P. R. Davies (ed.), *Second Temple Studies*, 1, *Persian Period*, JSOT Supp., 117, Sheffield, 1991, pp. 22–53. ('Achaemenid' is the name given by scholars to the Persian empire of this period, after the name of its rulers.) It is held that such communities could well operate within the overall political control of an externally administered empire. Blenkinsopp believes that such a community in Judah was established after the exile by Jews who returned from exile in Babylon, reclaimed their old homes and land, saw to the rebuilding of the temple, and established their own social structures. The result was what we might call a 'hierocracy' (rule by priests), but civil governors were also in office. It has to be said we do not know very much about the exact extent of territory, nor the precise kind of control over their own affairs which the Judeans exercised within the province of the Persian empire known as 'The Province Beyond the River'. Nor can we be sure of the exact balance of influence between civil governor and temple priests. The present form of the books of Haggai and Zechariah 1—8 seem to suggest a joint rule between the two.

3 The Hebrew of the opening verse of the Bible is ambiguous in that it can be read legitimately two ways. It can be taken to mean that there was a

pre-existent chaos before God began his work of imposing order on it, or that the first stage of God's creation was the forming of the state of chaos and then the ordering of it into the universe of light and fertility. Later theologians have often been concerned to take it the second way in order to safeguard the doctrine that God created all matter from nothing (*creatio ex nihilo*). It is doubtful if such matters were of much concern to the biblical writer, however.

4 It has often been argued that this Hebrew word has some etymological links to the name *Tiamat*, the dragon monster in the Babylonian *Enuma Elish* epic (see above, pp. 8f.). Even if this were so there is no echo in Genesis of the battle between Marduk and Tiamat (although there is elsewhere in the Old Testament) and it is far more likely that this myth influenced Israelite thought through its Canaanite versions. See J. Day, *God's Conflict with the Dragon and the Sea*, Cambridge, CUP, 1985, p. 4.

5 I have examined the 'speeches' in the books of Chronicles and the priests' part in them in my book *Preaching the Tradition: Homily and Hermeneutic after the Exile*, Cambridge, CUP, 1990.

6 See *Preaching the Tradition*, pp. 197–205.

7 Again, in *Preaching the Tradition* I have examined this issue more fully, and some general conclusions may be found on pp. 123–33.

8 Berger, *The Social Reality of Religion*, pp. 42f.

9 Mary Douglas, *Purity and Danger: An Analysis of the Concepts of Pollution and Taboo*, London, Routledge and Kegan Paul, 1966.

10 Daniel L. Smith, *The Religion of the Landless: The Social Context of the Babylonian Exile*, Bloomington, Ind., Meyer Stone Books, 1989.

4   *Propaganda and* Subversion – the Deuteronomists

1 The term 'Holy War' has long been associated with G. von Rad, who wrote a study *Der Heilige Krieg im Alten Testament*, Zürich, Zwingli-Verlag, 1951, ET *Holy War in Ancient Israel*, by M. J. Dawn, Grand Rapids, Mich., Eerdmans; Leominster, Gracewing, 1991. Others have preferred the term 'Yahweh War'. See, for example, D. H. Jones, '"Holy War" or "Yahweh War"?', *VT*, 25, 1975, pp. 642–58. Other studies have included R. Smend, *Yahweh War and Tribal Confederation: Reflections upon Israel's Earliest History*, Nashville, Abingdon Press, 1970; P. D. Miller, Jr, *The Divine Warrior in Early Israel*, Harvard, HUP, 1973; and M. C. Lind, *Yahweh is a Warrior: The Theology of Warfare in Ancient Israel*, Scottdale, Pa., and Kitchener, Herald Press, 1980.

2 For example, this is largely the view of M. Weippert, *The Settlement of the Israelite Tribes in Palestine*, SBT 2nd series, 21, London, SCM Press, 1971.

3 This view is particularly associated with N. K. Gottwald, *The Tribes of Yahweh*, New York, Maryknoll, Orbis Books, 1979; London, SCM Press, 1980. Gottwald applied his own avowedly Marxist views to such a sociological interpretation of the origins of Israel. Somewhat similar views were expressed by G. E. Mendenhall, although he stressed more the continuity

of the Israelites with the Canaanite population and saw the religion of Yahwism as the determining factor in the emergence of that group of tribes which came to form 'Israel'. See 'The Hebrew Conquest of Palestine', *Biblical Archaeologist*, 25, 1962, pp. 66–87.

4 C. H. G. de Geuss, *The Tribes of Israel: An Investigation into some of the Presuppositions of Martin Noth's Amphictyony Hypothesis*, Studia Semitica Neerlandica, 18, Assen, Van Gorcum, 1976.

5 N. P. Lemche, *Early Israel: Anthropological Studies on the Israelite Society Before the Monarchy*, Supp. VT, 37, Leiden, Brill, 1985. See also his later *Ancient Israel: A New History of Israelite Society*, Biblical Seminar 5, Sheffield, JSOT Press, 1988.

6 Adrian H. W. Curtis, *Joshua*, Old Testament Guides, Sheffield, Sheffield Academic Press, 1994.

7 See the strong tradition to this effect in the possibly early 'Song of the Sea' in Exodus 15, especially with its emphatic, 'Yahweh is a man of battle' (v. 3). Again, the 'Song of Deborah' in Judges 5, often thought to be a very early composition, represents Yahweh as marching out from the region of Edom to the military help of (some of) the Israelite tribes. There would be nothing strange in such an early belief about Yahweh, for the Canaanite literature shows clearly that Ba'al was similarly regarded.

8 We cannot explore this extensive subject in any detail here. A good general introduction to the subject was provided by A. S. Kapelrud, *The Ras Shamra Discoveries and the Old Testament*, Oxford, Blackwell, 1965. A work already cited, John Day, *God's Conflict with the Dragon and the Sea: Echoes of a Canaanite Myth in the Old Testament*, Cambridge, CUP, 1985, contains an intensive investigation into the influence of Canaanite religious mythology on Israel. Another study is provided by Mark S. Smith, *The Early History of God: Yahweh and the Other Deities in Ancient Israel*, San Francisco, Harper & Row, distributed by T & T Clark, Edinburgh, 1990. An earlier study which saw a very complex development of early Yahwism was that of Morton Smith, *Palestinian Parties and Politics that shaped the Old Testament*, New York and London, Columbia University Press, 1971. Each of these books provides further bibliographical details of the extensive literature on the topic for those who would like to explore it further.

9 There are some problems with the Hebrew text in verses 28 and 29, which read rather like a short trading memorandum, perhaps part of original palace documents. These questions over the text make it difficult to be sure of the exact trading process which is being described here, but the general thrust, that Solomon's officials imported and exported horses, seems clear. The issues are addressed in all the commentaries.

10 The historicity of the account in 2 Kings 22f. has been much debated. Have the Deuteronomists inflated the importance of the lawbook in instigating the reform? The Chronicler, for example, reduces its influence by stating that Josiah had begun the process of reform almost from the time he ascended the throne as a boy (2 Chron. 34.1—35.19, esp. 34.3). That may, equally, be due to particular theological interests of the Chronicler

himself. Some have wondered whether there ever really was such a religious reform at all. Others have stressed the likely *political* purpose of the reform. It was a means by which Josiah could break free of Assyrian overlordship and at the same time assert his claim to rule over *all* Israel, north as well as south. There is no reason why religious and political motives may not have intermingled. The whole thrust of this book is to suggest that they nearly always do. The issues of Josiah's reform are discussed by J. McKay, *Religion in Judah under the Assyrians 732–609 BC*, SBT, 2nd series, 26, London, SCM Press, 1973. The argument here is not affected by issues of historicity or motive. What matters is how the present account in 2 Kings expresses the Deuteronomists' views and beliefs.

11 See P. Kyle McCarter, Jr, *1 Samuel*, The Anchor Bible, New York, Doubleday & Co., 1980, pp. 178f., for references.

12 Literally, 'your house' or 'your household', but for the deeper significance the term 'house' can have, see A. R. Johnson, 'Psalm 23 and the Household of Faith', in J. I. Durham and J. R. Porter (eds.), *Proclamation and Presence: Old Testament Essays in Honour of Gwynne Henton Davies*, London, SCM Press, 1970, pp. 261–71. The relevance of this in application to David's 'house' is seen in the way Yahweh is depicted as responding to David's wish to build a 'house' for God by the assurance that, on the contrary, it is he, Yahweh, who will build a 'house' for David (2 Sam. 7.11). The reference is to far more than a palace, as verse 12 makes clear with its immediate assurance that God will provide him with a successor, a point further confirmed by the linking in verse 16 of the promise that his 'house' will last for ever to the eternal nature of David's kingdom and throne.

13 This view is particularly associated with the American scholars, Cross and Nelson. See n. 9, p. 178 above.

14 Nelson's suggestion in the work referred to above that these three sayings are an attempt to explain merely the loss of the northern kingdom to the house of David is ingenious but implausible. The text carries no such implication.

15 It was P. R. Ackroyd who made the comparison, only, quite rightly, to modify it considerably. Speaking of the Priestly writer's emphasis on the provision in the cult for the means of expiation and renewal he goes on, 'It would be an oversimplification to describe this as the "Catholic" element in Old Testament religion where Deuteronomy and the prophets might represent the "Protestant" element. In fact, the two are complementary ways of approaching the same truths – the reality of the divine grace and the reality of the divine indwelling.' *Exile and Restoration: A Study of Hebrew Thought in the Sixth Century BC*, London, SCM Press, 1968, p. 100.

16 E. W. Nicholson, 'Deuteronomy's vision of Israel', in D. Garrone and F. Israel (eds.), *Storia e tradizioni di Israele: Scritti in onore di J. Alberto Soggin*, Brescia, Paideia Editrice, 1991, pp. 191–203. The quotation is from pp. 202f.

17 So, for example, G. von Rad, *Studies in Deuteronomy*, SBT, 9, London, SCM Press, 1953.

18 So, for example, E. W. Nicholson, *Deuteronomy and Tradition*, Oxford, Blackwell, 1967.

19 So, for example, M. Weinfeld, *Deuteronomy and the Deuteronomic School*, Oxford, Clarendon Press, 1972.

5 The Subversion of the Prophets

1 Berger, *The Social Reality of Religion*, p. 42. See above, p. 4.

2 The Deuteronomistic theology of prophecy can be seen in such verses as one of their additions to the book of Amos: 'For the Lord Yahweh does no deed without [first] revealing his secret plan to his servants the prophets' (Amos 3.7). It is seen in the way the Deuteronomistic History is shaped so as to show that events exactly fulfil a word spoken to a prophet earlier. So, for example, when Rehoboam, after the death of his father, Solomon, rejects the advice of his older counsellors to show lenient treatment towards his discontented northern subjects, the resulting fatal split between the northern and southern kingdoms is seen, not primarily as the working out of human character, personality and motive, but as an act of God already determined by an earlier prophetic word: 'The king paid no heed to the people, but this was a turn of affairs brought about by Yahweh in order to fulfil his word which he had spoken through Ahijah the Shilonite' (1 Kings 12.15, cf. 1 Kings 11.29–39). Two classic Deuteronomistic statements about prophecy are found in Deuteronomy 13.1–11, and 18.15–22. Both these show prophecy as a divine institution, but they also reflect a problem which grew with time. When different prophets predicted different things, how could one tell who was the 'genuine' prophet? None of the suggested answers, whether the word comes true, whether it leads hearers towards or away from Yahweh, whether the prophet has 'stood in the council of Yahweh' before speaking, whether it is genuinely a first-hand oracle or merely one stolen from others (both these occur in a very Deuteronomistic section of the book of Jeremiah, in chapter 23) is satisfactory, probably because there is no possible external 'rule-of-thumb' method by which truth claims in matters of religion can be established. Other relevant passages are the fascinating story of the two prophets in 1 Kings 13.1–32 and the equally fascinating story of Micaiah and the prophets in 1 Kings 22.1–36.

3 There is a vast bibliography on the subject, but some books which have been particularly influential are A. Haldar, *Associations of Cult Prophets among the Ancient Semites*, Uppsala, Almqvist and Wiksell, 1945; A. R. Johnson, *The Cultic Prophet in Ancient Israel*, 2nd edn, Cardiff, University of Wales Press, 1962 and *The Cultic Prophet and Israel's Psalmody*, Cardiff, University of Wales Press, 1979; S. Mowinckel, *The Psalms in Israel's Worship*, 2 vols., Oxford, Blackwell, 1962.

4 So, for example, E. W. Heaton, *The Old Testament Prophets*, London, Penguin Books, 1961, a revised reprint of his original, *His Servants the Prophets*, London, SCM Press, 1949.

5 e.g. J. Lindblom, *Prophecy in Ancient Israel*, Oxford, Blackwell, 1962. A useful survey of the whole question can be found by J. R. Porter, 'The origins of prophecy in Israel', in R. Coggins, A. Phillips and M. Knibb (eds.), *Israel's Prophetic Tradition: Essays in Honour of Peter Ackroyd*, Cambridge, CUP, 1982.

6 Cited by H. Ringgren, 'Prophecy in the Ancient Near East', in R. Coggins et al., *Israel's Prophetic Tradition*, p. 3.

7 There is a seventh, that against Judah in 2.4f. However, that is certainly a later addition to the book, couched as it is in strongly Deuteronomistic language, lacking all the vivid description of specific sins of war atrocities in the other oracles, and addressing the southern kingdom whereas Amos's message was directed to the northern kingdom of Israel. No doubt later editors in the south added it as a warning to their own people. They were saying in effect, 'See how all that Amos threatened would happen to Israel for their sins *did* happen. So let us make sure we do not persist in the same ways or the same fate may befall us.' Some scholars have also questioned the originality of the oracles against Tyre and Edom for various reasons which need not detain us here. The issue of their originality to Amos does not affect the nature and function of the series as a whole. An excellent study of these oracles is that of John Barton, *Amos's Oracles against the Nations: A study of Amos 1.3—2.5*, The Society for Old Testament Study Monograph Series, 6, Cambridge, CUP, 1980.

8 The verb in Hebrew carries a third person masculine singular pronominal suffix which can mean either 'I will not revoke/turn back *it* or *him*.' This can be taken either that God will not hold back 'it', i.e. the judgement in general, or 'him', referring to some specific threat from a particular person. Either is possible. I have taken it that at the time of Amos no one would have doubted from whom any military threat would have come – it could only have come from the king of Assyria. There was no need to be specific. It is rather like the German propaganda broadcasts by William Joyce (Lord Haw-Haw) after Dunkirk in the Second World War. They assured the English that they should not be fooled by the growing delay in the German plans for invasion of England. '*He* is coming' we were assured. There was no need to spell out for anyone in England at that time who or what was meant by 'he'.

9 As Hans Barstad has vigorously reminded us, 'The Religious Polemics of Amos', Supp. VT, 34, 1984.

10 G. I. Davies, *Hosea*, New Century Bible: London, Marshall Pickering; Grand Rapids, Eerdmans, 1992.

11 Grace Emmerson, *Hosea: An Israelite Prophet in Judean Perspective*, JSOT Supp., 28, Sheffield, 1984.

12 P. S. Fiddes, 'The Cross of Hosea Revisited', *Review & Expositor*, 90, 1993, pp. 175–90. The title refers to an earlier work by H. Wheeler Robinson, 'The Cross of Hosea', first published in 1925 but later reissued in a work entitled *Two Hebrew Prophets*, London, Lutterworth Press, 1948.

13 The matter is discussed by R. E. Clements, *Isaiah 1—39*, New Century Bible: London, Marshall, Morgan and Scott; Grand Rapids, Eerdmans, 1980, pp. 11–14.

14 This aspect of Isaiah's teaching is discussed by John Barton, *Isaiah 1—39*, Old Testament Guides, Sheffield, Sheffield Academic Press, 1995, pp. 46–9.

15 There are a number of problems with the Hebrew text in the two verses quoted here. I have taken a few liberties, as every other interpreter has to do! Even if some of my liberties are different from those of other scholars, I think I have offered something near the meaning.

16 I have spelled this out in detail and dealt with the 'originality' of the themes of hope in the book of Micah in *Micah, Nahum, Obadiah*, Old Testament Guides, Sheffield, Sheffield Academic Press, 1991, pp. 43–53.

17 The literature on the subject is vast, but a good general study is that by J. McKay, *Religion in Judah under the Assyrians*, SBT, 2nd series, 26, London, SCM Press, 1973. There is also a good discussion by A. D. H. Mayes, *Deuteronomy*, New Century Bible: London, Marshall, Morgan and Scott; Grand Rapids, Eerdmans, 1979, pp. 85–103.

18 I have discussed this further, together with other aspects of Zephaniah's ministry and message, in my introductory study to the book in *Zephaniah, Habakkuk, Joel*, Old Testament Guides, Sheffield, Sheffield Academic Press, 1994.

19 This is the view of E. W. Nicholson, *Preaching to the Exiles: A Study of the Prose Tradition in the Book of Jeremiah*, Oxford, Blackwell, 1970.

20 Such a view has been vigorously expressed by R. P. Carroll, *From Chaos to Covenant: Uses of Prophecy in the Book of Jeremiah*, London, SCM Press, 1981; *Jeremiah*, Old Testament Library, London, SCM Press, 1986 and, more recently and more accessibly for the general reader, *Jeremiah*, Old Testament Guides, Sheffield, Sheffield Academic Press, 1989.

21 For the expression of a more conservative view, see J. G. McConville, *Judgment and Promise: An Interpretation of the book of Jeremiah*, Leicester, Apollos; Winona Lake, Ia., Eisenbrauns, 1993.

22 The particular works of Carroll to which he referred were his articles on several prophets, (Amos, Micah, Habakkuk, Jeremiah, Obadiah and Joel) in R. J. Coggins and J. L. Houlden (eds.), *A Dictionary of Biblical Interpretation*, London, SCM Press; Philadelphia, Trinity Press International, 1990. In addition to these I also reread Carroll's article 'Prophecy and Society', in R. E. Clements (ed.), *The World of Ancient Israel: Sociological, Anthropological and Political Perspectives*, Cambridge, CUP, 1989, pp. 203–26. The article by David Clines is 'Metacommentating Amos', in H. E. McKay and D. J. Clines (eds.), *Of Prophets' Visions and the Wisdom of Sages: Essays in Honour of R. Norman Whybray on his 70th Birthday*, JSOT Supp., 162, Sheffield, JSOT Press, 1993, pp. 142–60.

6   The Subversion of the Visionaries

1 A study of just such 'millenarian' movements in western Europe between the eleventh and sixteenth centuries is offered by N. Cohn, *The Pursuit of the Millennium: Revolutionary Millenarians and Mystical Anarchists of the Middle Ages*, rev. edn, London, Temple Smith, 1970. He stresses that the roots of

such movements and ideologies were complex and varied, but begins his work by tracing them back to Jewish apocalyptic literature with its own roots in the prophetic literature of the Old Testament (see esp. pp. 19–25).

2 The literature on all this is immense and, in line with my stated policy in this book, I am not going even to try to be comprehensive. Here, however, is some literature on the subject, spanning many years, in which fuller bibliographies can be found by any wishing to follow further this fascinating subject: S. B. Frost, *Old Testament Apocalyptic: Its Origin and Growth*, London, Epworth Press, 1952; H. H. Rowley, *The Relevance of Apocalyptic*, London, Lutterworth Press, 1963; D. S. Russell, *The Method and Message of Jewish Apocalyptic*, Old Testament Library, London, SCM Press, 1964; O. Plöger, *Theocracy and Eschatology*, Oxford, Blackwell, 1968; K. Koch, *The Rediscovery of Apocalyptic*, SBT 2nd series, London, SCM Press, 1972; P. D. Hanson, *The Dawn of Apocalyptic*, Philadelphia, Fortress Press, 1975; D. S. Russell, *Apocalyptic: Ancient and Modern*, Philadelphia, Fortress Press; London, SCM Press, 1978; E. W. Nicholson, 'Apocalyptic', in G. W. Anderson (ed.), *Tradition and Interpretation*, Oxford, Clarendon Press, 1979, pp. 189–213; J. J. Collins, 'Towards the Morphology of a Genre', 'The Jewish Apocalypses', in *Apocalypse: The Morphology of a Genre*, Semeia 14, Missoula, Mont., 1979, pp. 1–20, 21–59; M. A. Knibb, 'Prophecy and the Emergence of the Jewish Apocalypses', in R. Coggins, A. Phillips and M. Knibb (eds.), *Israel's Prophetic Tradition*, Cambridge, CUP, 1982, pp. 155–80; C. Rowland, *The Open Heaven: A Study of Apocalyptic in Judaism and Early Christianity*, London, SPCK, 1982; P. D. Hanson (ed.), *Visionaries and their Apocalypses*, Philadelphia, Fortress Press; London, SPCK, 1983; D. Hellholm (ed.), *Apocalypticism in the Mediterranean World and the Near East: Proceedings of the International Colloquium on Apocalypticism, Uppsala, August 12–17, 1979*, Tübingen, Mohr, 1983; J. J. Collins, *The Apocalyptic Imagination: An Introduction to the Jewish Matrix of Christianity*, New York, Crossroad, 1984; P. R. Davies, 'The Social World of the Apocalyptic Writings', in R. E. Clements (ed.), *The World of Ancient Israel: Sociological, Anthropological and Political Perspectives*, Cambridge, CUP, 1989, pp. 251–71; J. J. Collins and J. H. Charlesworth (eds.), *Mysteries and Revelations: Apocalyptic Studies since the Uppsala Colloquium*, Sheffield, JSOT Press, 1991; D. S. Russell, *Divine Disclosure: An Introduction to Jewish Apocalyptic*, London, SCM Press; Minneapolis, Fortress Press, 1992.

3 I have dealt with this, and other matters to do with the books of Haggai and Zechariah, more fully in 'The Prophets of the Restoration', in R. Coggins, A. Phillips and M. Knibb (eds.), *Israel's Prophetic Tradition*, Cambridge, CUP, 1982, pp. 137–54, and *Preaching the Tradition: Homily and Hermeneutic after the Exile*, Cambridge, CUP, 1990, pp. 185–234.

4 R. N. Whybray, *Isaiah 40—66*, New Century Bible, London, Oliphants, 1975, p. 192.

5 One who does give great prominence to the figures of David and Solomon and their successors is the Chronicler. There have certainly been those who believe that such a glowing picture of the line and God's promises

towards it coming after the exile shows that he had a strong hope for a restoration of the Davidic line. Readers will not be surprised to learn that the literature on this subject is enormous. Just one example of those who believe in the Chronicler's 'messianism' is R. G. North, 'Theology of the Chronicler', *JBL*, 82, 1963, pp. 369–81. Others, however, see the emphasis on David and Solomon to be almost exclusively on their activity as those who between them organized the building, worship and priestly orders of the temple, and that this was the function of the Davidic dynasty (just as in Zechariah 4.6b–10a Zerubbabel is reminded that his role is to be that merely of temple builder, not of military ruler). If this view is correct, then the whole point of the Chronicler's treatment is that the goal of the (interim) historical monarchy was the emergence after the exile of the temple-based community under the leadership of the priests. Most recently this view has been expressed by W. Riley, *King and Cultus in Chronicles: Worship and the Reinterpretation of History*, JSOT Supp. 160, Sheffield, JSOT, 1993. This was certainly the side I myself came down on in *Preaching the Tradition*. I also argued there that the figure of Nehemiah is depicted to some extent in royal terms in the book of Nehemiah, but, again, that there is no suggestion of the resumption of the old historic Davidic line through him. A mediating position between these two extremes is offered by H. G. M. Williamson, *Israel in the Books of Chronicles*, Cambridge, CUP, 1977, see esp. p. 135. But, whatever judgement each of us comes to in this matter, I could not deal with the Chronicler in this chapter because, for one thing, he can hardly be described as one of the 'visionaries' and, for another, whatever else the Chronicler may or may not be, he is not 'subversive' towards the leadership of priests and others whom he sees as appointed by God. He may well express hope for an end to Persian control, but he sees that as a result to be brought about entirely by God without any help from human arms.

6 After a long period of neglect these chapters are now receiving a good deal of attention, and there has been a number of commentaries on them recently. Two of the most recent are D. L. Petersen, *Zechariah 9—14 and Malachi*, Old Testament Library, London, SCM Press, 1995 and P. L. Redditt, *Haggai, Zechariah, Malachi*, New Century Bible: Grand Rapids, Eerdmans; London, Marshall Pickering, 1995.

7 This is my own point of view, expressed long ago in my commentary, *The Books of Haggai, Zechariah and Malachi*, The Cambridge Bible Commentary on the New English Bible, Cambridge, CUP, 1977. I hope to be dealing much more fully with Zechariah 9—14 in a forthcoming book.

8 I find the claim by P. D. Hanson that the chapter as a whole forms a unity and is to be viewed as a 'Divine Warrior Hymn' to be forced. See 'Zechariah 9 and the Recapitulation of an Ancient Ritual Pattern', *JBL*, 92, 1973, pp. 37–59, and *The Dawn of Apocalyptic: The Historical and Sociological Roots of Jewish Apocalyptic Eschatology*, 2nd edn, Philadelphia, Fortress Press, 1979.

9 The idea is fully explored by A. R. Johnson, *Sacral Kingship in Ancient Israel*, 2nd edn, Cardiff, University of Wales Press, 1967.

10 Following a widely accepted emendation of the text which, as it stands, reads, 'the dwellers of the wilderness'.

11 There is a difficulty over the last phrase of 2.3. The Hebrew reads, 'he will carry you away to it'. This is often amended on the basis of the Syriac Version to read, 'I will put you out of my presence' (RSV). Very reasonably, B. Glazier-McDonald suggests a passive understanding of the construction, 'one will take you away' = 'you will be taken away', *Malachi: The Divine Messenger*, SBL Dissertation Series, 98, Atlanta, Scholars Press, 1987, p. 68. The meaning is clear whichever reading we choose.

12 I have discussed them briefly in my small commentary, *The Books of Haggai, Zechariah and Malachi*, The Cambridge Bible Commentary, Cambridge, CUP, 1977, and this would be adequate for anyone unfamiliar with the material who needs just a general introduction. Naturally the larger and more recent commentaries, such as those I indicated above (see n. 6) take their discussion farther.

13 Again, I have discussed such issues in *Zephaniah, Habakkuk, Joel*, Old Testament Guides, Sheffield, Sheffield Academic Press, 1994.

14 The numbering of the chapters differs between our English versions and the Massoretic Text. The first two chapters of the Hebrew text equal 1.1—2.27 in the English text. The English 2.28–32 forms chapter 3 in the Hebrew while the English chapter 3 is the Hebrew chapter 4. To avoid littering the text with numbers in brackets I give the English references only.

15 P. L. Redditt, 'The Book of Joel and Peripheral Prophecy', *CBQ*, 48, 1986, pp. 225–40.

7 The Subversion of the 'Universalists'

1 The Hebrew text actually reads 'he established national boundaries according to the number of the sons of Israel'. But it is widely agreed that this represents a watering down of the original text, which is best preserved in the Greek version (LXX). It is the text of the LXX which alone gives the sense required by the context.

2 A well-informed and readable study of polytheism and the movements towards monotheism in early Israel is to be found in Mark S. Smith, *The Early History of God: Yahweh and the Other Deities in Ancient Israel*, San Francisco, Harper & Row; Edinburgh, T & T Clark, 1990.

3 See Pritchard, *Ancient Near Eastern Texts*, p. 320.

4 A study of the idea of 'the Heavenly Council' can be found in R. N. Whybray, *The Heavenly Counsellor in Isaiah xl 13–14: A Study of the Sources of the Theology of Deutero-Isaiah*, SOTS Monograph Series 1, Cambridge, CUP, 1971. Significantly, Whybray sees Second Isaiah as rejecting the idea. Yahweh does not need 'counsellors' to advise him. Of that, more below.

5 This is the version found in Micah. The Isaiah form of it does not include the last two lines.

6 This is the way C. L. and E. M. Meyers take it in their commentary *Haggai, Zechariah 1—8*, The Anchor Bible, New York, Doubleday, 1987, p. 169.

7 The reasons for the almost unanimous verdict of scholars that Isaiah 40—55 are from a different prophet than Isaiah of Jerusalem (as the prophet behind Isaiah 1—39 is often termed) are set out in all the commentaries. A fascinating recent study of the reason why the two collections may have become joined has been offered by H. G. M. Williamson, *The Book Called Isaiah: Deutero-Isaiah's Role in Composition and Redaction*, Oxford, Clarendon Press, 1994. As the title suggests, Williamson argues that Second Isaiah was consciously setting out to edit and comment on the earlier teachings of the prophet Isaiah in the light of the later, exilic situation. In all discussion of the relation between chapters 1—39 and 40—55 (as well as the rest of the book) we have to remember it is probably an oversimplification to talk as if the work of just *two* individual prophets have become joined. Both sections are themselves clearly of composite authorship and origin.

8 The four passages usually so designated are customarily identified as 42.1–4; 49.1–6; 50.4–9; 52.13—53.12. The literature on these passages is vast, and opinions on just exactly who the 'servant' is meant to be are numerous and widely different. I have cut through all this by simply stating, without much defence, my view that the 'servant' in the songs, as throughout these chapters, is Israel. I am tempted to say (with outrageous immodesty) that it is the most plausible view, but many of my fellow scholars would have plenty to say about that! A brief introduction to the critical debate can be found by R. N. Whybray, both in the article 'Servant Songs' in R. J. Coggins and J. L. Houlden (eds.), *A Dictionary of Biblical Interpretation*, London, SCM Press; Philadelphia, Trinity Press International, 1990, pp. 628–31 and also in *The Second Isaiah*, Old Testament Guides, Sheffield, JSOT Press, 1983, esp. pp. 65–78.

9 There has been a great deal of discussion over the complex issue of Second Isaiah's attitude to the nations. A very detailed account and full bibliography is given by G. I. Davies, 'The Destiny of the Nations in the Book of Isaiah', in J. Vermeylen (ed.), *The Book of Isaiah*, Leuven, 1989, pp. 93–120. He shows that some have attributed the mixed signals from these chapters to various layers of redaction. He cites D. W. Van Winkle, 'The Relationship of the Nations to Yahweh and to Israel in Isaiah XL—LV', *VT*, 35, 1985, pp. 446–58, esp. pp. 446f. Van Winkle claims that a '... vision of the ultimate salvation of the nations does not preclude their submission to Israel. The prophet does not envisage the co-equality of Jews and Gentiles. He expects that Israel will be exalted, and that she will become Yahweh's agent who will rule the nations in such a way that justice is established and mercy shown. This rule is both that for which the nations wait expectantly and that to which they submit' (p. 457). That is the position which I have outlined above, although it seems as though the 'mercy' the nations can expect is somewhat mixed and, even if Second Isaiah imagined they were longing eagerly for such a subordinate role to Israel, it is difficult to imagine many of their kings and subjects in fact voting for it in a referendum. Davies himself attributes the very

varied and various themes to be found as having their origin in Israel's liturgical worship in the Jerusalem temple.

10 Again it is widely held among scholars that these chapters, at least in their present form, show different authorship from that of Isaiah 40—55. They are often located back on Judean soil after the exile. Perhaps it is fair to say there is not quite the unanimity over this that there is on the issue of Isaiah 40—55 being of different authorship from that of Isaiah 1—39. Nor is there anything like agreement on the 'unity' of chapters 56—66. There is much disparate material within them, disparate in tone, form, theology and future expectation, and the way each section relates to another presents a series of critical problems. Again there is a good recent introduction to these issues, this one by Grace I. Emmerson, *Isaiah 56—66*, Old Testament Guides, Sheffield, JSOT Press, 1992.

11 A most useful summary of recent scholarly discussion of the book is offered by R. B. Salters, *Jonah and Lamentations*, Old Testament Guides, Sheffield, JSOT Press, 1994.

Suggestions for Further Reading

Brettler, M. Z., *The Creation of History in Ancient Israel*, London and New York, Routledge, 1995.

Carroll, R. P., *Wolf in the Sheepfold: The Bible as a Problem for Christianity*, London, SPCK, 1991.

Coote, R. B. and M. P., *Power, Politics and the Making of the Bible*, Minneapolis, Fortress Press, 1990.

Ellul, J., *Propaganda: The Formation of Men's Attitudes*, tr. K. Kellen and J. Lerner, New York, Knopf, 1965.

Katz, D. et al. (eds.), *Public Opinion and Propaganda: A Book of Readings*, New York, Holt, Rineheart and Winston, 1954.

Larsen, M. T., *Power and Propaganda: A Symposium on Ancient Empires*, Mesopotamia, Copenhagen Studies in Assyriology, 7, Copenhagen, Akademisk Forlage, 1979.

van Seters, J., *In Search of History*, New Haven and London, YUP, 1983.

Walsh, J. P. M., SJ, *The Mighty from their Thrones: Power in the Biblical Tradition*, Philadelphia, Fortress Press, 1987.

Index of Modern Authors